GCSE 9–1 PHYSICS

AQA REVISION & EXAM PRACTICE

Alessio Bernardelli
and Sam Jordan

Authors Alessio Bernardelli and Sam Jordan
Editorial team Haremi Ltd
Series designers emc design ltd
Typesetting York Publishing Solutions Pvt. Ltd. and Newgen KnowledgeWorks (P) Ltd, Chennai, India
Illustrations York Publishing Solutions Pvt. Ltd. and Newgen KnowledgeWorks (P) Ltd, Chennai, India
App development Hannah Barnett, Phil Crothers and Haremi Ltd

Designed using Adobe InDesign
Published by Scholastic Education, an imprint of Scholastic Ltd, Book End, Range Road, Witney, Oxfordshire, OX29 0YD
Registered office: Westfield Road, Southam, Warwickshire CV47 0RA
www.scholastic.co.uk

Printed by Bell & Bain Ltd, Glasgow
© 2017 Scholastic Ltd
1 2 3 4 5 6 7 8 9   7 8 9 0 1 2 3 4 5 6

British Library Cataloguing-in-Publication Data
A catalogue record for this book is available from the British Library.
ISBN 978-1407-17677-2

Acknowledgements

The publishers gratefully acknowledge permission to reproduce the following copyright material:

p11 top styleuneed.de/Shutterstock; p11 bottom left DSBfoto/Shutterstock; p11 bottom right ersin ergin/Shutterstock; p13 Gearstd/Shutterstock; p14 top left Ian Duffield/Shutterstock; p14 bottom left Maxisport/Shutterstock; p14 right Nicola Bertolini/Shutterstock; p15 Aleks Kend/Shutterstock; p22 garagestock/Shutterstock; p23 first image Viktorija Reuta/Shutterstock; p23 second image johavel/Shutterstock; p23 third image Aleksandr Petrunovskyi/Shutterstock; p23 fourth image Serz_72/Shutterstock; p24 first image BigMouse/Shutterstock; p24 second image monicaodo/Shutterstock; p24 third image all_is_magic/Shutterstock; p24 fourth image KittyVector/Shutterstock; p24 fifth image VectorBand/Shutterstock; p25 anweber/Shutterstock; p26 Valentyn Volkov/Shutterstock; p30 Icon Craft Studio/Shutterstock; p31 Artur Synenko/Shutterstock; p32 your/Shutterstock; p35 photosync/Shutterstock; p38 Guschenkova/Shutterstock; p39 Edgewater Media/Shutterstock; p40 Gwoeii/Shutterstock; p46 M. Unal Ozmen/Shutterstock; p49 MIGUEL GARCIA SAAVEDRA/Shutterstock; p52 ducu59us/Shutterstock; p55 Joe White/Shutterstock; p57 Panimoni/Shutterstock; p60 top wellphoto/Shutterstock; p60 bottom Andreas Prott/Shutterstock; p64 top Everett Historical/Shutterstock; p64 bottom Milosz Maslanka/Shutterstock; p67 Vadim Sadovski/Shutterstock; p70 Thipawan kongkamsri/Shutterstock; p72 Igor Bukhlin/Shutterstock; p75 MASTER PHOTO 2017/Shutterstock; p76 Bonita R. Cheshier/Shutterstock; p80 Alexandru Nika/Shutterstock; p82 Tatiana Popova/Shutterstock; p83 Pete Niesen/Shutterstock; p83 PHOTOMDP/Shutterstock; p86 Bruce Ellis/Shutterstock; p99 Fouad A. Saad/Shutterstock; p100 Jose Carlos Alexandre/Shutterstock; p108 Olga Miltsova/Shutterstock; p109 Coprid/Shutterstock; p111 A. and I. Kruk/Shutterstock; p127 top Vadim Sadovski/Shutterstock; p127 bottom Cristian Cestaro/Shutterstock; p128 3Dsculptor/Shutterstock; p130 Designua/Shutterstock; p131 Vadim Sadovski/Shutterstock.

Every effort has been made to trace copyright holders for the works reproduced in this book, and the publishers apologise for any inadvertent omissions.

Note from the publisher:

Please use this product in conjunction with the official specification and sample assessment materials. Ask your teacher if you are unsure where to find them.

The marks and star ratings have been suggested by our subject experts, but they are to be used as a guide only.

Answer space has been provided, but you may need to use additional paper for your workings.

How to use this book

Inside this book you'll find everything you need to help you succeed in the new GCSE 9–1 AQA Physics specification. It combines revision and exam practice in one handy solution. Broken down into topics and subtopics, it presents the information in a manageable format. Work through the revision material first or dip into the exam practice as you complete a topic. This book gives you the flexibility to revise your way!

Refer to the AQA Physics GCSE specification for which equations you need to remember and which will be provided on the equation list in the exam for you.

SNAPIT!

Use the Snap It! feature in the revision app to take a picture, film a video or record audio of key concepts to help them stick. Great for revision on the go!

DOIT!

Activities that get you to turn information from one form into another so that it really embeds in your memory.

Callouts Step-by-step guidance to build understanding.

WORKIT!

Worked examples with model solutions to help you see how to answer a tricky question.

NAILIT!

Tips written by subject experts to help you in the revision process.

MATHS SKILLS

To help you with those tricky bits of maths that you need to know and remember.

Practical Skills

Revisit the key practicals in the specification.

STRETCHIT!

Questions or concepts that stretch you further and challenge you with the most difficult content.

CHECKIT!

Check your knowledge at the end of a subtopic with the Check It! questions.

Consolidate your revision with the Review It! questions at the end of every topic.

REVIEW IT!

H Higher Tier only content is highlighted helping you to target your revision. **H**

MARKS (5 marks)

Each question has the number of marks available to help you target your response.

EXAM-STYLE QUESTIONS

Exam-style questions for each subtopic ramped in difficulty.

★ STAR RATING ★

A quick visual guide to indicate the difficulty of the question, with 1 star representing the least demanding and 5 stars signposting the most challenging questions.

▮ PRACTICE PAPERS

Full mock-exam papers to enable you to have a go at a complete paper before you sit the real thing! Find Paper 2 online at www.scholastic.co.uk/gcse

Revision Guide contents

Topic 1

ENERGY

Energy stores and systems	10
Changes in energy stores	12
Energy changes in systems: specific heat capacity	15
Power	18
Energy transfers in a system	19
Efficiency	21
National and global energy resources	23
Review It!	26

Topic 2

ELECTRICITY

Standard circuit diagram symbols	27
Electrical charge and current	29
Current, resistance and potential difference	30
Resistors	32
Series and parallel circuits	34
Mains electricity	36
Electrical power, energy transfers in appliances and the National Grid	37
Static charge and electric fields	40
Review It!	42

Topic 3

PARTICLE MODEL

Particle model and density of materials	43
Changes of state and internal energy	45
Particle model and pressure	47
Review It!	50

Topic 4

ATOMIC STRUCTURE

The structure of the atom	51
Developing a model of the atom	53
Radioactive decay and nuclear radiation	54
Nuclear equations	56
Half-life of radioactive elements	58
Hazards and uses of radioactive emissions	61
Nuclear fission and fusion	63
Review It!	65

Topic 5

FORCES

Forces and their interactions	66
Resultant forces	68
Work done and energy transfer	71
Forces and elasticity	73
Moments, levers and gears	76
Pressure and pressure differences in fluids	78
Distance, displacement, speed and velocity	80
Distance–time relationship	82
Acceleration	84
Newton's laws of motion	87
Stopping distance	90
Momentum	92
Review It!	94

WAVES

Transverse and longitudinal waves	95
Reflection and refraction	98
Sound waves	100
Electromagnetic waves	102
Lenses	105
Visible light	108
Emission and absorption of infrared radiation and black body radiation	110
Review It!	112

ELECTROMAGNETISM

Magnetism	113
Motor effect	115
Electromagnetic induction	119
Transformers	123
Review It!	126

SPACE PHYSICS

Our solar system	127
Life cycle of a star	129
Red-shift	130
Review It!	132

Glossary/Index for Revision Guide	133
Answers for Revision Guide	137

Topic 6

Topic 7

Topic 8

Exam Practice contents

Topic 1

ENERGY

Energy stores and systems	144
Changes in energy stores: kinetic energy	145
Changes in energy stores: elastic potential energy	147
Changes in energy stores: gravitational potential energy	148
Energy changes in systems: specific heat capacity	149
Power	150
Energy transfers in a system	152
Efficiency	153
National and global energy resources	154

Topic 2

ELECTRICITY

Standard circuit diagram symbols	156
Electrical charge and current	157
Current, resistance and potential difference and resistors	159
Series and parallel circuits	162
Mains electricity: direct and alternating potential difference (ac/dc)	164
Mains electricity	165
Electric power (with electrical devices)	166
Energy transfers in appliances	167
The National Grid	168
Static charge and electric fields (1)	170
Static charge and electric fields (2)	171

Topic 3

PARTICLE MODEL

Particle model of matter and density of materials	172
Changes of state and internal energy	173
Changes of temperature and specific latent heat	175
Particle motion in gases (1)	176
Particle motion in gases (2)	177

Topic 4

ATOMS

The structure of the atom (1)	178
The structure of the atom (2)	179
Developing a model of the atom	181
Radioactive decay and nuclear radiation	182
Nuclear equations	183
Half-life of radioactive elements	184
Hazards and uses of radioactive emissions (1)	185
Hazards and uses of radioactive emissions (2)	186
Hazards and uses of radioactive emissions (3)	188
Nuclear fission and fusion	189

Topic 5

FORCES

Forces and their interactions	190
Gravity	192
Resultant forces	193
Work done and energy transfer	194
Forces and elasticity	195
Moments, levers and gears	197
Pressure and pressure differences in a fluid (1)	198
Pressure and pressure differences in a fluid (2)	199

Distance, displacement, speed and velocity 201
Acceleration 203
Newton's laws of motion 205
Stopping distance 208
Momentum (1) 210
Momentum (2) 211
Momentum (3) 212

WAVES

Transverse and longitudinal waves 213
Properties of waves 214
Reflection and refraction 216
Sound waves (1) 217
Sound waves (2) 218
Electromagnetic waves (1) 219
Electromagnetic waves (2) 220
Lenses 221
Visible light 223
Emission and absorption of infrared radiation and black body radiation 225

ELECTROMAGNETISM

Magnetism 228
Electromagnetism 229
Motor effect 230
Electromagnetic induction 232
Transformers 234

SPACE PHYSICS

Our solar system 236
Life cycle of a star 238
Orbital motion, natural and artificial satellites 239
Red-shift 241

PAPER 1 243

ANSWERS FOR EXAM PRACTICE 253

Topic 6

Topic 7

Topic 8

7

HOW TO REVISE!

PLAN YOUR REVISION

Get ahead by planning your revision!

Work out the **time** you have available for revising.

Think about when you work at your best. Are you a morning or an evening person?

Allocate **MORE TIME** for the topics you struggle with.

Revision works best in **SMALL BURSTS**, so keep sessions **SHORT AND SWEET**!

Remember to allow time to **PRACTISE** applying what you have revised.

Use your **revision app** to put together a revision timetable.

LOOK AFTER YOURSELF

Help your brain by looking after your whole body!

Take regular **breaks** from revising – your brain needs time to digest information in order to retain it.

★ HOTEL ★

Keep **hydrated** by drinking plenty of water – dehydration stops your brain from working at its full capacity.

Regular **exercise** helps stimulate the brain and will help you relax.

Get plenty of **sleep**, especially the night before an exam.

EAT WELL and limit unhealthy snacks – your brain needs fuel for memory and concentration.

Find methods of **relaxation** that work for you throughout the revision period.

BE PREPARED!

Limit potential stress on the day of an exam by getting everything you need ready the night before.

30

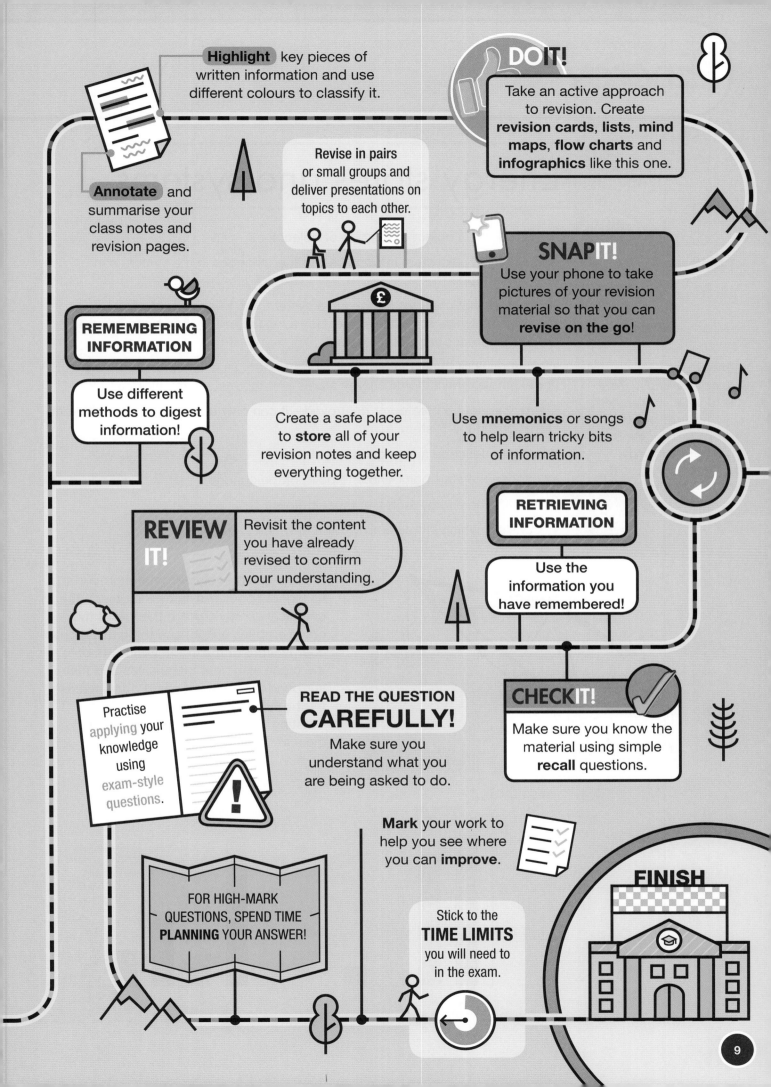

Highlight key pieces of written information and use different colours to classify it.

DO IT!

Take an active approach to revision. Create **revision cards, lists, mind maps, flow charts** and **infographics** like this one.

Annotate and summarise your class notes and revision pages.

Revise in pairs or small groups and deliver presentations on topics to each other.

SNAP IT!

Use your phone to take pictures of your revision material so that you can **revise on the go!**

REMEMBERING INFORMATION

Use different methods to digest information!

Create a safe place to **store** all of your revision notes and keep everything together.

Use **mnemonics** or songs to help learn tricky bits of information.

RETRIEVING INFORMATION

Use the information you have remembered!

REVIEW IT!

Revisit the content you have already revised to confirm your understanding.

CHECK IT!

Make sure you know the material using simple **recall** questions.

Practise *applying* your knowledge using *exam-style questions.*

READ THE QUESTION CAREFULLY!

Make sure you understand what you are being asked to do.

Mark your work to help you see where you can **improve**.

FOR HIGH-MARK QUESTIONS, SPEND TIME **PLANNING** YOUR ANSWER!

Stick to the **TIME LIMITS** you will need to in the exam.

FINISH

Energy

Energy stores and systems

NAILIT!

It is always better to say **dissipated energy** instead of wasted energy.

Energy is **not** an object. Never use the word 'heat' as a noun. For example, say 'The energy is dissipated to the surroundings by work done against friction', not 'Heat is produced by friction'.

A **system** is an object or a group of objects.

The **energy** in a system informs us whether changes in the system can or cannot happen.

No matter what changes happen in a system, the total amount of energy in the system always stays the same. However, the energy can be transferred around different parts of the system.

We can think of these different parts of a system as **energy stores** (for example, gravitational energy stores and thermal energy stores).

Energy cannot be created or destroyed – it can only be transferred to different stores within the system.

When you describe a change in a system:

- choose the start point and end point of the change
- identify the energy stores at those points
- consider which stores empty out and which stores fill up.

A crane lifts an object from the ground to its highest point. As it lifts the object, the chemical energy store in the fuel of the crane empties a little, and the gravitational energy store of the crane fills. Parts of the crane also heat themselves and their surroundings by work being done against **friction**, filling the thermal store and 'wasting' some energy (dissipating it to the surrounding air).

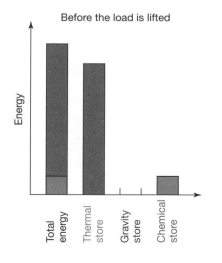

Before the load is lifted

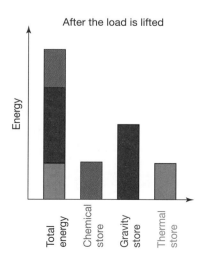

After the load is lifted

Changes in a system can happen by:

- heating
- **work done** by **forces**
- work done when an electric current flows.

SNAP**IT!**

Use your phone to film a ball being dropped.

DO**IT!**

Play your video back and pause it randomly. Starting from the drop and ending at the point you pressed pause, describe the changes in the system and how energy is transferred from one energy store to other stores.

CHECK**IT!**

1 You are asked to describe a change in a system as a series of energy transfers.

What are the three steps you need to do?

2 How is energy transferred when:

  a a lamp is switched on

  b an electric kettle is boiling water

  c a car is accelerated

  d chips are fried in a pan over the hob?

3 Think of two more examples of how energy is transferred.

Changes in energy stores

Kinetic energy

There is a kinetic store of **energy** associated with a moving object.

The greater the **mass** and the faster it is moving, the greater the energy in the kinetic store.

We can calculate the kinetic energy of a moving object using the equation:

$$\textbf{kinetic energy} = \textbf{0.5 mass} \times \textbf{(speed)}^2$$

$$E_k = \frac{1}{2}mv^2$$

- E_k = kinetic energy (unit: **joule**, J)
- m = mass (unit: **kilogram**, kg)
- v = **speed** (unit: **metre** per second, m/s)

WORKIT!

A car and a lorry are both travelling on the motorway at 70 mph (31.3 m/s). The car has a mass of 2650 kg, and the lorry has a mass of 5230 kg. Calculate the kinetic energy of the car and the kinetic energy of the lorry. (3 marks)

$E_k = \frac{1}{2}mv^2$

$E_k \text{ (car)} = 0.5 \times 2650 \times 31.3^2 = 1298089 \text{ J} \quad (1)$

$E_k \text{ (lorry)} = 0.5 \times 5230 \times 31.3^2 = 2561889 \text{ J} \quad (1)$

When they travel at the same speed, the kinetic energy store is 'fuller' for the lorry than for the car. This is because the lorry has more mass than the car. (1)

Gravitational potential energy

There is a gravitational potential store of energy associated with the height of an object.

The **higher** the object and the **greater** its **mass**, the greater the **energy** in the **gravity store**.

We can calculate the gravitational potential energy of a raised object using the equation:

$$\textbf{gravitational potential energy} = \textbf{mass} \times \textbf{gravitational field strength} \times \textbf{height}$$

$$E_p = mgh$$

- E_p = gravitational potential energy (unit: joule, J)
- m = mass (unit: kilogram, kg)
- g = **gravitational field strength** (unit: **newton** per kilogram, N/kg)
- h = height (unit: metre, m)

WORKIT!

A cricket ball is batted vertically upwards with an initial speed of 28.5 m/s. The mass of the ball is 155.9 g. What height will the ball reach? Assume the gravitational field strength is 10 N/kg. (3 marks)

$E_k = \frac{1}{2} m v^2$

$E_k = 0.5 \times 0.1559 \times 28.5 = 63.3$ J (1)

Don't forget to convert the mass into kg first.

Find the kinetic energy the ball started with.

At its highest point the kinetic store is empty as the ball stops just before falling back down again, so the gravity store is full with the same amount of energy when the ball was batted. (1)

$(E_k = E_p = 63.3$ J$)$

$E_p = m g h$

Remember the question states that g = 10 N/kg

$h = \dfrac{E_p}{mg} = \dfrac{63.3 mg}{0.1559} \times 10 = 40.6$ m (1)

Elastic potential energy

There is an elastic potential store of energy associated with an object that can be stretched, twisted, or compressed.

The greater the **extension** of a spring, the greater the **energy** in the **elastic store**.

We can calculate the elastic potential energy of a stretched or compressed spring using the equation:

elastic potential energy = 0.5 × spring constant × (extension)²

$$E_e = \frac{1}{2} k e^2$$

- E_e = elastic potential energy (unit: joule, J)
- k = **spring constant** (unit: newton per metre, N/m)
- e = extension (unit: metre, m)

DOIT!

Start making a list of the equations you will need to remember for physics.

This equation only works if a spring is not stretched too much. If it is overstretched, it will pass its **limit of proportionality**, and this equation will not work.

NAILIT!

Only the elastic potential energy equation will be given to you in the exam. You will need to remember both the kinetic energy equation and the gravitational potential energy equation.

DOIT!

Write a short paragraph that describes the similarities and differences between the E_k and E_e equations.

WORKIT!

The spring of a fishing scale extends by 8 cm when a fish is hung on it. What is the elastic potential energy associated to the spring, if the spring constant is 28.9 N/m? (2 marks)

$e = 8$ cm $= 0.080$ m ← Remember to convert the units.

$E_e = \frac{1}{2} k e^2$ (1)

$\quad = 0.5 \times 28.9 \times 0.080$

$\quad = 0.09$ J (1)

✓ CHECKIT!

1 An eagle of mass 5.2 kg dives to catch a rat on the ground from a height of 58 m.

What was the gravitational potential energy associated to the eagle before diving?

2 Mo Farah can run 10 000 m in about 26 minutes and 47 seconds. His mass is 58 kg.

Calculate the average energy in the kinetic store when Mo Farah is running a 10 km race.

3 Cyclist A rides the same bike as cyclist B and they both have the same mass. Cyclist B rides at one third of the speed of cyclist A. How much greater is E_k for cyclist A compared to cyclist B? Explain how you calculated your answer.

Energy changes in systems: specific heat capacity

Specific heat capacity is the **energy** needed to increase the temperature of 1 kg of a substance by 1°C.

The **higher** the specific heat capacity of a substance, the **more** energy is needed to increase its temperature.

Materials with high specific heat capacity can store large amounts of energy in their associated **thermal** store when they are hot. This means these materials can give out more energy when they cool down.

Water has a very large specific heat capacity, therefore it is a good substance to use in central heating systems.

NAILIT!

Make sure you know how to write and read numbers in **standard form**. For example, 1 150 000 in standard form is 1.15×10^6.

Water is often used in central heating systems.

We can calculate the thermal energy put into a **system**, or the thermal energy given out from a system, when its temperature changes using the equation:

change in thermal energy = mass × specific heat capacity

× temperature changes

$$\Delta E = m\,c\,\Delta\theta$$

- ΔE = change in thermal energy (unit: **joule**, J)
- m = **mass** (unit: **kilogram**, kg)
- c = specific heat capacity (unit: joule per kilogram per degree Celsius, J/kg °C)
- $\Delta\theta$ = temperature change (unit: degree Celsius, °C)

NAILIT!

This equation will be given to you. Make sure you know how to use it.

Practical Skills

You will have investigated in class how to find out the specific heat capacity of a substance. Think about the apparatus and method you used. Depending on the substance tested, it may have looked like the diagrams below.

- How did you link the decrease in one energy store (or work done) with the increase in temperature?

- How did you link this with an increase of energy in the thermal store?

With the data you collected, you can find out the specific heat capacity of the substances you tested.

To calculate the specific heat capacity, rearrange the equation $\Delta E = m\,c\,\Delta\theta$:

$$c = \frac{\Delta E}{m \times \Delta\theta}$$

Substance	Energy supplied (J)	Mass (kg)	Initial temperature (°C)	Final temperature (°C)	Temperature change $\Delta\theta$ (°C)	Specific heat capacity (J/kg °C)
Aluminium	18 000	0.250	23	102	79	911
Water	18 000	0.385	22	33	11	4250
Steel	18 000	1.000	24	61	37	

- Use the rearranged equation and the data in the table to calculate the specific heat capacity of steel.

- Suggest three ways to improve the accuracy of your results.

MATHS SKILLS

We could use an energy meter to measure the energy supplied by an immersion heater. But we can find out this energy from the power rating of the heater.

$$power = \frac{energy}{time}$$

$$energy = power \times time \quad \longleftarrow \quad \text{Rearrange the equation so energy is the subject}$$

$$60\,W \times 300\,s = 18\,000\,J$$

So each calorimeter is supplied with 18 000 J of energy in 5 minutes (300 seconds).

WORKIT!

A fish and chip shop needs to warm up 5.00 kg of oil from 22°C to 160°C to fry some cod fish. The specific heat capacity of the oil is 1670 J/kg°C.

How much energy needs to be transferred from the chemical store in the gas hob providing the flame to the thermal store associated with the oil to make this change in temperature? (2 marks)

$\Delta E = m\,c\,\Delta\theta$ (1)

$\quad = 5.00 \times 1670 \times (160 - 22)$

$\quad = 5.00 \times 1670 \times 138 = 1152\,300$ J

$\quad = 1.15 \times 10^6$ J (1)

> Remember to put units in your answer.

✓ CHECKIT!

1 300 g of water is brought to boiling temperature. The water is then left to cool to room temperature (25°C). The specific heat capacity of water is 4200 J/kg°C. How much energy is released by the thermal energy store associated with the water as it cools?

2 The specific heat capacity of water is 4200 J/kg°C. The chemical energy store from the fuel in the diagram will decrease by 4200 J as the temperature of 1 kg of water increases by 1°C. What will be the increase in the thermal energy store of the water?

3 Material A has twice the mass of material B, but half the specific heat capacity of material B. Choose the correct statement.

  a Material A will need more energy to raise its temperature by 1°C.

  b Material B will need more energy to raise its temperature by 1°C.

  c Both materials will need the same amount of energy to raise their temperature by 1°C.

1°C rise

1 kg water

4200 J

Power

Power is the amount of **energy** transferred or **work done** by, or to, a **system** every second.

One **joule** of energy transferred in one second = one **watt** of power.

We can calculate the power in a system using the equation:

- P = power (unit: watt, W)
- E = energy (unit: joule, J)
- t = time (unit: second, s)

$$power = \frac{energy\ transferred}{time}$$

$$P = \frac{E}{t}$$

$$power = \frac{work\ done}{time}$$

$$P = \frac{W}{t}$$

- P = power (unit: watt, W)
- W = work done (unit: joule, J)
- t = time (unit: second, s)

NAILIT!

Have you noticed that both energy and work done are measured in joules (J)? In physics, work done is just another way of transferring energy between the energy stores of a system. They both cause changes in the system. You can find more about work done in the Forces chapter.

MATHS SKILLS

You will need to remember and apply the equations on this page.

WORKIT!

Jasmine was late for school yesterday, so she ran upstairs to her classroom which was 15 m up from the ground floor. It took her 5 seconds. Today, Jasmine is on time, so she walks to her classroom and takes 20 seconds to climb the stairs. What was Jasmine's power output on both days, if her mass is 52 kg? Assume the gravitational field strength is 10N/kg. (3 marks)

Use the equation for gravitational potential energy to work out the energy as

$E_P = mgh = 52\ kg \times 10\ N/kg \times 15\ m$

$= 7800\ J$ (1)

So, her power is:

$g = 10\ N/kg$

When Jasmine goes upstairs the same amount of energy is transferred from the chemical store associated to her body to the gravity store when she's on top of the stairs.

$P\ (running) = \frac{E_P}{t} = \frac{7800}{5} = 1560\ W$ (1)

$P\ (walking) = \frac{E_P}{t} = \frac{7800}{20} = 390\ W$ (1)

CHECKIT!

1 You need to boil a glass of water using a microwave oven. Which power rating will be the quickest? Explain your answer.

   a 650 W   b   850 W

2 How much energy is transferred by an 11 W light bulb every second when it is turned on?

3 An 1100 W electric drill takes 6.3 seconds to drill a hole in a wall. How much energy has been transferred to the kinetic energy store and the thermal energy store in that time?

Energy transfers in a system

Conservation of energy and dissipated energy

The principle of **conservation of energy** says that **energy** is always conserved. Energy can be transferred usefully, stored or **dissipated**, but it cannot be created or destroyed.

In other words, the total energy in a **system** is the same before and after a change happens in the system. The energy just gets redistributed to different energy stores in the system. So, there is *no net change* in the total energy of the system.

Every time a change happens in a system, some energy is dissipated. This dissipated energy gets stored in less useful ways. For example, when water evaporates from a hot bath it increases the amount of energy in the **thermal** store associated with the bathroom.

WORKIT!

Explain why a ball never bounces higher than the height it is dropped from. (3 marks)

When the ball hits the floor part of the kinetic store (where energy is stored usefully) empties and the thermal store associated with the ball and surroundings increases. (1) The total energy in the system is still the same, but the energy in the thermal store is too spread out (dissipated) to be transferred back to the kinetic store (1) – this energy is 'wasted' and the ball cannot bounce back to where it was dropped from. (1)

A thermal infrared image of a ball before (left) and after (right) being bounced

Reducing unwanted energy transfers

It is important to reduce unwanted energy transfers in a system so that less energy is 'wasted'.

Car engines and other machines reduce the 'wasted' energy transferred by heating by using lubricants like engine oil between mechanical parts. This reduces the **friction** between moving parts of the car so less work is done against friction.

Thermal insulation is used in houses to reduce 'wasted' energy transferred by heating from the house to its surroundings.

Different materials have different thermal conductivity. The higher the thermal conductivity of a material, the quicker energy can be transferred by **conduction** through that material.

DOIT!

Take a metal tray and a plastic tray that are about the same size. Feel both trays with your hands, then place an ice cube on each tray. Which ice cube melts first? Is this what you were expecting? Can you explain what happened in terms of thermal conductivity?

The rate a house cools depends on the thickness of its walls and on the thermal conductivity of the walls. The thinner the bricks, the quicker the energy is conducted through them from the inside of the house to the outside. Cavity wall insulation is sometimes used between the inner and outer walls of houses. It reduces the amount of energy conducted through the walls because it has low thermal conductivity.

Inner wall

Insulation

Outer wall

Practical Skills

You will have investigated in class the effectiveness of different materials as thermal **insulators**.

You might have used hot water and a copper container like the one in the diagram. When the copper container is filled with water, it can be wrapped with different materials to test the temperature of the water at the start and after a set time.

Think about how you carried out your investigation.

You might have used layers of bubble wrap, foam, and then left the copper container without any wrapping.

- Why is it important to use the same amount of water each time you test a different material?
- Which material did you conclude was the best thermal insulator? Why?
- What does this tell you about the thermal conductivity of each material?
- What do you think makes bubble wrap and foam good thermal insulators? What do you think makes copper a poor thermal insulator?

CHECKIT!

1 Describe three features Olympic cyclists use to reduce unwanted energy transfers.

2 How is energy dissipated in a toaster?

3 Describe two advantages of reducing unwanted energy transfers from a car engine.

Efficiency

Devices and machines are designed to do specific jobs. A specific amount of **energy** needs to be transferred into a device so that it can do its job. This is called the total input energy.

But only some of the total input energy is transferred into the device in a useful way that lets it do its job.

The rest of the total input energy is **dissipated**. It gets **stored** in less useful ways. This is because all changes to a **system** result in some energy being dissipated.

The energy put in (total input energy transfer) compared with the useful energy given out (useful energy output transfer) is called the efficiency of the device or system.

$$\text{efficiency} = \frac{\text{useful output energy transfer}}{\text{total input energy transfer}}$$

We can also calculate efficiency using the useful **power** output and the total power input:

$$\text{efficiency} = \frac{\text{useful power output}}{\text{total power input}}$$

NAILIT!

Efficiency can only be a number between 0 and 1. So if you get something bigger than 1, check your equation and that you have put the right numbers into it.

NAILIT!

Make sure you can remember and use these equations.

WORKIT!

In a 100 W light bulb, 93 W of its power goes to increase the thermal energy store of the room. In a 11 W LED, only 1 W of its power goes to increase the thermal energy store of the room. Calculate the efficiency of both lights, and explain which light is more efficient. (4 marks)

The useful power output of the 100 W light bulb is only
100 W − 93 W = 7 W (1)
But the useful power output of the LED is 11 W − 1 W = 10 W.

So, the efficiency of each light is:

Efficiency (100 W light bulb) $= \dfrac{\text{useful power output}}{\text{total power output}} = \dfrac{7}{100} = 0.07$

$= 0.07 \times 100$

$= 7\%$ efficient (1)

Efficiency (11 W LED) $= \dfrac{\text{useful power output}}{\text{total power output}} = \dfrac{10}{11} = 0.91$

$= 0.91 \times 100$

$= 91\%$ efficient (1)

The LED is much more efficient than the 100 W light bulb because most of the total input energy is transferred in a useful way. (1)

> Raising the temperature of the room is not the job a light bulb is designed to do. So increasing the thermal energy store is an unwanted energy transfer.

MATHS SKILLS

Efficiency can also be written as a percentage. So if a device has an efficiency of 0.23, you can also say that it is 23% efficient. To get the percentage, just multiply the efficiency by 100.

H

Devices and systems can be made more efficient. In Higher Tier exams you could be asked to describe ways to increase the efficiency of an intended energy transfer. So:

- Think about what the 'job' of the system is and identify the associated energy transfer, i.e. the intended energy transfer.

- Identify the unwanted energy transfers and suggest ways to reduce them.

H

DO IT!

Take photos of different devices in your house and make a short narrated slideshow or video where you describe how unwanted energy transfers are, or could be, reduced.

Keeping track of how efficient appliances are, can save money

CHECK IT!

1 Why is only some of the total input energy transferred to a system in useful ways?

2 Look at the equation for efficiency. Why can the efficiency of a device never be more than 1?

3 Your body is about 25% efficient at transferring energy from the chemical store of the food you eat by mechanical work when you exercise. Why is this low efficiency an advantage if you are trying to lose weight?

National and global energy resources

Earth has many **energy** resources. Different **energy stores** are associated to energy resources and this energy can be shifted (or transferred) where it is needed.

Renewable energy resources can be replaced (replenished) as they are used. Examples of renewable energy resources are biofuel, wind, hydroelectricity, geothermal, the tides, the Sun and water waves.

Non-renewable energy resources cannot be replenished. If we keep using them, they will eventually run out. Examples of non-renewable energy resources are fossil fuels and nuclear fuels.

NAILIT!

Do not confuse 'replenished' with 'recycled'. **Replenished** means that when a resource is used, more of it is replacing it. **Recycled** means that one object or resource is **reused** in a useful way again.

Energy resource	Energy store	Renewable or non-renewable	Main uses	Reliability	Environmental impact
Fossil fuels (coal, oil and gas)	Chemical energy store	Non-renewable Estimated to run out by 2080	Transport Heating Generating electricity	Very reliable and high power output	Releases carbon dioxide, which is partly responsible for global warming
Nuclear fuel (mainly uranium)	Nuclear energy store	Non-renewable Estimated to be available for more than 200 years	Generating electricity	Very reliable and very high power output	Makes dangerous radioactive waste that needs to be buried underground for thousands of years
Biofuel	Chemical energy store	Renewable	Transport Heating Generating electricity	Very reliable and medium power output	Low negative impact because it is 'carbon neutral' (it releases the same amount of carbon dioxide as it absorbed when the organisms the fuel is made of were alive)
Wind	Kinetic energy store	Renewable	Generating electricity	Unreliable because it depends on the weather, and very low power output	Windmills take up big areas that could be used for farming Birds can be killed by windmill blades

Energy resource	Energy store	Renewable or non-renewable	Main uses	Reliability	Environmental impact
Hydroelectricity	Gravitational potential energy store	Renewable	Generating electricity	Very reliable and medium power output	Big areas need to be flooded to build dams, which can have a negative effect on the local ecosystem, landscape and people
Geothermal	Thermal energy store	Renewable	Generating electricity Heating	Reliable, but only available in some areas In some geothermal sites, the thermal energy store might empty out completely Medium power output	Very low negative impact
Tides	Kinetic energy store	Renewable	Generating electricity	Very reliable and potentially very high power output, but difficult to harness	Tidal barrages can negatively affect birds that feed on mud flats that are exposed when the tide goes out, and block sewage and other waste from being carried out to sea
Sun	Nuclear energy store	Renewable	Generating electricity Heating	Very unreliable because the weather, which dictates light levels, can be highly changeable. It is only available during daylight hours Low power output	Low negative impact, but big areas are needed to harness it
Water waves	Kinetic energy store	Renewable	Generating electricity	Unreliable because it depends on the weather Low power output	Very low negative impact

SNAP**IT!**

Take photos of the table of energy resources on the previous pages and use them to revise wherever you are.

STRETCH**IT!**

Fossil fuels, as well as being non-renewable, release harmful gases into our atmosphere and the environment, like carbon dioxide and sulfur dioxide. Fossil fuels still make up about 87% of the world's energy use.

How do you think these percentages have changed in the past 30 years? How could they change in the future?

Research the environmental, political, social, ethical and economic issues of using different energy resources.

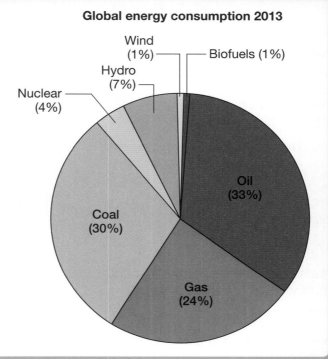

Global energy consumption 2013

Wind (1%)
Biofuels (1%)
Hydro (7%)
Nuclear (4%)
Oil (33%)
Coal (30%)
Gas (24%)

CHECK**IT!**

1 What is the difference between renewable and non-renewable energy resources?

2 What is one advantage of using fossil fuels to generate electricity?

3 Suggest one disadvantage of using the Sun to generate electricity in the UK.

1 Which of the following are renewable and non-renewable energy resources?

a Nuclear fuels

b Water waves

c Coal

d Biofuel

e Hydroelectricity

f The Sun

g Geothermal

h Oil

i The tides

j Natural gas

2 Rearrange the following equations to find m, e and h respectively:

a *kinetic energy = 0.5 × mass × (speed)²*

$$E_k = \frac{1}{2}mv^2$$

b *elastic potential energy = 0.5 × spring constant × (extension)²*

$$E_e = \frac{1}{2}ke^2$$

c *gravitational potential energy = mass × gravitational field strength × height*

$$E_p = mgh$$

3 In the equation *change in thermal energy = mass × specific heat capacity × temperature change* $[\Delta E = mc\Delta\theta]$ the temperature is normally expressed in degrees Celsius (°C). Explain why expressing $\Delta\theta$ in degrees kelvin (K) would not affect the results of your calculations.

4 a Describe the difference between lift A which lifts a 70 kg load up three floors in 20 seconds and lift B which can lift the same load up three floors in 15 seconds.

b Assuming the lifts are operated in the same building and that the power of lift B is 343 W, what is the height of each floor in this building? ($g = 9.8$ m/s²)

5 Two ice cubes are placed on two blocks of equal size, but different materials. One block is made of aluminium and the other block is made of plastic. Which ice cube will melt first? Explain why this happens.

6 A battery powered toy car has a total power input 1.5 W. The mass of the car is 520 g and reaches a top speed of 2.2 m/s. Calculate the percentage efficiency of the toy car.

Electricity

Standard circuit diagram symbols

A **switch** can break or complete an **electric circuit**. A switch allows a device to be used only when we need to, by switching it on or off.

switch (open)

switch (closed)

cell

battery

Cells and **batteries** are power supplies for a circuit. They provide the **potential difference** (p.d.), which drives the **charges** around the circuit. A battery is a collection of cells connected in **series** with each other.

NAILIT!

Make sure you know how to draw and interpret circuit diagrams.

A **lamp** has a very thin filament (wire), usually made of tungsten. This gets very hot when a **current** flows through it, so it glows and emits **visible light**.

lamp

A **fuse** is a safety component. It is made of a wire that has lower melting point than other components. This means that if too much current is flowing through the circuit, the wire in the fuse will melt, breaking the circuit and stopping the high current from flowing and damaging other components or devices on the circuit.

fuse

Voltmeters measure the potential difference (p.d.) across components in a circuit. They always need to be connected in series with other components. Voltmeters need to have a very big **resistance** so that hardly any current flows through them.

voltmeter

ammeter

Ammeters measure the current through a circuit. They always need to be connected in series with other components. The resistance of an ammeter needs to be as close to zero as possible so that the current reading is not affected by its presence in the circuit.

A **diode** lets current flow through it in one direction only. It is useful when we want to direct the current in some parts of the circuit but not in others. The diode points from +ve to –ve.

diode

LED

A **light-emitting diode** (LED) lets current flow through it in one direction only, just like a diode, but when current flows through an LED, it emits light.

Fixed **resistors** and variable resistors oppose (resist) the flow of current with a particular resistance. This means they can be used to set the current in a circuit to the value that we want. Fixed resistors have a fixed value of resistance. However, variable resistors can be set to different values of resistance within a particular range.

resistor

variable resistor

A **thermistor** is a resistor that changes its resistance when its temperature changes. Generally, the resistance of a thermistor decreases when its temperature increases.

thermistor

The resistance of a **light-dependent resistor** (LDR) changes when the amount of light shone on it changes. Normally, LDRs have very high resistance; when light is shone on them, their resistance drops a lot.

LDR

SNAP**IT!**

Make flash cards showing the standard circuit diagram symbols to test your knowledge of each component. Take pictures on your phone so you can revise on the go.

CHECK**IT!**

1 What is the main difference between a voltmeter and an ammeter?

2 Explain the main difference and similarity between LEDs and diodes.

3 What components would you use in a circuit that needs to switch on when it gets dark, but only when the current flows through it in one particular direction?

Electrical charge and current

MATHS SKILLS

You need to remember and be able to apply this equation.

An electric **current** is a rate of the flow of **charge**. Whenever a charge is flowing, there is a current.

So an electric current is a measure of the rate of flow of electrical charge over time.

We can calculate the electrical charge flowing through a point of a **circuit** in a given time using the equation:

charge flow = current × time $Q = I\,t$

- Q = charge flow (unit: **coulomb**, C)
- I = current (unit: **ampere**, or amp, A)
- t = time (unit: second, s)

For electrical charge to flow through a circuit, the circuit must be closed and at least one of its components must be a source of **potential difference** (p.d.).

In a single closed loop of a circuit, the current is the same at any point.

The free **electrons** in a circuit fill all wires and components of the circuit all the time, even when the circuit is broken (or open). So, when a potential difference is applied to a circuit, the charges (electrons) will all start flowing along the circuit at the same time, wherever they are in the circuit. That is why a light bulb lights up almost straight away after the switch is turned on.

The free electrons move inside the circuit at a speed of about 1 cm per minute, so if you had to wait for them to go from the **battery** to the light bulb every time you turned the switch on you would be in darkness for quite a long time.

SNAPIT!

Draw a flow chart to show what happens when the switch in a simple circuit containing a cell, a light bulb, a switch and wires in series is turned on. Take a photo of your flow chart to use as a revision tool.

Switch open
0.00 Amps

Switch closed
0.90 Amps

WORKIT!

A charge of 0.24 C flows through a **resistor** in a circuit over a time of 14 seconds. What is the current in the circuit? Write your answer in milliamps. (2 marks)

To find out the current (I), we need to rearrange the equation $Q = I\,t$ to $I = \dfrac{Q}{t}$.

So, $I = \dfrac{0.24}{14} = 0.017$ A. (1)

$0.017 × 1000 = 17$ mA (1) ◀ ─── Remember to convert your answer to milliamps 1A = 1000 mA

CHECKIT!

1 What is an electrical current?

2 Why does a light bulb light up almost straight away after a switch has been turned on?

3 How much charge flows through a light bulb in a circuit with 0.205 A current if the circuit is closed for 2 minutes and 33 seconds and then opened again?

Current, resistance and potential difference

The value of electrical current (I) in a circuit is determined by the value of **potential difference** (V) we choose for our power supply and by the value of the **resistance** (R) of the components we add to the circuit.

We can calculate p.d., resistance or electric current using the equation:

potential difference = current $\times$ resistance

$$V = IR$$

- V = potential difference, p.d. (unit: **volt**, V)
- I = current (unit: **ampere**, or amp, A)
- R = resistance (unit: **ohm**, Ω)

You cannot change electrical current (I) in a circuit directly, because its size depends on both the resistance (R) of the components and the potential difference (V) across those components.

> ## MATHS SKILLS
>
> You need to remember and be able to apply the equation above. The bigger the potential difference across the components of a circuit, the bigger the current. The bigger the resistance of the components, the smaller the current. We can get a better idea of this if we rearrange the equation to:
>
> $$I = \frac{V}{R}$$
>
> A good way to describe the relationship between I, V and R is to say that the current (I) is **directly proportional** to the potential difference (V) and **inversely proportional** to the resistance (R) at a constant temperature.

NAILIT!

You might have heard your teacher using the word 'voltage' to mean potential difference (p.d.), but only potential difference (or p.d.) will be used in questions.

DOIT!

Find out about conductive ink and how this can be used in special pens and printers to make 'DIY' circuit boards on paper.

Practical Skills

You should have done practical work to investigate how different components affect the resistance of electrical circuits.

How the length of a wire changes the resistance in a circuit

The **longer** the wire, the **bigger** the resistance. This makes sense because every component has a certain resistance, so adding a longer wire in **series** with the other components increased the resistance.

In this investigation, the wire had to be at a constant temperature.

Why was this important?

It is important because, if you had changed the length of the wire and the temperature together, you could not be sure which of these two changes caused a change in resistance. So the test would not have been fair.

How different combinations of resistors in series and parallel affect the resistance in the circuit

- Adding more resistors in series **increased** the resistance in the circuit.

- Adding more resistors in **parallel** decreased the resistance in the circuit.

In both investigations you need to be able to read **circuit diagrams** and know how to set up a circuit.

Make sure you know which way around the **ammeter** and **voltmeter** go. The ammeter is always in series with the components, and the voltmeter is always in parallel with the components.

Ammeter in series with resistors

Voltmeter in parallel with resistors

Ammeter in series with both resistors

Voltmeter in parallel with both resistors

CHECKIT!

1 What is the relationship between electric current, potential difference and resistance?

2 A current of 1.2 A flows through an appliance of resistance 1.3 kΩ. What is the p.d. across the appliance?

3 A torch uses two 1.5 V AA cells. When it is switched on, the current through the light bulb is 150 mA. Calculate the resistance of the light bulb in the torch.

Resistors

The electric **current** through an **ohmic conductor** (at constant temperature) is **directly proportional** to the **potential difference** across the ohmic conductor (**resistor**).

So the **resistance** stays constant as the current changes.

This means that a graph of current against potential difference (called an I–V graph) for an ohmic conductor is a straight line going through the origin (through zero), like the graph to below.

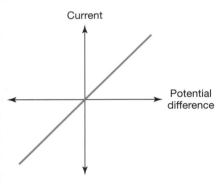

Current against potential difference for an ohmic conductor

MATHS SKILLS

You should know that the equation of a straight line is $y = mx + c$ and that $I = \dfrac{V}{R} = \dfrac{1}{R}V + 0$

So, if R is constant:

$y = I$

$m = \dfrac{1}{R} \rightarrow$ the gradient of your graph is $\dfrac{1}{R}$, and $R = \dfrac{1}{Gradient}$

$x = V$

$c = 0$ because the line goes through 0.

I–V characteristics of non-ohmic components

Non-ohmic components like **lamps**, **diodes**, **light-emitting diodes** (LEDs), **light-dependent resistors** (LDRs), and **thermistors** do not have constant resistance. Their resistance changes when the current through them changes.

Filament lamp

Filament bulbs contain a thin coil of wire, this is called the filament. When an electric current passes through the filament it heats up and emits light. When the temperature of the filament in a lamp increases due to the electric current passing through it, its resistance increases too. The graph to the right shows that the current is not directly proportional to the voltage.

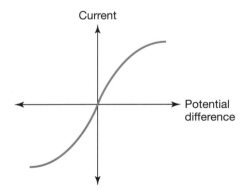

Current against potential difference for a filament lamp

STRETCHIT!

Draw the I–V graph for a filament lamp. Show in which parts of the graph the resistance is fairly constant, and where the temperature of the filament starts to increase.

Hint: where the resistance is constant, the graph should look like the I–V graph for an ohmic conductor, in other words, it should be linear.

Diode and LED

The *I–V* graph for a diode and an LED is very similar – see graph to the right. Diodes and LEDs both let current flow in only one direction. This means that the resistance of diodes and LEDs is very high in the reverse direction.

Thermistor

The resistance of a thermistor decreases when its temperature increases.

Thermistors are used in thermostats in your home to 'tell' your heating system when to turn on/off, or in your computer to turn on its fan when it is getting too hot.

LDR

The resistance of an LDR decreases when the amount (intensity) of **light** shone on it increases.

LDRs are used in street lamps to turn them on at night.

Current against potential difference for a diode or an LED

Practical Skills

You should have done practical work to investigate the *I–V* graphs of ohmic conductors (resistors), filament lamps, and diodes (the graphs on this page and on page 32).

Remember that to measure the resistance of an electrical component, you measure the current through it and the potential difference across it.

You need to be able to draw and use this **circuit diagram** when investigating how the resistance of a component changes.

You also need to be able to use *I–V* graphs to describe the properties and functions of a circuit component and to say whether each property is **linear** or **non-linear**.

Just remember that the **ohmic** component of an *I–V* graph is **linear**, and the others that are not a straight line are non-linear.

But remember that some parts of *I–V* graphs can be both linear and non-linear. This means that a component can be linear over a particular range of potential difference, but become non-linear for another range, like the filament lamp that is nearly linear for some values of potential difference.

DO IT!

Stretch your legs perpendicularly to your body and imagine your body to be the y-axis and the line formed by your legs as the x-axis. Now use your hands to make the shape of the graphs for each of the components in this topic.

CHECK IT!

1 Describe the relationship between current through and potential difference across an ohmic conductor.

2 Look at the *I–V* graph of a diode and describe how its resistance changes as

the potential difference goes from negative values to positive and increasing values.

3 Describe the difference between a linear and a non-linear relationship between two variables.

Series and parallel circuits

Electrical **circuits** can be wired in **series** or **parallel**. Circuits might have some electrical components in series with each other *and* some in parallel with others, which can be very useful.

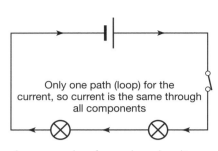

Only one path (loop) for the current, so current is the same through all components

An example of a series circuit

For components in series with each other:

- All components are in the same loop.

- The **current** is the same through each component.

- The total **potential difference** from the power supply is shared between the components.

- The total **resistance** of all components is the sum of the resistance from each component $R_{total} = R_1 + R_2$.

- The current through all components can be changed by adding or removing components (for example, adding a resistor in series with a component would decrease the current through that component).

WORKIT!

The diagram shows two 40 Ω light bulbs in series with a 1.5 V cell and two ammeters. What value of current will ammeter A_1 and ammeter A_2 measure? (2 marks)

The light bulbs are in series, so their combined resistance (total resistance) is

$R_{total} = 40 + 40 = 80\ \Omega$ (1)

The current through both ammeters and light bulbs is:

$$I = \frac{V}{R}$$

$$I = \frac{1.5}{80} = 0.019\,A\ (1)$$

This is a series circuit (single loop), so the current is the same in all parts of the circuit.

V = 1.5V

A_2

A_1

$A_1 = A_2$

An example of a parallel circuit

components can be operated separately

For components in parallel with each other:

- Each component is individually connected to the power supply in its own loop – this means that the potential difference is the same across each component.

- The total current through the circuit is the sum of the currents through each branch/loop of the circuit.

- The total resistance of two components in parallel is less than the smallest resistance from individual components.

- Switching individual loops (circuits) in parallel on/off will not affect other loops (houses are wired with parallel circuits so that we can turn different appliances on/off separately from each other).

NAIL IT!

At GCSE, you do not need to calculate the total resistance of two resistors joined in parallel. You just need to explain why adding more components in parallel will decrease the total resistance of the circuit.

The potential difference across each branch in a parallel circuit is the same. So each loop acts as an individual circuit with the power supply. The individual currents from each loop are $I = V/R$. These all sum up before the circuit splits in individual loops and where the loops join together again at the other terminal of the power supply. This means that the total current through the circuit increases, and because $V = I \times R$, the total resistance in the circuit must decrease.

DO IT!

Fill your lungs with air, and blow through two straws 'in series' (one straw stuck inside the other as in the picture).

Then, put the two straws side by side 'in parallel', and empty the air from your lungs through them.

Which setting emptied your lungs more quickly? How does this compare with electrical components in series and in parallel?

WORKIT!

In the circuit shown in the diagram, the current measured by the ammeter is 0.5 A. Resistor R_1 has a resistance of $15\,\Omega$. What is the current through R_1 and R_2, and what is the resistance of R_2? (3 marks)

The potential difference is the same across both resistors (6 V), so we can find the current through R_1 using the relationship

$$I = \frac{V}{R} \rightarrow I_1 = \frac{V}{R_1}$$

$$I_1 = \frac{6}{15} = 0.4\,A \ (1)$$

$$I_{total} = I_1 + I_2 \rightarrow I_2 = I_{total} - I_1 \longleftarrow$$

The total current through the circuit is the sum of the currents through the individual resistors.

$$I_2 = 0.5 - 0.4 = 0.1\,A \ (1)$$

Now we can calculate R_2 using $R = \frac{V}{I} \rightarrow R_2 = \frac{V}{I_2}$

$$R_2 = \frac{6}{0.1} = 60\,\Omega \ (1)$$

STRETCH IT!

Christmas lights are wired in series with each other. Why could it be dangerous if they were wired in parallel?

CHECK IT!

1 Look at the series circuits in the Work It! example and state what potential difference there is across each of the two light bulbs.

2 Explain why the potential difference across each component in a parallel circuit is the same.

3 A 9 V battery is connected in series with two resistors R_1 and R_2. The resistance of R_1 is twice as large as the resistance of R_2. What is the potential difference across R_1 and R_2 individually?

Mains electricity

dc and ac current

Most **circuits** you use in school are connected to a **direct current** (dc) **battery**/power supply. This means that the **potential difference** provided by the battery does not change in direction (sign) or in value.

Steady dc
from a battery or regulated power supply.
This is ideal for electronic circuits

To transfer **energy** efficiently across the country from power stations to homes, schools, and workplaces, an **alternating current** (ac) potential difference must be used. This is why the **mains electricity** in your home is ac. An ac potential difference continually alternates in direction (sign) and changes value.

The ac supply in the mains electricity in your home has a **frequency** of 50 Hz and a potential difference of 230 V.

SNAPIT!

Write the difference between ac and dc current and take a photo of it to revise later.

ac from a power supply

Mains electricity

Most appliances are connected to the mains electricity with a **three-core cable** plug. To make them easy to tell apart, the **insulation** around each of the three wires is colour coded.

Rubber or plastic case · Earth Wire Green/Yellow · Fuse · Neutral Wire Blue · Live Wire Brown · Cable grip · Brass Pins

- **Live wire** – *brown*. This carries the ac potential difference from the power supply. The potential difference between the live wire and the earth wire is about 230 V.

- **Neutral wire** – *blue*. This completes the circuit. It is at, or close to, the same potential as the earth wire (0 V).

- **Earth wire** – *green and yellow stripes*. This is a safety wire. It is at 0 V potential. It carries **current** only if a **fault** happens in the circuit, to stop the appliance operating (stop it becoming 'live').

NAILIT!

If a fault happens and the live wire becomes connected to the case around an appliance, the earth wire will let a big current flow through the live wire and the earth wire. This 'overflow' of current will heat the **fuse**, which melts away, breaking the circuit. This is why exposed metal parts of appliances should always be connected to the earth wire – to make sure the current does not flow through anyone using it, which is very dangerous.

Circuits in the mains electricity supply are wired in **parallel**. This means that the live wire of an appliance could still be connected (and dangerous) even if a **switch** in the mains circuit is open (off).

CHECKIT!

1 Explain why the live wire in the cable of a kettle could still be dangerous even if the electric kettle is turned off.

2 What is the difference between ac and dc?

3 How would the current through an appliance designed to work in the UK be affected if you used the same device in the USA, where the mains potential difference is 110 V?

Electrical power, energy transfers in appliances and the National Grid

Power

The **power** of an electrical device or appliance depends on the **potential difference** across the appliance and the current through it.

We can calculate the power transferred in an appliance using the equations:

power = potential difference × current
P = VI

power = (current)² × resistance)
P = I² R

- P = **power** (unit: **watt**, W)
- V = **potential difference** (unit: **volt**, V)
- I = **current** (unit: **ampere**, or **amp**, A)
- R = **resistance** (unit: **ohm**, Ω)

The power of an appliance is the rate of **energy** (unit: **joule**, J) transferred by the appliance. In other words, how much energy is transferred each second.

So, a 40 W light bulb transfers 40 J of energy each second.

MATHS SKILLS

You need to recall and apply these two equations. If you remember that $V = IR$, you can see how both equations are the same. In fact, we have substituted IR (V) instead of V in $P = VI$ to get $P = I²R$.

NAILIT!

Always remember that the potential difference from your mains electricity (household sockets in the UK) is 230 V.

WORKIT!

What current will flow through an 800 W microwave oven when it is operating? (1 mark)

By rearranging the power equation $P = VI$, we get

$$I = \frac{P}{V} = \frac{800}{230}$$

$$= 3.5 \text{ A (1)}$$

 Remember that the mains potential difference is 230 V.

SNAPIT!

Take photos of the power labels from at least three of your home appliances. Then try to calculate the current flowing through them. How does their stored energy change?

NAILIT!

You need to be able to describe, and give examples of, how the power ratings for some home appliances relate to changes in stored energy when you are using them.

Energy transfers in circuits

Every time a **charge** flows in a **circuit**, electrical work is done.

The amount of energy transferred by an appliance changes depending on:

- the time the appliance is operating
- the power of the appliance.

We can calculate the amount of energy transferred by electrical work using the equations:

$$\text{energy transferred} = \text{power} \times \text{time}$$
$$E = Pt$$

$$\text{energy transferred} = \text{charge flow} \times \text{potential difference}$$
$$E = QV$$

- E = energy transferred (unit: **joule**, J)
- P = **power** (unit: **watt**, W)
- t = time (unit: second, s)
- Q = **charge flow** (unit: **coulomb**, C)
- V = **potential difference** (unit: **volt**, V)

WORKIT!

A 9 V battery is used in series with a 1200 Ω resistor and a 340 Ω resistor. How much energy is transferred by the resistors if the switch is closed for 2 minutes? (3 marks)

The total resistance in the circuit is $R_{total} = R_1 + R_2 = 1200 + 340 = 1540\ \Omega$

$I = \dfrac{V}{R} = \dfrac{9}{1540}$ ◄—— Rearrange $V = IR$

$\quad = 0.006\,A$ (1)

The total power of both the resistors is

$P = VI = 9 \times 0.006$

$\qquad = 0.053\ W$

The circuit is operating for time

$t = 2\ minutes = 60 \times 2 = 120\ s$ (1)

So, the energy transferred in that time is

$E = Pt = 0.053 \times 120$

$\qquad = 6.3\ J$ (1) ◄—— Don't forget to put units in your answer!

Everyday appliances are designed to transfer energy in **useful** ways. For example, energy is shifted from the chemical store in a power station to the **kinetic** store in a drill connected to the **mains** via electrical working, or to the **thermal** store in the heating element of a kettle via electrical working.

The National Grid

Energy is transferred from power stations to homes, schools and workplaces through a system of **transformers**, cables and pylons called the **National Grid**.

There are two types of transformers:

- **step up**

- **step down**.

A transformer changes the value of potential difference in a circuit, but it keeps the electrical power the same.

Transformers can work only if the current is **alternating current** (ac).

Step-up transformers increase the potential difference across the circuit they are connected to.

1 This decreases the current through the circuit.

2 Fewer heating effects.

3 Less energy dissipated (wasted).

Step-down transformers decrease the potential difference across the circuit they are connected to. This increases the current through the circuit → useful for industrial and home appliances that need bigger currents.

NAILIT!

Some questions may give an amount of power in terms of megawatts (see question 3 in the Check It! below). Remember that a megawatt (MW) is a unit of power equal to one million watts.

The National Grid

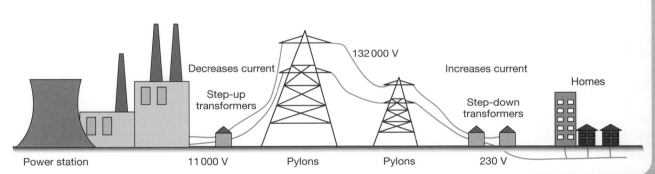

Power station   11 000 V   Pylons   Pylons   230 V

CHECK**IT!**

1 What does the power of an appliance depend on?

2 Describe the energy transfers and the changes in **energy stores** when a car engine is working.

3 The safety guidelines for laser pointers are that their power should not be greater than 1 mW. If a safe laser pointer uses two AAA cells, which each have a voltage of 1.5, what will be the current through its laser diode?

Static charge and electric fields

DO IT!

Cut some paper into small pieces and spread them on your table. Then, rub a balloon against a woolly jumper, or your hair, and put it closer to the bits of paper. Describe what you are observing using the term **non-contact** force.

When some **insulating** materials are rubbed against each other, they can become **electrically charged**. **Electrons** (negatively charged) move from one material onto the other material. Positive charges are left on the material that lost electrons.

Only the electrons move. The positive charges stay in their place (they don't move).

* The material that gains electrons becomes negatively charged.
* The material that loses electrons is left with an equal positive charge.

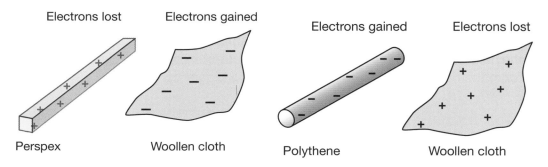

Electrons lost — Perspex   Electrons gained — Woollen cloth   Electrons gained — Polythene   Electrons lost — Woollen cloth

NAIL IT!

Electric field lines are always drawn with the direction of the force that a positive charge would experience in that field. In other words, an attractive force if the charge generating the field is negative, and a repulsive force if the charge generating the field is positive.

When two charged objects are brought close together, they exert a **force** on each other as a consequence of Newton's third law, which is discussed on page 89.

Like charges repel each other (for example, positive and positive). Opposite charges (positive and negative) attract each other.

The forces between charges are an example of non-contact forces.

Static electricity can cause small shocks and sparks on skin

Sometimes rubbing materials together can build up big charges. For example, if you wear a woolly jumper against the seat of a car. When this happens, big **potential differences** can form across these materials. If they get near a **conductor**, air molecules might lose electrons to the positively charged material. So there will be positively charged **ionised** air molecules between the material and the conductor. The high potential difference and the ionised air between the material and the conductor make a path for the electrons. They jump between the conductor and the charged material, and cause a spark. This is an effect of static electricity.

Electric fields

A charged object generates an electric field around itself.

An electric field is a force field that can be felt by another electric charge that is inside the field.

The further away from the charged object, the weaker the electric field. So if you place a second charged object in its field, the force experienced by the second object gets weaker the further away it is from the first object.

The electric field from an isolated charged sphere can be drawn like the diagrams on the right, depending on whether the charge of the sphere is positive or negative, with field lines drawn as straight lines coming from the centre of the sphere.

The non-contact forces between charged objects can be explained with electric fields. In fact, any charged object will generate a field of 'force lines' that can affect any other charged object placed in a region reached by the electric field.

Electric fields can also explain why sparks are formed between two electrically charged objects. As concentrations of opposite charges build on two objects close to each other, the electric field between the two objects increases until the forces on the negative charges become strong enough to drag them away from the negatively charged object onto the positively charged object.

Electric fields around charged spheres

 ## SNAP**IT!**

Take a picture of the electric field diagrams above to revise from later.

DO**IT!**

Think about how the forces in electric fields change. Come up with some examples and describe the forces present.

 ### STRETCH**IT!**

The electric field generated by a charged object gets weaker as we move further away from the object because the force field lines get more spread out. So there are fewer and fewer field lines 'hitting' it.

 # CHECK**IT!**

1 When two insulators are rubbed against each other, what moves and what stays stationary?

2 How are sparks of static electricity formed?

3 What direction would the force on a negative charge have if it were placed in the electric field of a negatively charged sphere?

Electricity

1 Match the component with the correct symbol and the symbol with the correct description.

Light Dependent Resistor	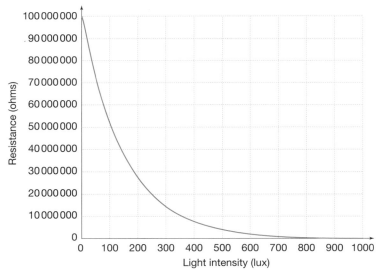	It lets current flow through it in one direction only, but when current flows through it, it emits light.
Light Emitting Diode		It is a collection of cells connected in series with each other.
Lamp		It opposes the flow of current with a certain resistance and it can be set to different values of resistance within a specific range.
Variable Resistor		It is a resistor that changes its resistance depending on how much light is shone on it.
Battery		It is a resistor that changes its resistance depending on its temperature.
Thermistor		It has a very thin filament (wire), usually made of tungsten, which gets very hot when a current flows through it, so it glows and emits visible light.

2 a What is electric current?

  b Explain why an ammeter needs to have resistance as close to zero as possible.

3 Rearrange the equation **charge flow = current × time** to the formula that would allow you to calculate the time taken by a certain amount of charge to flow through a point in a circuit.

4 a From the relationship $V = IR$ show what the gradient of a graph of Current vs Potential Difference would be.

  b Using the same relationship what would be the current flowing through a 12 kΩ resistor when a p.d. of 9 V is applied across it?

  c An electronic circuit connected to an LDR is set to turn a set of garden lights on when the resistance of the LDR increases beyond 40 MΩ. The graph to the right shows how the resistance of this LDR changes with light intensity. What is the minimum light intensity needed for the garden lights to automatically switch off at dawn?

  d A light bulb of resistance 2.5 kΩ is connected to three 1.5 V cells in series. What charge would flow through the bulb, if the circuit is switched on for 1.5 minutes?

Particle model

Particle model and density of materials

The **density** of a material tells us how much **mass** of that material is in one unit of **volume** ($1\ m^3$).

Materials denser than water will sink. Materials less dense than water will float.

We can calculate the density of a material using the equation:

$$density = \frac{mass}{volume}$$

$$\rho = \frac{m}{V}$$

- ρ = density (unit: **kilogram** per metre cubed, kg/m^3)
- m = mass (unit: kilogram, kg)
- V = volume (unit: **metre** cubed, m^3)

The particle model

Everything is made of particles (atoms and molecules). Materials that have more massive particles that are closer together are more dense than other materials.

The same material can change density as it **changes state**. For example, ice is made of water molecules that are in a **solid state**. The solid state of water is less dense than its **liquid state** (ice molecules are spread out over a bigger volume than water molecules). This is why ice floats in water.

Molecules of water
(liquid state)

Molecules of water as ice
(solid state)

Most materials expand when the temperature increases, so become less dense. The red water in the image to the right is at much higher temperature than the cold (blue) water at the bottom, so the red dyed water floats on top of the blue dyed water.

NAILIT!

You need to recall and apply this equation. If you struggle to remember which way around the mass and volume go in the equation, think of the units of density, kg/m^3, which is a mass divided by a volume.

You might be asked to calculate the volume of regular shapes. For example, the volume of a cube is
$V = l \times l \times l = l^3$,
or in other words the length of its side multiplied by itself three times.

DOIT!

Think about what you would see as the red liquid cools down.

SNAPIT!

Find a small irregular object denser than water and drop it gently inside a measuring jug filled to the 300 ml mark with water. Take a photo of the jug before and after adding your object and calculate the density of your object in kg/m³.

WORKIT!

What is the density of the irregular rock in the diagram? (2 marks)

Remember to put mass into kg.

The mass of the rock is $m = 25\ g = 0.025\ kg$, and its volume is the difference in the volumes recorded in the measuring cylinder before and after dropping in the rock,

$V = 10\ cm^3 = 0.00001\ m^3$ (1)

So, using the density equation, we get

$\rho = \dfrac{m}{V} = 0.0025/0.00001$

$\qquad = 2500\ kg/m^3$ (1)

Practical Skills

You might have used micrometers and vernier callipers to measure the dimensions of regular objects and to calculate their volume in density investigations.

Reading vernier and micrometer scales can be tricky.

The Vernier scale in the diagram reads 2.6 mm.

The 0 mark on the lower scale is between 2 mm and 3 mm on the upper scale, so we know that the vernier calliper is measuring an object that is 2 mm and something wide. To find out the tenth of millimetres measured by the calliper, we need to check that the mark on the lower 0–10 scale aligns exactly with one of the marks on the top scale. In our diagram, this is mark 6, so the reading is 2.6 mm, or 0.0026 m.

Most micrometers can measure objects' thicknesses and diameters to the nearest 100th mm (0.01 mm). A full turn of the thimble measures a length of 0.5 mm.

So, you first read the numbers on the sleeve (in our example, 5.50 mm).

Then, read which mark on the thimble aligns with the middle line on the sleeve (in our example, 0.12 mm).

Finally, add the two readings together (5.50 + 0.12 = 5.62 mm).

Can you convert all these readings to cm or m?

Sleeve reading   = 5.50 mm
Thimble reading   = 12 divisions
                           = 0.12 mm
Total reading   = 5.62 mm

✓ CHECKIT!

1 What does the density of a material depend on?

2 The density of the element mercury is 13 534 kg/m³. What volume would 2.3 kg of mercury have?

3 0.250 kg of fresh water has a volume of 250 cm³. The average density of the human body is 985 kg/m³. Explain (with calculations) why a person would float better in the Dead Sea than in a fresh water lake, knowing that 0.250 kg of Dead Sea water has a volume of about 202 cm³.

Changes of state and internal energy

Changes of state

The mass of a substance is always conserved when it changes state of matter, i.e. the total mass **before** the change is equal to the total mass **after** the change.

Changes of state are reversible which means that the material gets back to its original state, if the change is reversed.

When a substance changes state its internal energy changes too.

Internal energy

The total energy in the kinetic and potential stores associated with the particles that make up a system (their movement and interactions) is the internal energy of that system.

Heating a system changes the energy stored within the system by increasing the energy associated with the particles that make up the system.

This increase in internal energy either raises the temperature of the system or causes a change of state.

Specific latent heat

The **latent heat** is the **energy** needed for a substance to change state.

When a substance changes state, the energy supplied changes the internal energy of the system (the **energy stored**), but not its temperature.

This is why heating and cooling curves for different substances show that the temperature remains **constant** during a change of state.

MATHS SKILLS

In this topic you will need the equation to calculate the change in thermal **energy** of a **system** again. This depends on the **specific heat capacity** of a substance (page 15).

change in = mass × specific × temperature
thermal energy   heat capacity   change

$$\Delta E = mc\,\Delta\theta$$

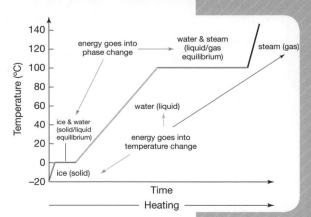

These graphs show state change compared to temperature change

The **specific latent heat** of a **material** is the amount of **energy** needed for 1 kg of that substance to **change state** (without a change in temperature).

SNAPIT!

Take a photo of the cooling and heating graphs on the previous page and keep it with you to revise their features wherever you are.

The equation to find the energy needed to change the state of a substance is:

energy for a change of state = mass × specific latent heat

$$E = mL$$

- E = energy (unit: **joules**, J)
- m = **mass** (unit: **kilogram**, kg)
- L = specific latent heat (unit: **joules per kilogram**, J/kg)

Specific latent heat of fusion – change of state from solid to liquid.

Specific latent heat of vaporisation – change of state from liquid to vapour.

WORKIT!

108 800 J are supplied to 320 g of ice at 0°C for it to melt completely. Calculate the specific latent heat of fusion of water.

The mass of the ice is

$m = 320 \text{ g} = 0.320 \text{ kg}$.

$L = \dfrac{E}{m} = \dfrac{108\,800}{0.320}$

$= 340\,000 \text{ J/kg}$

Use the equation $E = mL$ and rearrange

CHECKIT!

1 What is the difference between specific heat capacity and specific latent heat?

2 How would the sections where the ice is melting and the water is boiling in the heating curve above change if a larger amount of water were used, but the same power were provided to the system over time?

3 The specific latent heat of vaporisation of alcohol is 896 kJ/kg. How much energy needs to be supplied to 2.3 kg of alcohol for it to completely evaporate?

Particle model and pressure

Particle motion in a gas

The particles of a **gas** always move with **random** motion. This means they move in all directions and at different speeds (random **velocity**).

The temperature of a gas depends on the average **kinetic energy** of its particles.

For a gas at constant **volume**, increasing the temperature will increase the **pressure** exerted by the gas. This is because the gas particles collide against (hit) each other and the walls of their container with a bigger average **force**.

So, the higher the temperature of a gas (at constant volume), the higher its pressure.

A pressure cooker works by keeping most of the steam from boiling water inside the fixed volume of the container. So, as the temperature increases, the pressure increases too. Temperatures higher than 100°C can be reached, and so the food cooks faster.

Low pressure   High pressure

This image shows how particles move at different pressures

The gas particles on the right have more kinetic energy than those on the left. So, the gas on the right is at a higher temperature.

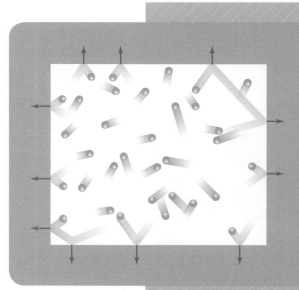

Pressure cookers reach higher temperatures so food cooks faster

Pressure in gases

Gas particles keep colliding against (hitting) the walls of their container. Each collision exerts a tiny force on the walls of the container, but there are lots and lots of particles colliding at high velocities. So, if we add together all the collisions, we can measure a net force produced by the pressure perpendicular (at right angles, 90°) to the wall of the container, or to any other surface that the gas is in contact with. The image on the right shows how gas particles behave within a container.

If the temperature of a gas stays constant, but its volume changes, its pressure changes too.

The bigger the volume of a gas (at constant temperature), the lower its pressure.

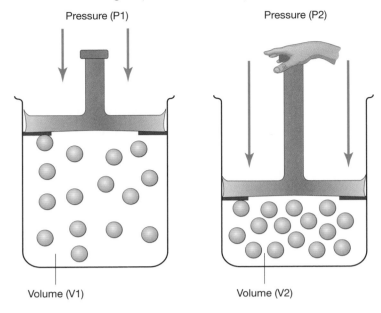

Pressure (P1)   Pressure (P2)

Volume (V1)   Volume (V2)

For a gas at the same temperature (same average kinetic energy):

- In a bigger volume, fewer collisions will happen per second. This is because there is more space for the gas particles to move around. So the pressure of the gas decreases. We say that the gas 'expanded'.

- In a smaller volume, more collisions will happen per second. This is because each particle has less space to move before it hits a wall. So the pressure of the gas increases. We say that the gas is 'compressed'.

The equation linking the volume and pressure of a gas kept at constant mass and temperature is:

$$pressure \times volume = constant$$
$$[pV = constant]$$

- p = pressure (unit: **pascal**, Pa)
- V = volume (unit: **metre** cubed, m^3)

WORKIT!

A diver is exploring the sea bed at a depth where the water pressure is 3.5×10^5 Pa. At that depth, the air bubbles that come out of her mouth have a volume of 1.7 cm^3. The pressure at the surface of the water is about 1.0×10^5 Pa. What will be the volume of the bubbles at the surface (assuming the temperature of the air inside the bubbles stays the same)? (3 marks)

First convert the volume to m^3

$1.7 \text{ cm}^3 = 1.7 \times 10^{-6} \text{ m}^3$ (1)

Now use the equation pV = constant

$P_1 V_1 = P_2 V_2 \rightarrow V_1 = \dfrac{P_1 V_1}{P_2}$ (1)

$$= \frac{3.5 \times 10^5 \times 1.7 \times 10^{-6}}{1.0 \times 10^5}$$

$$= 6.0 \times 10^{-6} \text{ m}^3 \text{ (1)}$$

Increasing the pressure of a gas

Work done is the transfer of energy by a force.

Applying a force on the particles of a gas increases the **internal energy** of the gas.

For example, if you use a pump to force air into a car's tyre, you increase the number of particles in the tyre and the average velocity of the air particles. So you increase the average kinetic energy of the air particles, or in other words, you increase the temperature of the gas.

> Remember that everything is made of particles, and particles are atoms and molecules (see page 43).

> **DO IT!**
>
> Summarise the content in this subtopic using no more than 50 words.

 STRETCH IT!

Look at this thermal image. Notice how just a few pushes with the foot pump increases the temperature of the air inside the tube.

Temperature in the tube before pumping ~16.7 °C

The temperature in the tube increased after a few pumps ~18.1 °C

CHECK IT!

1 Describe how the particles of a gas move.

2 Explain why pV might not be constant when the volume of a bicycle tyre is increased by pumping air into it with a foot pump.

3 A gas is contained inside a sealed syringe with a movable piston at an initial volume V_1 and initial pressure p_1. If the piston of the syringe is moved to a final volume $V_2 = 3 V_1$, what will be the difference between p_1 and the final pressure p_2?

1 a What are the units of density?

b The density of olive oil is $\rho_o = 812$ kg/m³ and the density of ethanol is $\rho_o = 785$ kg/m³.

   i Which fluid will float on top of the other, if they are both poured in a glass cylinder?

   ii What is the ratio of the mass of ethanol and the mass of oil ($m_e : m_o$) for an equal volume of ethanol and oil?

c The equation for the volume of a cylinder is $\pi r^2 h$. What is the density of a cylinder of steel of height 12 cm, diameter 24 mm and mass 0.437 kg?

2 a What changes of state are associated with latent heat of fusion and latent heat of vaporisation?

b A toy soldier made of tin 185 g, is melted in a fire. The specific latent heat of fusion for tin is 59 000 J/kg. Calculate the energy transferred to increase the internal energy of the tin when the toy soldier melts.

3 Complete the boxes in the graph below to label the different areas of the cooling curve with reference to change of state.

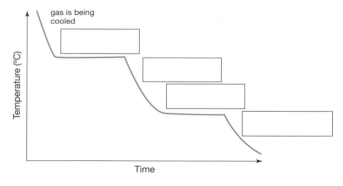

4 Explain why increasing the temperature of a gas in a gas cylinder causes the pressure of the gas to increase as well. Use the particle model of matter in your answer.

5 The image below shows the same syringe with trapped air inside it in two different situations – in hot water and in icy water. Explain why the volume of air inside the syringe is different in the two situations.

Hot water   Ice water

6 The volume of air trapped in a syringe at room temperature is measured to be 20 ml. The piston is very slowly pulled to allow the air inside the syringe to expand to 55 ml. The piston is then held in that position.

a Calculate the pressure of air inside the syringe when the volume is 55 ml, knowing that atmospheric air pressure is 101 325 Pa.

b Which assumption did you have to make to complete your calculation in part a?

Atomic structure

The structure of the atom

Atoms are the building blocks of matter. They have a very small radius (1×10^{-10} m).

Atoms have a positively charged nucleus, which has a tiny radius – smaller than 1/10 000 the radius of an atom.

The nucleus is made of neutrons (neutral particles) and protons (positive particles).

Electrons are negatively charged particles that orbit the nucleus. As the radius of these orbits (or electron clouds) is much bigger than the radius of the nucleus, most of the volume of an atom is empty space.

Electrons are arranged at different energy levels (different distances) from the nucleus. Electrons can move further from or closer to the nucleus by taking in (absorbing) or giving out (emitting) electromagnetic radiation.

- When an electron **absorbs** electromagnetic radiation, it will move to a **higher** energy level (further from the nucleus).

- When an electron **emits** electromagnetic radiation, it will move to a **lower** energy level (closer to the nucleus).

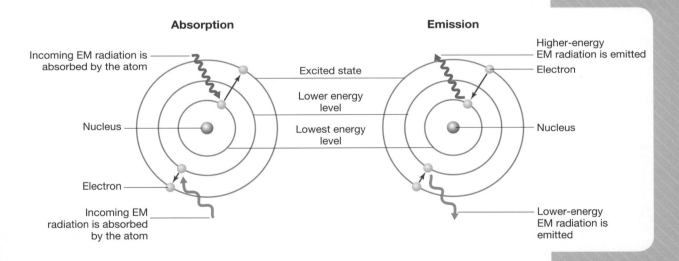

Mass number, atomic number and isotopes

The number of electrons and protons in an atom is the same, so the overall **electrical charge** of an atom is zero.

Atoms of the same element have the same number of protons. This is the atomic number of the element. For example, the atomic number of carbon is six because all carbon atoms have six protons in their nucleus.

The sum of the number of protons and neutrons in an atom is the **mass number** of the atom.

The atomic and mass numbers can be represented like this:

(Mass number)   23
(Atomic number) 11 **Na**

The same element can have different isotopes. These are atoms that have the same atomic number, but different mass numbers. This means that they have the same number of protons, but different numbers of neutrons. An example is below showing the three isotopes of hydrogen:

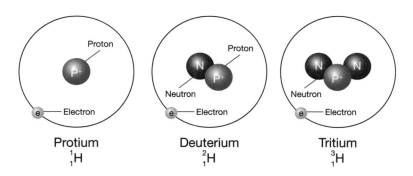

| Protium | Deuterium | Tritium |
| $^{1}_{1}H$ | $^{2}_{1}H$ | $^{3}_{1}H$ |

Sometimes atoms can lose some outer electrons, so the atoms become positively charged ions.

SNAPIT!

Take a picture on your phone of the ways to find the atomic number, mass number and number of neutrons.

Number of protons = atomic number = mass number − number of neutrons

Number of neutrons = mass number − atomic number

Mass number = number of neutrons + atomic number

CHECKIT!

1 What is the overall charge of an atom that has lost two outer electrons?

2 Uranium-238 has a mass number of 238 and atomic number of 92. What is the number of neutrons and protons in its nuclei?

3 The radius of an atom is bigger than the radius of its nucleus by how many orders of magnitude?

Developing a model of the atom

The flow chart below shows some of the different discoveries that scientists have made to create the model of the atom that we use today.

As new discoveries are made and checked using experiments, scientists might suggest even more accurate models of the atom in the future.

SNAPIT!

Make a copy of this flowchart and take a picture with your phone, so that you can revise the development of the model of the atom wherever you are.

Before the discovery of the electron — Greek philosophers believed that the atom was the most basic building block of all things, and that it could not be divided into smaller components.

Thompson's atomic model (1897) — the electron was discovered and the plum pudding model was developed. This suggested that the atom is a sphere of positive charge with negative electrons embedded in it, like raisins in a plum pudding.

Sphere of positive charge — Electron

Rutherford's model (1912)— alpha particles (positive nuclei of helium) were shot at high speed at gold atoms. Some went through undisturbed, some were deflected slightly, but some were bounced back at very large angles. This suggested that most of the mass of an atom is concentrated in a very small, positively charged nucleus, with electrons orbiting around it.

Gold Foil

Detecting Screen   Slit

Chadwick proves the existence of neutrons (1932) — the mass of nuclei was too large to be made only of protons, James Chadwick proved another neutral particle called a neutron is inside the nucleus of atoms with the protons.

Discovery of the proton (1919) — more experiments showed that the charge of a nucleus could be divided into a whole number of smaller charges called protons, all with the same positive charge.

Bohr's energy levels (1913) — Rutherford's model was adapted by showing that electrons could only orbit the nucleus of an atom at specific distances (radii). This was important because this new model agreed with experimental measurements.

Electron
Shell
Positive charged nucleus
Energy levels

x
$2x$
$3x$

NAILIT!

Remember that the development of a model of the atom is a good example of how scientific methods and theories change over time.

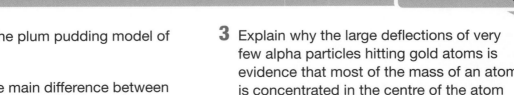

CHECKIT!

1 Describe the plum pudding model of the atom.

2 What is the main difference between Rutherford's nuclear model of the atom and Bohr's model?

3 Explain why the large deflections of very few alpha particles hitting gold atoms is evidence that most of the mass of an atom is concentrated in the centre of the atom (the nucleus).

Radioactive decay and nuclear radiation

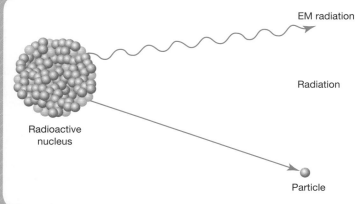

EM radiation

Radiation

Particle

Radioactive nucleus

Some elements are unstable. To become more stable, the nuclei of their atoms give out (emit) **radiation**.

By emitting radiation, the nucleus changes. This is a random process called radioactive decay.

To become more stable, a nucleus can:

- emit some of its mass (particle emissions) as nuclear radiation, or
- decrease its internal energy by emitting high-frequency electromagnetic radiation.

Each type of nuclear radiation emitted by unstable nuclei is **ionising**. This means that it can remove electrons from the outer orbits of other atoms, leaving them positively **charged**. If atoms in your cells are ionised, it can be very damaging to your body.

The types of nuclear radiation emitted by unstable nuclei are shown in the table below:

	Alpha (α)	Beta (β)	Gamma (γ)	Neutron (n)
Nature	A nucleus of helium $^4_2$He. Two protons and two neutrons	An electron e⁻	An electromagnetic wave	A neutral particle inside the nucleus of an atom
Charge	+2	−1	0	0
Mass	Relatively large	Very small	No mass	Large ($\frac{1}{4}$ of mass of α)
Range in air	3–5 cm	17 m	100s of metres	100s or 1000s of metres
Ionising effect	Very strong	Weak	Very weak	Very strong

Both alpha particles (α) and neutrons are heavy particles and have very high ionising power. As alpha particles are blocked by skin, they are most dangerous when the radioactive source is inside you. Neutrons are more dangerous when the source is outside your body, because neutrons have very high penetration power.

Gamma rays have no mass or charge, so do not interact with other particles as strongly as alpha particles. This means that gamma rays are not very ionising, but they are also not easily decelerated, so they are more penetrating than alpha particles. Neutrons are not typically able to ionize an atom directly because of their lack of charge, but they are indirectly ionizing, as they are absorbed by stable nuclei. These nuclei will become unstable by the absorption of a neutron, and more likely to emit ionizing radiation of another type. Neutrons are, in fact, the only type of radiation that is able to turn other materials radioactive.

DO IT!

Imagine what an atom in a patient's body would say if it were ionised by nuclear radiation.

Different nuclear radiation has different penetration power.

Types of radiation and penetration

Paper

Thin plates
made of wood
aluminium, etc.

Lead, iron and
other thick metal
plates

Thick layer
of water,
concrete, etc.

A Geiger counter can
detect and measure
ionising radiation - alpha,
beta and gamma

Neutrons can easily pass through (penetrate) most materials, even iron.
But they are slowed and blocked by materials that are rich in hydrogen, such
as hydrocarbons and water. Thick concrete walls are good radiation shields
because they can block both neutrons and gamma rays (γ).

WORKIT!

Why are thick concrete walls a good radiation shield? (3 marks)

Alpha particles (α) are blocked by paper, and beta particles (β) are
blocked by aluminium, so a layer of concrete will be good at shielding
people from them. (1)

Fewer gamma rays can pass through a heavy material like lead or
concrete, so a concrete wall would give good protection from gamma
rays. (1)

Neutrons are the most penetrating type of radiation, but they can be
absorbed by hydrogen-rich materials. This is because concrete is made
by mixing cement and water (which contains a lot of hydrogen atoms),
thick concrete will give good protection from neutron radiation too. (1)

NAILIT!

For this question you
need to compare the
penetration power of
the different types of
radiation.

CHECKIT!

1 What are the main types of nuclear
radiation?

2 Why are neutrons the most dangerous
type of radiation?

3 Why is gamma radiation more
penetrating than alpha particles?

Nuclear equations

As chemical equations represent chemical reactions, nuclear equations represent radioactive decay.

The symbols for representing alpha particles and beta particles are:

- $^4_2$He or α particle is a nucleus of helium, so it has an atomic number of 2 (2 protons) and mass number of 4 (2 protons and 2 **neutrons**).

- $^0_{-1}$e or β particle is a fast-moving electron from the nucleus, so it has an atomic number of −1 to represent its negative **charge**, but mass number of 0 because it does not have a nucleus.

When nuclear radiation is emitted from a nucleus, it can change the **mass** and/or the charge of the nucleus.

This nuclear equation shows how **alpha decay** changes both the charge and the mass of a nucleus:

$$^{219}_{86}\text{radon} \longrightarrow \, ^{215}_{84}\text{polonium} \; + \; ^4_2\text{He}$$

The α emission takes away two protons and two neutrons from the nucleus of the radon atom. This means that its atomic number falls by 2 and its mass number falls by 4. Both charge and mass in its nucleus fall, and so the radon changes into a different element.

This nuclear equation shows how beta decay increases the charge, but does not change the mass of a nucleus:

$$^{14}_{6}\text{carbon} \longrightarrow \, ^{14}_{7}\text{nitrogen} \; + \; ^0_{-1}\text{e}$$

NAIL IT!

At GCSE, you don't need to remember these two examples. You only need to know what happens in alpha decay and beta decay and how to balance atomic numbers and mass numbers.

DO IT!

Draw a table showing the general rules of how the atomic and mass numbers change when a nucleus emits alpha or beta particle, or gamma radiation.

NAIL IT!

Make sure you know the Greek letters used for the different types of radioactive decay:

α alpha

β beta

γ gamma

WORKIT!

Complete the following nuclear equations. (2 marks)

$$^{60}_{27}\text{Co} \rightarrow \underline{}\text{Co} + \gamma \qquad ^{42}_{19}\text{K} \rightarrow \underline{}\text{Ca} + \underline{}\text{e}$$

γ-rays have no atomic number and no mass, so there is no change in the atomic number and mass number of cobalt in the equation.

$$^{60}_{27}\text{Co} \rightarrow ^{60}_{27}\text{Co} + \gamma \ (1)$$

β particles have atomic number = −1 and mass number = 0, so the atomic number of potassium (K) will increase by 1 (and become a calcium nucleus), and the mass number will not change.

$$^{42}_{19}\text{K} \rightarrow ^{42}_{20}\text{Ca} + ^{0}_{-1}\text{e} \ (1)$$

NAILIT!

The proton/atomic number of a nucleus tells you what the element is in the periodic table. So, a change in atomic number in nuclear equations always means that the nucleus has become a different element, even if its mass number has not changed.

Periodic table of the elements

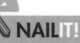

NAILIT!

Make sure you can find information from the periodic table, it will be useful when completing nuclear equations.

CHECKIT!

1 What tells you which element in the periodic table a nucleus belongs to?

2 How would you represent a neutron in a nuclear equation?

3 What changes would a neutron emission cause in a nucleus?

Half-life of radioactive elements

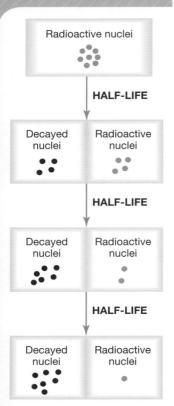

Half-life measured in terms of radioactive nuclei, look at how the numbers of radioactive and decayed nuclei change every half-life

Radioactive decay is a **random** process. This means that it is impossible to predict which of the nuclei in a sample of a radioactive isotope will decay next, or when a nucleus will decay. However, we can make predictions about decay when there are lots of unstable nuclei.

The decay rate of a radioactive isotope depends on:

- The element in the sample.
- How many undecayed nuclei are in the sample.

The *more* undecayed nuclei there are, the bigger the decay rate. This means that, on average, more nuclei decay per second when we start measuring the radiation of an isotope sample than when we *stop* measuring the radiation.

The decay rate of a radioactive isotope does not depend on the temperature and pressure of the sample. Even at very high temperatures and pressures the radioactive decay rate of an element is not affected.

We can define the half-life of a radioactive isotope in two ways:

- The time taken for the number of nuclei in a sample of a radioactive isotope to halve.
- The time taken for the count rate (or **activity**) from a sample of a radioactive isotope to fall to half its original level.

Half-life in terms of count rate halving

STRETCH IT!

The random nature of radioactive decay is linked to the half-life of different isotopes. So, other random events also behave like a sample of decaying nuclei.

For example, the level of foam on top of a fizzy drink will fall in a random way. We can find its 'half-life' by plotting a graph of the height of the foam against time.

DO IT!

Take a big plastic bottle and pierce a hole at the bottom. Then fill the bottle with water, covering the hole with your finger. Let the water out into your sink and make a mark on the bottle every 5 seconds. Use your marks to draw a graph of the level of water left against time. You should get a curve that looks like the one for the fizzy drink foam.

NAIL IT!

You can find the half-life of a sample of radioactive nuclei from a graph which shows the number of undecayed nuclei against time. Just find the point on the activity axis (y-axis) where the activity/number of undecayed nuclei has dropped to half the original value. Then, go across the x-axis to see at what time that happened. That time is the half-life of the radioactive isotope.

SNAP IT!

Take a video of the foam from a fizzy drink and count how many seconds it takes for the level of foam to halve each time. You should notice a similar pattern to the graph on page 58.

WORK IT!

The remains of an animal found frozen in a glacier on the Alps contains $\frac{1}{32}$ the amount of carbon-14 found in living animals today. Carbon-14 is a radioactive isotope of carbon and has a half-life of 5730 years. How old might this animal be? (3 marks)

The net decline of the radioactive emission is:

1 half-life → $\frac{1}{2}$ original amount

2 half-lives → $\frac{1}{4}$ original amount

3 half-lives → $\frac{1}{8}$ original amount

4 half-lives → $\frac{1}{16}$ original amount

5 half-lives → $\frac{1}{32}$ original amount (1) ◄──

Each half-life is 5730 years long, so 5730 × 5 = 28650 years. (1)

This means that the animal was probably alive 28650 years ago. (1)

> If the amount of carbon-14 is $\frac{1}{32}$ of the original amount when the animal was alive, and because the amount of carbon-14 halves every half-life, this means that 5 half-lives have gone by since it died.

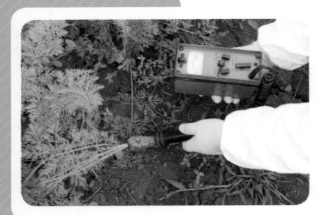

Radioactive contamination and irradiation

Soil, food and other materials can become contaminated by unwanted materials that have radioactive isotopes.

Dust and gases that have radioactive isotopes are the most dangerous, because they are very difficult to remove from the environment. Dust and gases can also be breathed into your body.

The hazard from radioactive contamination comes from the decay of the contaminating atoms.

The level of hazard is affected by how many contaminating atoms there are and the type of radiation emitted.

People working with radiation or in hazardous areas wear protective suits.

An object can be **irradiated** if it is exposed to nuclear radiation, but the irradiated object does **not** become radioactive itself.

Irradiation can be useful, for example, to make medical equipment and food safe by sterilising them, or to destroy cancer cells in patients' bodies. But the amount of irradiation a human body is exposed to should be as small as possible. That is why precautions, like lead screening, must be taken against the hazards from the radioactive sources that are used in irradiation. People who are often around radiation because of their jobs, for example, people who operate x-ray machines, may wear a radiation monitoring badge to make sure they stay within the recommended dose limits.

CHECK**IT!**

1 What does the rate of radioactive decay depend on?

2 Define the half-life of a radioactive isotope.

3 The activity of a sample drops to a quarter of its original activity after 146 days. What is the half-life of the radioactive isotope in the sample?

Hazards and uses of radioactive emissions

Background radiation

A **radiation** detector measures some radiation even when there are no radioactive sources nearby. What the detector measures is the background radiation that is surrounding us all the time and that comes from:

- rocks and cosmic rays from space – **natural sources**
- testing of nuclear weapons and nuclear accidents – **man-made sources**.

The amount of background radiation absorbed by a person is called the **dose**. It changes depending on where the person lives and on what the person does for a living.

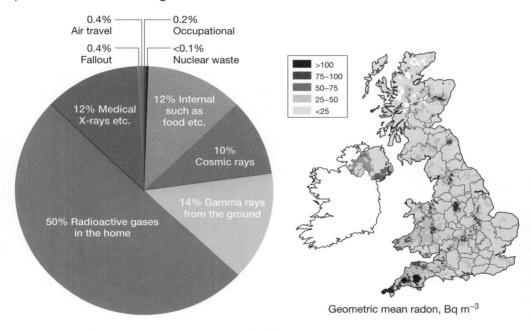

Geometric mean radon, Bq m^{-3}

The unit to measure the dose of radiation absorbed is called the sievert (Sv).

$$1 \text{ Sv} = 1000 \text{ mSv}$$

Different half-lives of radioactive isotopes

The half-life of different radioactive isotopes can be very different. For example, the half-life of uranium-235 is 700 million years, but the half-life of iodine-131 is only 8.02 days.

The hazard level of different radioactive isotopes depends on their half-life. For example, polonuim-209 is a powerful poison, because it is an alpha emitter and has a half-life of 138 days, so if a powder of polonium is ingested by a person it will cause a lot of damage. Plutonium-239 has a half-life of 24 100 years, so if the soil of a residential area gets contaminated by plutonium it will affect crops and animals for a very long time.

NAILIT!

At GCSE, you don't need to remember the unit of radiation dose. Just make sure you understand the different doses and can convert between sieverts and millisieverts.

Uses of nuclear radiation

Nuclear radiation can be useful in medical applications such as:

- Exploring internal organs. For example, a patient could be asked to ingest an iodine-131 tablet so that a gamma-probe can be used to measure the amount of radioactive iodine the thyroid gland takes in, to check if the gland is working properly.

Radioactive iodine
is ingested

Gamma probe measuring
thyroid gland radioactivity

- Killing some or all the cells of unwanted tissue, like tumours. For example, a machine can be used to focus intense beams of gamma rays, or γ-rays, on a tumour inside a patient's body to remove the tumour.

NAIL IT!

Make sure you can evaluate the risks and the perceived risks of nuclear radiations, as well as their consequences. For example, treating a patient with γ-ray therapy can affect other organs in the body, but the risk is kept small by focusing the beam of γ-rays only on the area affected by cancer.

Also, the risks of not removing the cancer cells may outweigh the risks of irradiation from γ-rays.

γ-rays

Tumor

CHECK IT!

1 What are the sources of background radiation?

2 Why is a radioactive isotope with a long half-life, more hazardous than one with a short half-life?

3 Iodine-131 has a half-life of 8.02 days, and it emits γ-rays. Explain why these two properties make it useful for internal organ exploration.

Nuclear fission and fusion

Nuclear fission

Nuclear fission happens when one big and unstable nucleus, such as uranium or plutonium, splits into two smaller nuclei of about the same size.

Spontaneous fission is very rare. Normally, for fission to happen, a neutron first has to be absorbed by the unstable nucleus.

When fission happens, the unstable nucleus releases large amounts of energy and two or three neutrons and gamma rays.

Meanwhile, the nuclear **energy stores** associated with the original nuclei empty, and the **kinetic energy** stores associated with the split (fissioned) nuclei and the released neutrons fill.

The neutrons released by each fission reaction can go on to start other reactions and create a chain reaction.

NAILIT!

Make sure you know how to draw and interpret nuclear fission chain reaction diagrams.

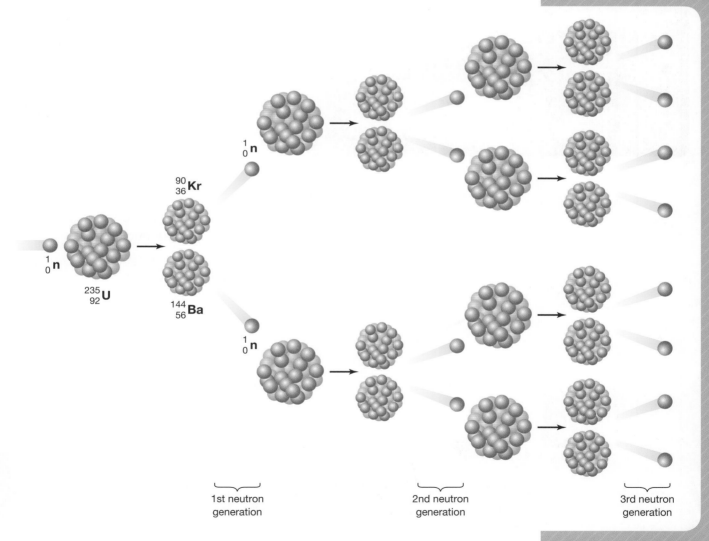

1st neutron generation   2nd neutron generation   3rd neutron generation

This image shows a nuclear fission chain reaction when uranium-235 absorbs a neutron

63

In nuclear reactors, some of the emitted neutrons are absorbed by non-fission material. This is used to control both the chain reaction and the energy released.

Nuclear weapons cause uncontrolled chain reactions that result in devastating explosions.

This picture shows the explosion caused by testing nuclear weapons in 1946, this particular explosion was caused by the Baker test which detonated 90 ft underwater and caused extensive radioactive contamination through radioactive sea-spray.

The city of Chernobyl has restricted access since the explosion of a nuclear reactor in 1986. The nuclear reactor was enclosed in a semi-circular sarcophagus to reduce further radioactive contamination of the environment. The sarcophagus can be seen in this picture.

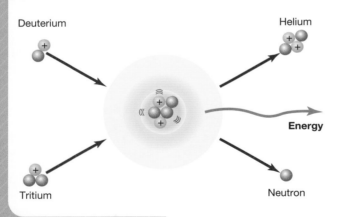

Nuclear fusion

Nuclear fusion happens when two light nuclei join (fuse together) to form a heavier nucleus.

In this process some of the **mass** of the light nuclei is converted into energy, which is transferred by **radiation**. We know this conversion happens because the mass of the heavier fused nucleus is smaller than the sum of the mass of each of the original nuclei.

CHECK**IT!**

1 What is nuclear fission?

2 Explain how a nuclear chain reaction can start.

3 Explain why the products of a nuclear fusion reaction are lighter overall than the combined mass of the original nuclei.

Atomic structure

1 Write the number of electrons, protons and neutrons for the following elements.

a $_{11}^{23}Na$ d $_{84}^{208}Po$

b $_{7}^{14}N$ e $_{4}^{9}Be$

c $_{92}^{235}U$ f $_{6}^{14}C$

2 Explain how Bohr's model of the atom is different from Rutherford's model.

3 Fill the gaps and balance the fission equation below:

$$_{0}^{1}n + _{92}^{235}U \longrightarrow _{56}^{\_\_}Ba + _{\_\_}^{92}Kr + _{0}^{1}n + Energy$$

4 The two graphs below show the activity of elements A and B changes over time. Look at the graphs and answer the questions.

Element A

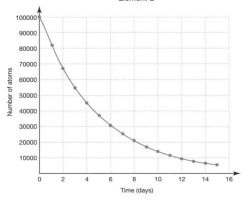

Element B

a What are the half-lives of element A and element B?

b After how many half-lives does the count per minute reading drop to 6 counts per minute in element A?

c How many days does it take for the number of radioactive atoms in element B to drop to a quarter of their original value?

5 Explain the difference between radioactive contamination and irradiation.

6 The map below shows the typical annual radiation dose in various regions of Europe due to background radiation. Look at the map and answer the questions below it.

a Which areas of Europe have the least annual radiation doses from background radiation?

b Which areas are exposed to annual doses higher than 10 mSv/year?

c What is the typical annual radiation dose in Italy?

Typical annual doses (mSv/year)

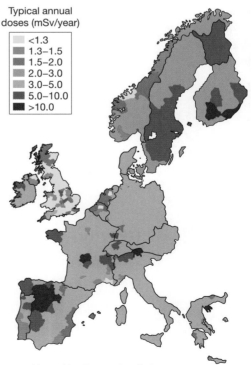

	<1.3
	1.3–1.5
	1.5–2.0
	2.0–3.0
	3.0–5.0
	5.0–10.0
	>10.0

Natural background radiation exposure

Forces and their interactions

Scalar and vector quantities

Scalar quantities have only magnitude. Some examples of scalar quantities are **speed**, **mass** and **energy**.

Vector quantities have magnitude and direction. Some examples of vector quantities are **velocity**, **pressure** and **forces**.

An arrow is a useful way to represent a vector quantity. The length of the arrow shows the magnitude (the size) of the vector quantity. The direction of the arrow shows the direction of the vector quantity.

8N

12N

Contact and non-contact forces

When two objects interact with each other, they experience a force caused by this interaction.

Forces can be described as pushes or pulls acting on an object. All forces between objects are either:

- **contact forces** – when the objects are touching (for example, **friction**, air resistance, tension and the 'normal' contact force)

- **non-contact forces** – when the objects are not touching (for example, gravitational force, electrostatic force (from static electricity) and magnetic force).

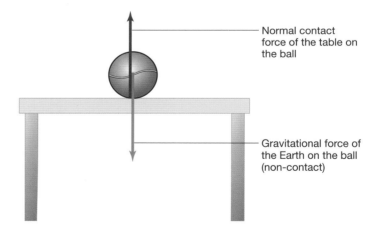

Normal contact force of the table on the ball

Gravitational force of the Earth on the ball (non-contact)

Gravity

The mass of an object is a scalar quantity measured in **kilograms** (kg). The mass of an object stays the same wherever it is in the universe.

The weight of an object on the Earth is the gravitational force caused by the pull of the Earth on the object.

NAILIT!

Get used to saying and writing 'the force of the object on the other object'.

For example, 'the pull of the rope on the climber'. This will help you to identify all the forces applied to an object.

The direction of the pull (weight) is always towards the centre of the Earth. We can think of the weight of an object, which is a vector quantity, as the gravitational force acting at a single point called the centre of **mass** of the object.

The magnitude of weight on the Earth is caused by the **gravitational field** around the Earth. The magnitude depends on the gravitational field strength at the point where the object is. The **further** away an object is from the Earth, the **smaller** its weight.

We can calculate the weight of an object using the equation:

weight = mass × gravitational field strength

$$W = m\,g$$

- W = weight (unit: **newton**, N)
- m = mass (unit: kilogram, kg)
- g = gravitational field strength (unit: newton per kilogram, N/kg)

Weight is measured using weighing scales made of a calibrated spring-balance (a **newtonmeter**).

DOIT!

Weighing scales show your mass not your weight. So, measure your mass in kg with your scales. What is your weight in newtons?

WORKIT!

The spacecraft *Juno* arrived in Jupiter's orbit on 4 July 2016. Its mass was 3625 kg when it was launched from Earth. What is its weight on Earth and on the surface of Jupiter? (2 marks)
(g = 9.8 N/kg on Earth, and g = 23 N/kg on Jupiter.)

The weight of Juno on Earth is $W = m\,g$ = 3625 × 9.8

= 35 525 N (1)

The weight of Juno on Jupiter is $W = m\,g$ = 3625 × 23

= 83 375 N (1)

The mass of *Juno* will still be 3625 kg on Jupiter, because the mass of an object stays the same wherever it is in the universe.

MATHS SKILLS

Weight and mass are **directly proportional** ($W \propto m$). Saying 'weight is directly proportional to mass' means that, if we double the mass, the weight also doubles.

Make sure you can recognise and use the symbol for direct proportionality ($\propto$).

CHECKIT!

1 Name one scalar quantity and one vector quantity not listed above.

2 What is the difference between contact and non-contact forces?

3 Explain the difference between mass and weight.

Resultant forces

When more than one **force** is acting on an object, we can replace all these forces with a single force that has the same effect as all of the forces acting together.

This single force is called the **resultant force**. It is the sum of all of the forces acting on an object.

When the resultant force is zero (0 N), all of the forces acting on an object are **balanced**.

WORKIT!

1 Look at the images. Which diagram best describes the forces acting on the tennis ball? Explain your choice. (3 marks)

(Note that the yellow arrows are only showing the direction the ball is moving and are **not** a force.)

Diagram C best describes the forces on the tennis ball because the ball is no longer in contact with the racket, so there is no forward force acting on the ball. (1) The only horizontal force on the ball is the air resistance in the opposite direction to the motion of the ball. (1) So the ball is decelerating. The force pointing downward is the weight of the ball. (1)

2 The truck in the diagram is travelling east. What is the resultant force F on the truck? (2 marks)

The thrust from the engine, F_t, and the drag, F_d, are in opposite directions.

$F = F_t - F_d = 3250 - 1050 = 2200$ N (1)

The truck is accelerating eastward with a force of 2200 N. (1)

1050 N

3250 N

STRETCH IT!

The resultant force on a ping-pong ball at rest on a table and the resultant force on the same ping-pong ball falling freely (when it has reached **terminal velocity**) is the same. In both situations, the forces on the ball are equal and in opposite directions. So the sum of the forces is zero, so the resultant force is 0 N.

In physics, the effect is the same because the velocity of the ball in both situations does not change. The ball when it is on the table stays at rest, and the ball when it is falling freely carries on falling at a constant velocity (at the same speed and in the same direction). So in both situations, all the forces on the ball are balanced.

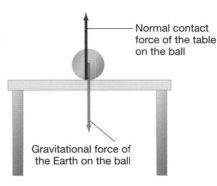

Ping-pong ball at rest on the table — Normal contact force of the table on the ball — Gravitational force of the Earth on the ball

Ping-pong ball in free fall — Air resistance of the air molecules on the ball — Gravitational force of the Earth on the ball

H   Components of forces

A single force can be broken down ('resolved') into two components acting at right angles (90°) to each other.

Just like for resultant forces, these two components together have the same effect as the single force.

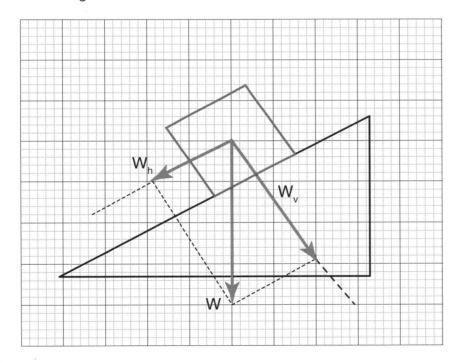

DO IT!

Draw each of these **vectors** on graph paper, and find their horizontal and vertical components:

- A force arrow of 6.5 N pointing right 30° above the horizontal line.
- A **velocity** arrow of 2.8 m/s pointing left 55° below the horizontal line.

Look at the diagram above. We can resolve the weight of the box on the ramp into two components:

- a component acting along the surface of the ramp (W_h)
- a component acting at 90° to the surface of the ramp (W_v).

We can draw a 'free body diagram' on graph paper to show all the forces acting on the box. If the weight of the box is 4 N, we can draw W 4 cm long. The **magnitude** of W_h = 3.5 N, so we can draw its arrow 3.5 cm long. And the magnitude of W_v = 2.2 N, so we can draw its arrow 2.2 cm long.

WORKIT!

A passenger plane is applying a thrust T = 63 000 N in a direction 70° north-west (70° to the left of the vertical line). The horizontal component of the drag is D = 28 000 N, and the weight of the plane is W = 14 000 N. Calculate the resultant horizontal force and the resultant vertical force on the plane. (2 marks)

> First, we need to find the horizontal and vertical components of the thrust, T_h and T_v.

Redraw the force arrows on graph paper (making sure we keep the same proportions). We will use 1 cm on the graph paper to represent 10 000 N. (1)

Our vector diagram shows that T_h = 60 000 N (because the length of this arrow is 6 cm) and T_v = 21 000 N (because the length of this arrow is 2.1 cm). (1)

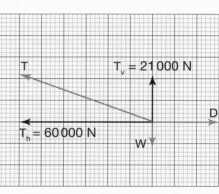

CHECKIT!

1 What is meant by a resultant force?

2 A skydiver of mass 75 kg opens his parachute. The air resistance from it is initially 1542 N. What is the magnitude and direction of the resultant force on the skydiver?

H 3 What are the horizontal and vertical components of a force of 5 N pulling an object to the left 45° above the horizontal line?

Work done and energy transfer

A **force** does work on an object when it causes that object to move a distance. In other words, when a force causes the **displacement** of an object, this means that the force has done work on the object.

We can calculate the work done by a force on an object using the equation:

work done = force × distance (moved along the line of action of the force)

$$W = F\,s$$

- W = work done (unit: **joule**, J)
- F = force (unit: **newton**, N)
- s = distance, or displacement (unit: **metre**, m)

One joule of work is done when a force of one newton causes a displacement of one metre. This means that:

one joule = one newton-metre → 1 J = 1 Nm

NAIL IT!

Make sure you can remember and use this equation.

You also need to be able to convert joules to newton-metres, and newton-metres to joules.

Whenever work is done by a force, **energy** is transferred. For example, when an apple is dropped, the **weight** of the apple does work as it pulls the apple to the ground. The gravitational potential energy store associated with the apple empties as the **kinetic energy** store of the apple fills.

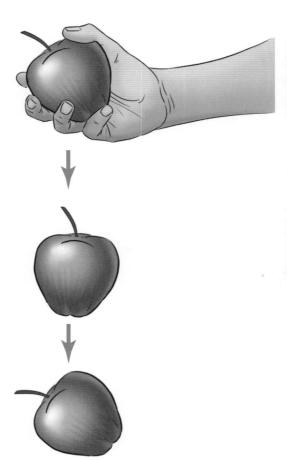

Work is also being done against another force that is acting on the falling apple. This is the frictional force of air resistance. Air resistance is a frictional force because the **particles** of air cause **friction** on the falling apple. The work done against air resistance increases the **thermal** energy store of the apple and increases the thermal energy store of the air around it.

So, the work done against a frictional force causes an increase in the temperature of an object.

WORKIT!

A ball of mass 10 kg is dropped from a height of 20 m. The same ball is then left free to roll down a ramp that is 20 m high and 50 m long. Calculate the work done by the weight of the ball in these two situations. (4 marks) (g = 9.8 N/kg)

Weight of the ball = $m g$ = 10 × 9.8 = 98 N (1)

When the ball is dropped from a height s = 20 m, the work done by the weight is:

$W = F × s$ = weight × s = 98 × 20

$\qquad\qquad$ = 1960 J (1)

When the ball is free to roll down the ramp, the work done by the weight is the same as when the ball is dropped (W = 1960 J). This is because the height of the ramp is 20 m (the same as the height of the drop), and the line of action of the weight is along the vertical. (1) So any horizontal movement does not count toward the work done by the weight. (1)

NAILIT!

It is useful to know that weight = mass × gravitational field strength when calculating the work done on an object.

DOIT!

Choose an object you can lift without too much effort and find its weight. Then, lift it to a height you have previously measured. Now, calculate how much work your pulling force did in lifting the object to that height.

CHECKIT!

1 What is the work done by a force?

2 How many joules are in 530 newton-metres?

3 A rocket has a mass of 22 000 kg. What is the minimum work that needs to be done by the thrust to lift the rocket 1.54 km? Assume that the mass of the rocket stays constant. In this question the gravitational field strength = 9.8 N/kg.

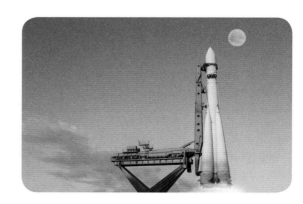

Forces and elasticity

To change the shape of a stationary object (stretch, compress or bend it), you always need to apply two **forces** on the object. If you applied only one force, you would only turn (rotate), pull or push the object.

When stretching a rubber band, one finger is pulling in one direction, while the other finger is pulling in the opposite direction.

When compressing Blu-Tack against a wall, the finger is pushing on the Blu-Tack, while the wall is exerting a force on the Blu-Tack in the opposite direction.

When bending a piece of Blu-Tack, one hand is twisting the block of Blu-Tack clockwise, while the other hand is twisting it anti-clockwise.

Objects that are stretched, compressed or bent can be warped from their original shape (deformed) either elastically or inelastically.

- **Elastic deformation** → the object returns to its original shape after being stretched.

- **Inelastic deformation** → the object does **not** return to its original shape after being stretched (its shape is changed permanently).

For an elastic object, we can see the relationship between the force on the object and how the object changes shape using the equation:

$$force = spring\ constant \times extension$$

$$F = k\,e$$

- F = force (unit: **newton**, N)

- k = spring constant (unit: newton per metre, N/m)

- e = extension, or compression (unit: metre, m)

DO IT!

Write a social media post describing the difference between elastic and inelastic deformation.

Practical Skills

In class, you will have investigated the relationship between force and extension for a spring. Think about how you calculated the spring constant of the spring from the data you collected. You could have drawn the graph linking the force and the extension as either a force–extension graph or an extension–force graph.

Force–extension graph:

If the graph is plotted with force on the y-axis and extension on the x-axis, the equation is:

$$F = k\,e$$

So, the spring constant k is the gradient of the line.

The gradient is always calculated as gradient $= \frac{\Delta y}{\Delta x} \rightarrow$ make sure you draw a big right-angled triangle on the graph to find Δy and Δx.

Force vs Extension

- $\Delta y \rightarrow$ highest y − lowest y (the height of your triangle)

- $\Delta x \rightarrow$ highest x − lowest x (the base of your triangle)

So, in our graph:

$$k = \text{gradient} = \frac{\Delta y}{\Delta x} = \frac{100 - 10}{1.20 - 0.12} = \frac{90}{1.08} = 83.3 \text{ N/m}$$

The spring constant of our spring is 83.3 N/m.

Extension–force graph:

If the graph is plotted with extension on the y-axis and force on the x-axis, the equation is:

$$e = \frac{F}{k}$$

So, the gradient of the line is $\frac{1}{k}$.

In the graph:

$$\text{gradient} = \frac{\Delta y}{\Delta x}$$
$$= \frac{10.80 - 0.100}{90 - 8}$$
$$= \frac{0.980}{82}$$
$$= 0.112$$

Extension Vs Force

But in this graph:

$$\text{gradient} = \frac{1}{k} \Rightarrow k = \frac{1}{\text{gradient}} = \frac{1}{0.012} = 83.3 \text{ N/m}$$

The symbol Δ is the Greek letter Delta, which can be used as an abbreviation for 'change in' or 'difference between'.

The spring constant of our spring is again 83.3 N/m.

MATHS SKILLS

The equation shows that the force on an elastic object, such as a spring, is **directly proportional** to the extension (or to the compression) of the object. However, the equation does not work any more if the spring goes above its **limit of proportionality** (because then it becomes permanently deformed).

The equation is a straight line (**linear**) relationship. So, you might be asked to find the spring constant (k) using experimental data plotted on a F-e graph and by calculating the gradient of the line.

If the spring extends above its limit of proportionality, its f-e relationship becomes **non-linear**. That is, its f to e relationship is no longer directly proportional.

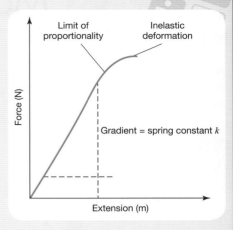

Work done and energy transfer

A force stretching or compressing a spring does work on the spring. So **energy** is transferred to the elastic potential energy store associated with the spring. If the spring has not exceeded its limit of proportionality (if it is not inelastically deformed):

• the work done on the spring = the elastic potential energy stored

We can calculate the work done on a spring when stretching or compressing it using the equation:

$$\textbf{\textit{elastic potential energy}} = \textbf{\textit{0.5}} \times \textbf{\textit{spring constant}} \times \textbf{\textit{(extension)}}^2$$

$$\mathbf{E_e = \frac{1}{2}ke^2}$$

This equation will be given to you, but make sure you know how to use it. It is also used in the Energy chapter (page 13).

CHECK**IT!**

1 What is the difference between elastic and inelastic deformation?

2 A rubber band extends by 5 cm when pulled with a force of 3.5 N. What is the spring constant of the rubber band?

3 What is the elastic potential energy of the rubber band in Question 2? What is the work done on it?

Moments, levers and gears

One or more **forces** might make an object turn (rotate). The turning effect of a force is called the moment of force. We can calculate the moment of a force using the equation:

$$\textit{moment of a force} = \textit{force} \times \textit{distance}$$

$$M = F\,d$$

- M = moment of a force (unit: newton-metre, N m)

- f = force (unit: **newton**, N)

- d = distance (the perpendicular (90°) distance from the pivot to the line of action of the force) (unit: **metre**, m)

If an object is **balanced**:

- the total clockwise moment about a pivot = the total anti-clockwise moment about that pivot

DOIT!

Tie a string around the handle of your door, and pull the moving door using the string. First, pull the string at 90°. Then gradually increase the angle between the string and the hinge up to 180°. What do you notice? How can you link this to the moments of a force?

WORKIT!

The beam in the diagram is balanced on its centre of mass by resting it on the pivot. Calculate the weight (W) of the block on the left-hand side of the beam. (3 marks)

When the beam is balanced,
total clockwise moment = total anti-clockwise moment (1)

The forces on the right-hand side produce a clockwise moment,
and the weight of the block on the left produces an anti-clockwise moment. (1)

Total clockwise moment = $(1 \times 300) + (1.5 \times 450) = 975$ N m

First, sum up the total clockwise moment.

= total anti-clockwise moment

Total anti-clockwise moment = $Fd = Wd \rightarrow 975 = W \times 1.5 \rightarrow W = \dfrac{975}{1.5} = 650$ N (1)

A see-saw is an example of how pivots are used in everyday life.

Levers and gears

Simple levers and gears can be used to transmit the rotational effects of a force.

The spanner is an example of a lever.

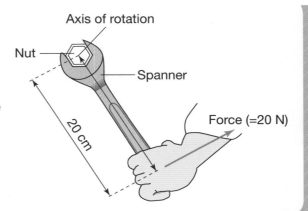

Look at the diagram. The pivot is the centre of the nut. The perpendicular distance from the pivot to the line of action of the force is the distance between the centre of the nut and the hand (0.200 m). The force is 20 N. So the moment of the force is:

$$M = F\,d = 20 \times 0.200 = 4.0 \text{ N m}$$

If the perpendicular distance from the pivot to the line of action of the force were halved (0.100 m), the moment would also halve. So:

- the *longer* the lever, the *bigger* the moment of the force.

Gears work in the same way as levers. Gears and levers are usually used to multiply a force.

10 teeth 20 teeth   20 teeth 10 teeth

In a gear system:

- a force is exerted (the 'effort') on the smaller wheel (the 'load')
- the rotational effect is transmitted to the bigger wheel
- the bigger wheel moves a smaller distance, but with a bigger force.

So, the original force on the smaller wheel is multiplied on the bigger wheel.

CHECK IT!

1 A crane lifts a load of 2300 kg at a distance of 15 m from the pivot. What is the moment of the force applied by the load? (g = 9.8 N/kg)

2 A girl is sitting on the end of the right-hand side of a see-saw, and a boy twice her weight is sitting in the middle of the left-hand side. Is the see-saw balanced? Explain your answer.

3 In a system of gears, a smaller wheel is connected to a bigger wheel. How does this multiply a force?

Pressure and pressure differences in fluids

DO IT!

Make three holes in a plastic bottle and cover them with Blu-Tack. Then, fill the bottle with water and remove the Blu-Tack, like in the diagram above. Make a video with your phone and describe what happens.

A fluid is a liquid or a **gas**.

The **pressure** in a fluid always causes a **force** that is 'normal' (that is at right angles, 90°) to any fluid surface.

We can calculate the pressure at the surface of a fluid using the equation:

$$\text{pressure} = \frac{\text{force normal to a surface}}{\text{area of that surface}}$$

$$P = \frac{F}{A}$$

- p = pressure (unit: **pascal**, Pa)
- F = force (unit: **newton**, N)
- A = area (unit: **metre** squared, m²)

NAIL IT!

Make sure you can remember and use this equation.

Columns of liquid

The demonstration with the bottle and three holes in the Do It! box shows the water leaving the bottle at right angles (90°) from the walls of the bottle.

So, pressure in liquids always acts at 90° to the surfaces of their containers or to objects that are immersed in them.

H

WORKIT!

A submarine that has about the same surface area at its top and bottom is emerging from the water. The pressure at the top of the submarine is p_t = 250 000 Pa, and the force 'normal' to the top surface is F_t = 60 000 kN. The pressure at the bottom of the submarine is p_b = 325 000 Pa. Calculate the resultant force on the submarine. (2 marks)

$$A_t = A_b = \frac{F_t}{P_t} = \frac{F_b}{P_b} \Leftrightarrow F_b = \frac{F_t \times P_b}{P_t}$$

The surface area is the same at the top and bottom of the submarine.

$$= \frac{6 \times 10^7 \times 3.25 \times 10^5}{2.50 \times 10^5}$$

$$= 7.8 \times 10^7 \text{N} \ (1)$$

Now that we know the force 'normal' to the bottom surface, we can calculate the resultant upward force on the submarine:

$$F = F_b - F_t = 7.8 \times 10^7 - 6.0 \times 10^7$$

$$= 1.8 \times 10^7 \text{ N (upward)} \ (1)$$

H Our investigation of the submarine ('Work It!') shows that any partly (or totally) submerged object experiences a bigger pressure on its bottom surface than on its top surface. This produces an upward force called the upthrust.

The pressure at any point in a liquid always increases when there is more liquid (the height of the column of liquid increases) above it. This is because there are more particles of liquid above the point pressing down on it, the deeper the object is in the liquid.

So, in a column of liquid:

- the deeper the column of liquid at any point, the bigger the pressure at that point
- the denser the liquid above any point, the bigger the pressure at that point.

We can calculate the pressure caused by a column of liquid using the equation:

pressure = height of the column × density of the liquid × gravitational field strength

$$P = h\rho g$$

- p = pressure (unit: pascal, Pa)
- h = height of the column (unit: metre, m)
- ρ = **density** (unit: **kilogram** per metre cubed, kg/m³)
- g = **gravitational field** strength (unit: newton per kilogram, N/kg)

Objects in a liquid will either sink or float depending on density and upthrust. The object will float if:

- It is less dense than the liquid.
- The upthrust (upward force) is greater than its weight (downward force).

Atmospheric pressure

The Earth has a thin layer of air surrounding it called the atmosphere. This atmosphere gets less dense as the altitude (height above the surface of the Earth) increases.

Atmospheric pressure is caused by air molecules hitting a surface.

The higher an object is above ground level, the fewer particles of air there are above pushing down on the surface of the object. Therefore, the higher up we go, the less atmospheric pressure we experience.

For example, a balloon filled with helium will rise (float) in air because its density is lower than the density of air and because the atmospheric pressure below it is greater than the atmospheric pressure above it.

NAILIT!

This equation will be given to you. But make sure you know how to use it.

CHECKIT!

1 Pressure in a fluid acts in which direction?

2 Atmospheric pressure at sea level is 101.325 kPa. What is the force exerted by air particles on 0.010 m² of your skin?

H 3 The density of mercury is 13 594 kg/m³. The column of mercury in a thermometer is 4.3 cm high. Calculate the pressure at the bottom of the column near the surface of the Earth and the pressure at the bottom of the column near the surface of the Moon (g = 9.8 N/kg on the Earth, and g = 1.6 N/kg on the Moon).

Distance, displacement, speed and velocity

Distance and displacement

Distance is a **scalar** quantity. This means that it does not have a direction.

For example, if you walked along a straight line of 100 m and then walked back to the start, you will have walked a distance of 200 m.

Displacement is a **vector** quantity. This means that it has both magnitude and direction.

Therefore, if you walked along the straight line of 100 m and then back to the start, your total displacement will have been 0 m. This is because the displacement in one direction cancels out the displacement in the other direction.

Speed and velocity

Speed is also a scalar quantity, so it does not have a direction.

Moving objects and people often change speed. The speed of a person walking, running or cycling depends on lots of factors, like the person's age, how hilly/flat the land is, how fit the person is and the distance travelled.

We can calculate the distance travelled by an object moving at a constant speed using the equation:

$$distance\ travelled = speed \times time$$
$$s = vt$$

s = distance (unit: metre, m)

v = speed (unit: metre per second, m/s)

t = time (unit: second, s)

NAILIT!

Make sure you can remember typical values of speed for walking (about 1.5 m/s), running (about 3 m/s), cycling (about 6 m/s) and different types of transportation (like cars).

The speed of sound and the speed of the wind also change in different conditions. A typical value for the speed of sound in air is 330 m/s.

NAILIT!

Make sure you can remember and use this equation.

MATHS SKILLS

The average speed of an object travelling with non-uniform motion (changing speed) can be thought as the constant speed the object would need to travel at to cover the distance travelled in the time taken to travel that distance.

To calculate average speed, you can rearrange the equation to:

$$v = \frac{s}{t}$$

WORKIT!

A girl usually takes 20 minutes to walk to school. Use suitable values and calculations to estimate the distance of the school from the girl's house. (1 mark)

Time taken in seconds is:

$t = 20 \times 60 = 1200 \text{ s}$

If the girl is travelling at a constant speed, the distance travelled can be calculated as:

$s = vt = 1.5 \times 1200 = 1800 \text{ m}$

> A typical value for the speed of a person.

Distance = 1.8 km (approximately) (1)

The **velocity** of an object is a vector quantity, so it has both magnitude and direction. It is the speed of the object in the direction it is moving.

Circular motion

An object moving at a constant speed in a circle has a changing velocity. This is because the direction of the object keeps changing.

When a sparkler is moved in a circle at high speed, it is constantly changing direction. However, the sparks that detach from the sparkler move in a straight line in the direction the sparkler was moving when these sparks were formed.

SNAPIT!

Push a tennis ball around the inside of a hula hoop. The contact force between the ring and the ball keeps the ball moving in a circle. After one or two circles, lift the hula hoop. Take a video with your phone, and explain why the ball moves in a straight line when the hoop is lifted.

✓ CHECKIT!

1 What is the difference between displacement and distance, and the difference between velocity and speed?

2 A builder takes 12 minutes to cycle to work. What is the estimated distance from his house to his place of work?

3 Mo Farah's time for the World Half Marathon in Cardiff 2016 was 59 minutes and 59 seconds. The distance of a half marathon is 21.098 km. What was Mo Farah's average speed in this competition?

Distance–time relationship

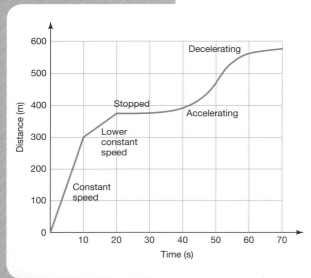

The distance travelled by an object moving in a straight line can be represented by a distance–time graph.

The gradient of a distance–time graph (how 'steep' the line is) represents the **speed** of the object. The greater the value of the gradient (the steeper the line), the faster the object.

In a distance–time graph, we can identify important features:

- A straight line means constant speed (constant gradient)
- A horizontal (flat) line means stationary (stopped)
- A steepening curve means **accelerating** object (increasing gradient)
- A flattening curve means **decelerating** object (decreasing gradient).

NAILIT!

Make sure you know how to find out the speed of an object from the gradient of a graph.

SNAPIT!

Push a toy car, or an object that can slide along a table, for 10 cm at steady speed in 2 seconds. Stop the object at 10 cm for 4 seconds and then move it further on the same line for 30 cm in 3 seconds. Take a video of the object moving and plot a distance-time graph of the object's motion.

WORKIT!

The graph shows the distance travelled by a cyclist over 70 seconds. Calculate the speed of the cyclist between 50 and 70 seconds.
(1 mark)

$$\text{Gradient} = \frac{\Delta y}{\Delta x} = \frac{\text{change in distance}}{\text{change in time}}$$

$$= \frac{400 - 100}{70 - 50} = \frac{300}{20} = 15\,\text{m/s} \ (1)$$

Remember that the symbol Δ is just a short way of saying 'change in' or 'difference between two values'.

To calculate the speed of the cyclist between 50 and 70 seconds, we need to calculate the gradient of the line for that time interval.

MATHS SKILLS

You might be asked to calculate the speed of an object that is accelerating or decelerating. To do this, you need to draw the **tangent** to the graph at the point needed. The tangent is a straight line that is at a right angle (90°) to the curve at a specific point.

For example, look at the distance–time graph of Usain Bolt breaking the 100 m world record in Beijing in 2008. If you want to calculate Bolt's speed 2 seconds into the race, you need to calculate the gradient of the curve at 2.00 seconds. So, first draw a long straight line that is 90° to the curve at 2.00 seconds (the red line in the diagram). Then work out the gradient of the straight line:

$$\text{Gradient} = \frac{\Delta y}{\Delta x} = \frac{52 - 0}{7.00 - 0.75} = \frac{52}{6.25} = 8.32 \text{ m/s}$$

Usain Bolt D-T graph (100 m world record breaking)

(H)

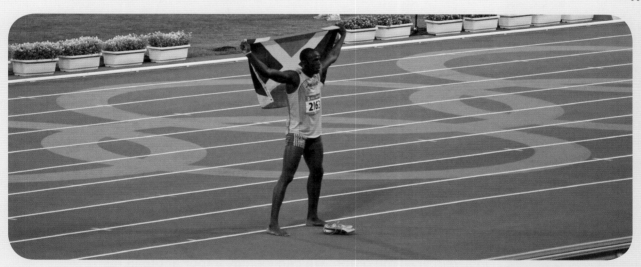

✓ CHECKIT!

1 What does the gradient of a distance–time graph tell you?

2 Why does a flattening curve show a decelerating object?

3 A distance–time graph for a racing car shows a horizontal line along the time axis between 0.00 and 0.62 seconds,

then a sharp curve of increasing gradient. What might the horizontal line mean?

Acceleration

We can calculate the average **acceleration** of an object using the equation:

$$acceleration = \frac{change\ in\ velocity}{time\ taken}$$

$$a = \frac{\Delta v}{t}$$

- a = acceleration (unit: **metre** per **second** squared, m/s²)
- Δv = change in **velocity** (unit: metre per second, m/s)
- t = time (unit: second, s)

In a velocity–time graph, the gradient represents the acceleration of the object.

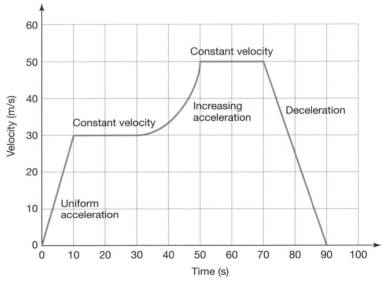

An example of a velocity-time graph

In a velocity–time graph, we can identify important features:

- A straight line means constant acceleration (constant gradient).
- A horizontal (flat) line means constant **velocity** (no acceleration).
- A steepening curve means increasing acceleration (increasing gradient).
- A straight line pointing down means slowing down (**deceleration**) (negative gradient).

MATHS SKILLS

You might be asked to use a velocity–time graph to calculate the distance travelled (the **displacement**) by an object. You can do this by calculating the area under the velocity–time graph.

In some velocity–time graphs, you might need to count the squares under the graph to estimate the displacement.

For example, to calculate the distance travelled in the first 30 seconds by the object in the graph, you can calculate the area under the line between 0 and 30 seconds (in the graph, the red triangle between 0 and 10 seconds and the red rectangle between 10 and 30 seconds).

Using a velocity–time graph to calculate displacement

Area of triangle $= \frac{1}{2} \times$ base $\times$ height

$= 0.5 \times (10 - 0) \times (30 - 0) = 0.5 \times 10 \times 30 = 150\,m$

area of rectangle = base $\times$ height $= (30 - 10) \times (30 - 0) = 20 \times 30 = 600\,m$

So, the total distance travelled is $150 + 600 = 750$ m.

When an object is moving with uniform acceleration, we can use the equation:

(final velocity)² − (initial velocity)² = 2 × acceleration × distance

$$v^2 - u^2 = 2\,a\,s$$

- v = final velocity (unit: metre per second, m/s)
- u = initial velocity (unit: metre per second, m/s)
- a = acceleration (unit: metre per second squared, m/s²)
- s = distance (unit: metre, m)

Near the surface of the Earth, all objects that fall freely because of **gravity** fall with a constant acceleration of about 9.8 m/s².

NAILIT!

This equation will be given to you, but make sure you know how to use it.

WORKIT!

A car accelerates with constant acceleration from 12 m/s to 17 m/s. If it took 13 m to reach 17 m/s, what is the acceleration of the car? (2 marks)

$a = \dfrac{v^2 - u^2}{2s} = \dfrac{17^2 - 12^2}{2 \times 13}$ (1)   ◄── Rearrange the equation $v^2 - u^2 = 2\,a\,s$

$= \dfrac{289 - 144}{26} = \dfrac{145}{26}$

$= 5.6\ m/s^2$ (1)

DOIT!

Search on the internet the typical acceleration of different objects, people and animals. For example, a fighter plane, a family car, a racing car, Usain Bolt, a cheetah, a bicycle, and so on.

Terminal velocity

An object falling through a fluid, like a ping-pong ball falling in air, will at first accelerate. This is because the gravitational pull of the Earth is greater than the air resistance on the object.

But as the velocity of the falling object increases, so does the upward **force** on the object (the air resistance), until the magnitude of the upward force becomes equal to the magnitude of the downward force on the object (its weight).

So, eventually, the **resultant force** on the object will be 0 N, and it will now fall at a constant speed. This is called the object's terminal velocity.

The velocity–time graph shows how the velocity of a skydiver changes during her fall.

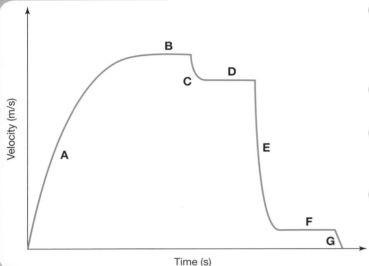

A The skydiver jumped and is accelerating. As her velocity increases, the air resistance on her body also increases, so the resultant force on her body decreases.

B The skydiver is moving at her terminal velocity.

C The skydiver spreads her arms and legs, increasing her surface area. This increases the air resistance, causing her to decelerate.

D The skydiver is moving at the terminal velocity for her spread-out body. (Her terminal velocity changed at C because the air resistance decreased when her velocity decreased).

E The skydiver opens her parachute. This increases her surface area dramatically, so the air resistance on her parachute also increases. She decelerates very quickly.

F The skydiver is moving at the terminal velocity for her increased surface area from her opened parachute.

G The skydiver decelerates as she lands on the ground.

CHECKIT!

1 Is acceleration a **scalar** quantity or a **vector** quantity?

2 A cheetah changes its speed from 18 m/s to 27 m/s in 8.2 seconds. What is its acceleration?

3 A professional racing car can go from 0 to 100 km/h with an acceleration of 2 m/s^2. Assume the acceleration is uniform. What distance will the car travel in performing this change in velocity?

Newton's laws of motion

Newton's first law

When the **resultant force** acting on an object is zero, the object will either:

- Stay stationary if the object was already stationary ('at rest').

- Continue moving with a constant **velocity** if the object was already moving. This means that it will continue moving both at the same **speed** and in the same direction.

So, the velocity will not change unless a resultant force (different from zero) is acting on the object.

Driving force Resistive forces

For example, when a car is travelling at constant speed along a straight line, resistive forces (like air resistance) are balancing the driving force.

So, if an object is at rest it will stay still unless acted upon by an unbalanced force. If an object is moving it will continue to move at the same speed with no acceleration or deceleration until acted upon by a resultant force.

STRETCH IT!

When you are on a bus and the bus starts moving, your body feels pulled backward. In the same way, when the bus stops, your body feels pushed forward. This happens because all objects have a tendency to stay in their state of rest or at constant motion. This tendency is called **inertia**.

SNAP IT!

Put a tennis ball on top of a skateboard and push the skateboard forward gently, but allow it to stop against a wall. Make a video with a smartphone and comment on how this explains the inertia of the tennis ball.

MATHS SKILLS

Remember that the symbol for proportionality is $\propto$. Therefore:

- $a \propto F$
- $a \propto \dfrac{1}{m}$

Newton's second law

Newton's second law can be shown as an equation:

$$\textit{resultant force} = \textit{mass} \times \textit{acceleration}$$

$$F = m\,a$$

- F = resultant force (unit: **newton**, N)

- m = **mass** (unit: **kilogram**, kg)

- a = **acceleration** (unit: **metre** per second squared, m/s²)

This equation can be rearranged to:

$$a = \frac{F}{m}$$

This shows that the acceleration of an object is **directly proportional** to the resultant force acting on it, and that the acceleration is inversely proportional to the mass of the object.

In other words, the effect of the **resultant force** (the **acceleration**) is the cause (resultant force) divided by the **resistance** to the cause (mass or **inertial** mass).

H

Inertial mass is a measure of how difficult it is to change the velocity of an object. You can see what this is when we rearrange the equation for Newton's second law to:

$$m = \frac{F}{a}$$

Inertial mass is defined as the ratio of force over acceleration.

 Practical Skills

You will have investigated in class how changing the force affects the acceleration of an object of constant mass, and how changing the mass of an object affects its acceleration caused by a constant force. Think about the method you used.

You might have used a data logging system to measure the velocity of a vehicle on an air track at two different points, while you changed the mass or the force on the vehicle. Whatever method you used, to increase the accuracy of your results, it is important to repeat the measurements of acceleration for different masses (or forces), and then to calculate a mean value from your measurements.

You might have calculated the mass (or force) from the gradient of a graph of your results. For example:

- For constant force and changing mass, if you plotted a graph of acceleration against $\frac{1}{\text{mass}}$, you could calculate the force as the gradient of your graph.

- For constant mass and changing force, if you plotted a graph of acceleration against force, you could calculate the mass as $\frac{1}{\text{gradient}}$ of the straight line. This is because gradient = $\frac{1}{m}$.

Newton's third law

When two objects interact, they exert forces on each other that are equal in magnitude and opposite in direction.

The weight of the book is balanced by the normal contact force of the table on the book. These two forces are equal and opposite, but they are **NOT** an example of **Newton's third law**.

Remember that **interaction pairs** (Newton's third law forces) must always:

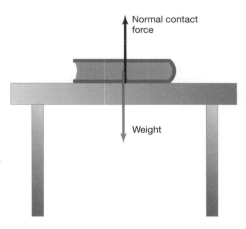

Normal contact force

Weight

MATHS SKILLS

The symbol ~ means that the value is an estimate (an approximate value). For example, ~3 N means 'approximately 3 N'. Make sure you know how to use this symbol in your answers.

- Act between two objects → the **gravitational pull** of the Earth on the book (**weight**) and the **gravitational pull** of the book on the Earth.

- Have the same nature → the **electrostatic repulsion** of the atoms of the table on the atoms of the book and the **electrostatic repulsion** of the atoms of the book on the atoms of the table.

In the example, both forces act on a single object (the book) and are different in nature – the **weight** is a **non-contact force** (**gravity**) and the **normal contact force** is an electrostatic force.

WORKIT!

A child of mass 35 kg jumps to the ground from a small wall. The child is pulled by the Earth with a force of 343 N. Use Newton's second and third laws to explain why the child moves toward the Earth, but the Earth does not seem to move toward the child at all. The mass of the Earth is 5.972×10^{24} kg. (3 marks)

Due to Newton's third law the Earth and the child attract each other with equal and opposite forces $F = 343$ N. (1)

If we use Newton's second law to calculate the acceleration of the child and the acceleration of the Earth caused by this force, we can see that the effect of the force (the acceleration) will be much bigger for the child than for the Earth, because of the much greater mass (inertia) of the Earth. (1)

a_c = child's acceleration m_c = child's mass

a_e = Earth's acceleration m_e = Earth's mass

$$a_c = \frac{F}{m_c} = \frac{343}{35} = 9.8 \text{ m/s}^2$$

$$a_c = \frac{F}{m_c} = \frac{343}{5.972 \times 10^{24}} = 5.7 \times 10^{-23} \text{ m/s}^2 \text{ (1)}$$

> Due to Newton's third law the Earth and the child attract each other with equal and opposite forces $F = 343$ N.

CHECKIT!

1 What needs to happen to change the velocity of an object?

2 What does Newton's second law tell you?

H 3 How are inertia and inertial mass related?

Stopping distance

The stopping distance of a vehicle is:

stopping distance = thinking distance + braking distance

- **Thinking distance** is the distance travelled by the vehicle during the driver's reaction time.

- **Braking distance** is the distance travelled by the vehicle because of the braking force.

The **speed** of the vehicle affects both the braking and stopping distance. In fact, the faster the vehicle, the longer it will travel during the reaction time of the driver, and the longer the distance needed to break with the same braking **force**. So, for a given braking force:

- the *faster* the vehicle, the *greater* the stopping distance.

The mind map below shows some factors that affect thinking distance and braking distance. Adverse road conditions include wet or icy roads. Vehicles might also have poor brakes and/or poor tyres.

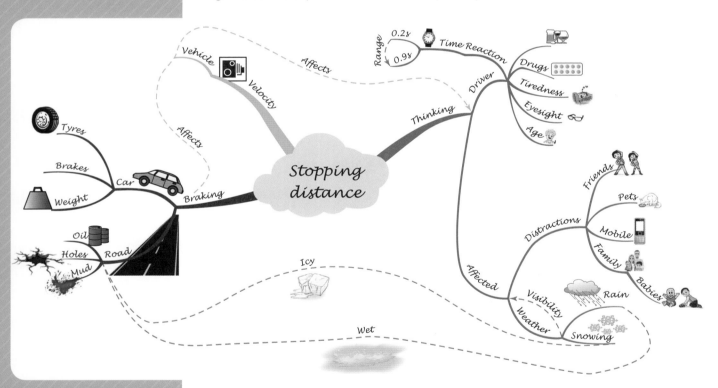

To reduce the **kinetic energy** of a vehicle, work is done by the **friction** force between the brakes and the wheels when the braking force is applied to the brakes. This causes the temperature of the brakes to increase.

For *higher* speeds, *greater* braking forces are needed to stop the vehicle within a given distance. *Greater* braking forces cause *greater* decelerations. These might cause brakes to overheat, due to increased friction, and/or the driver to skid and lose control of the vehicle.

WORKIT!

Distances

A car is travelling at 22 m/s on the motorway when the driver notices an accident ahead. Estimate the thinking distance travelled by the car after the driver notices the danger. (2 marks)

Typical reaction times are between 0.2 and 0.9 seconds. This means that the average reaction time of a person is ~0.6 s. (1) So:

$$s = vt = 22 \times 0.6$$

$$= 13.2 \text{ m (1)}$$

> The thinking distance is the distance travelled by the vehicle during the reaction time of the driver.

Forces and deceleration

A lorry travelling with kinetic energy 700 kJ performs an emergency stop in 124 m. Estimate the average braking force needed to stop the lorry. (2 marks)

The equation for work done is $W = Fs$. So:

$$F = \frac{W}{s} \text{ (1)}$$

$$= \frac{700\,000}{124}$$

$$= 5645 \text{N (1)}$$

> The work done by the braking force to stop the lorry needs to be at least equal to the kinetic energy of the lorry.

✓ CHECKIT!

1 What factors affect the stopping distance of a vehicle?

2 Explain the potential dangers of rapid decelerations of vehicles.

3 A young and healthy driver has a reaction time of 0.3 seconds. If the thinking distance after the driver noticed a danger was 6.5 m, at what speed was the driver's car travelling?

Momentum

H

Momentum is a property of moving objects. It can be defined using the equation:

$$Momentum = mass \times velocity$$

$$p = mv$$

- p = momentum (unit: **kilogram metre** per second, kg m/s)
- m = **mass** (unit: kilogram, kg)
- v = **velocity** (unit: metre per second, m/s)

In a system that is not affected by any external forces (closed system), momentum is always conserved.

This means that the total momentum before an event (like a collision) is always the same as the total momentum after the event.

This is called conservation of momentum.

MATHS SKILLS

The equation shows that:

- the *greater* the mass, the *greater* the momentum
- the *greater* the velocity, the *greater* the momentum

NAIL IT!

Momentum is a **vector quantity** because it depends on the object's velocity.

This explains why two identical balls that travel at the same **speed** in opposite directions (v and –v) and then hit each other head-on will stop after they collide. The momentum of each ball cancels out the momentum of the other ball. Therefore, the total momentum is zero before *and* after the collision.

Momentum mv   Momentum m(-v)

MATHS SKILLS

You can show this change in momentum by combining the equations for force (F) and acceleration (a)

$$F = m \times a \text{ and } a = \frac{\Delta v}{t}$$

to get: $F = \frac{m\Delta v}{\Delta t}$

- F = force
- m = mass
- Δv = change in velocity
- Δt = change in time, or the time taken

In our new equation, $m\Delta v$ = change in momentum.

So, the force applied on an object = the rate of change in momentum.

Changes in momentum

When a **resultant force** different from zero acts on an object that can move, or that is already moving, the velocity of the object changes.

When the velocity changes, the momentum changes too.

We can improve the safety of lots of things by reducing the rate of change in momentum. For example:

- Soft surfaces like crash mats in gyms and cushioned surfaces in play areas cause the change in velocity to happen over a longer time. If a fall or collision happens, the surface reduces the rate of change in momentum and therefore, the **force** applied on the body.

- Air bags and seat belts help to increase the time taken by the driver/ passengers to stop moving. This again results in a reduced rate of change in momentum.

- Cycle and motorcycle helmets reduce the rate of change in momentum of your head colliding with an obstacle, so the force on it is also reduced.

DO IT!

Find at least one object/tool used as a safety feature and explain how it works using rate of change of moment in your explanation.

WORKIT!

1 A toy car of mass $m_1 = 50$ g hits a stationary toy car of mass $m_2 = 78$ g at a velocity of 5 m/s. The stationary car has a bit of Blu-Tack on it, so the two cars stay attached to each other after they have collided. Calculate the total momentum of the two cars before and after the collision, and calculate the velocity of the two cars after the collision. (3 marks)

The total momentum is the same before and after the collision. The total momentum before the collision is:

$$P_{tot} = m_1 v_1 + m_2 v_2 = 0.050 \times 5 + 0.078 \times 0$$
$$= 0.25 + 0 = 0.25 \text{ kg m/s (1)}$$

So, the momentum of the two attached toy cars after the collision must also be 0.25 kg m/s, and their combined mass is now:

$$m_{tot} = m_1 + m_2 = 0.050 + 0.078$$
$$= 0.128 \text{ kg (1)}$$

and rearranging the momentum equation:

$$v = \frac{P}{m} = \frac{0.25}{0.128}$$
$$= 1.95 \text{ m/s (1)}$$

2 A bullet is fired at 420 m/s at a wooden target and it lodges itself in the wood in 0.12 seconds. If the mass of the bullet is 4.2 g, what is the force applied by the bullet on the target? (3 marks)

Change in speed $\Delta v = 0 - 420 = -420$ m/s. (1) (The negative sign just shows that the bullet has slowed down. It is not important here, so we will carry on without it).

The mass of the bullet in kg is m = 0.0042 kg. Therefore:

$$F = \frac{m\Delta v}{\Delta t}$$
$$= \frac{0.0042 \times 420}{0.12} \text{ (1)}$$
$$= 14.7 \text{ N (1)}$$

✓ CHECKIT!

1 What is the momentum of an object?

2 What is meant by conservation of momentum?

3 A tennis ball of mass 58.5 g moves at 17 m/s. What is its momentum?

1 a Draw the resultant force from the force arrows below.

b Resolve the force in its vertical and horizontal components, and label each component F_y and F_x, respectively.

2 Copy the diagram below and draw all the gravitational forces applied in this system, and explain why you drew those forces and with that size.

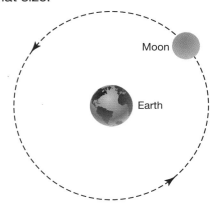

3 Draw and label the resultant force in this situation, making sure you draw the resultant force to the correct scale and label it with the correct value of force in newtons.

4 Two horses pull the Queen's carriage with a force of 523 N each. If the total work done by their forces is 378 652 J, calculate the distance they have travelled.

5 Usain Bolt takes 3.78 s to run the first 30 m from stationary, but he takes 3.95 s from the moment the starting gun is fired. Calculate the two average speeds to run 30 m from these two times, and suggest why there is a difference.

6 If the combined mass of this cyclist and bicycle is 81.5 kg, calculate the acceleration of the cyclist.

Waves

Transverse and longitudinal waves

Waves are **oscillations/perturbations** that travel through a **medium** (material).

Waves carry **energy** and can also carry information between different places.

It is the wave that travels, not the particles of the medium. We can see this because the water particles in a ripple tank only move up and down as the waves pass through a point, but they are not carried forward by the wave.

Transverse waves move up and down at right angles (90°) to the direction of travel of the wave. Examples of transverse waves are ripples in water and **electromagnetic waves**.

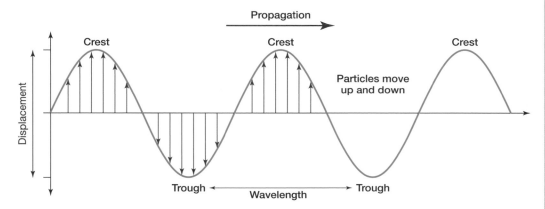

Longitudinal waves move along (parallel to) the direction of travel of the wave. Longitudinal waves have areas of compression and rarefaction. An example of longitudinal waves is **sound waves**.

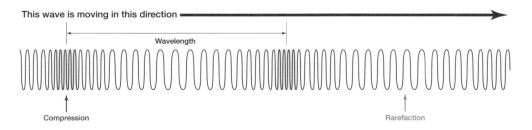

Properties of waves

Waves have four main properties that help us to describe how they move.

Amplitude is the maximum displacement of a point on a wave from its undisturbed position (from the horizontal middle line in the diagram).

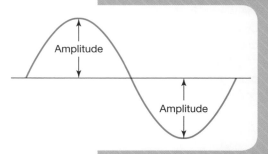

Wavelength (λ) is the distance between a point on a wave and the equivalent point on the adjacent wave (where the wave repeats itself). This is shown in the graph to the right.

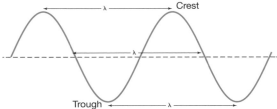

Frequency is the number of waves passing a point each second.

The wave speed is the speed the wave is moving through the medium or the speed the energy is being transferred in that medium.

The wave equation applies to all waves. It shows how wave speed, wavelength and frequency are related:

$$\textbf{wave speed} = \textbf{frequency} \times \textbf{wavelength}$$

$$v = f\lambda$$

- v = wave speed (unit: metre per second, m/s)
- λ = wavelength (unit: metre, m)
- f = frequency (unit: hertz, Hz)

The period of a waves is the time taken for a full wave to pass through a point. The relationship between the period of a wave and its frequency is show in the equation:

$$\textbf{Frequency} = \frac{1}{\textbf{period}}$$

$$f = \frac{1}{T}$$

- T = period (unit: second, s)
- f = frequency (unit: hertz, Hz)

MATHS SKILLS

When waves go from a less dense medium to a denser medium, they slow down and their wavelength decreases. However, their frequency stays the same.

The diagram shows that the wavelength decreases as the ripples go into shallower water (denser medium). As the wave equation informs us, due to the frequency staying the same, the wavelength decreases and therefore the wave speed (the velocity) must decrease too.

One way to measure the speed of sound in air is to put two microphones at a known distance between each other (the further, the better). Then, strike together two metal rods above one of the microphones. If we connect both microphones to an oscilloscope, or to a computer and use sound recording software, we can then calculate the time it took for the sound to travel from the microphone below the rods to the microphone further away.

We can calculate the speed of sound in air using the speed equation $v = \frac{s}{t}$ (from page 80 in the Forces chapter).

Practical Skills

You will have investigated in class how to find the speed of water waves in a ripple tank and the speed of waves in a solid medium. Think about what apparatus you needed and why it was suitable for measuring the frequency and wavelength of the waves.

For example, using the set up in the diagram to the right, putting a ruler on the white screen below the tank and using the stroboscope should let us take fairly accurate readings of the wavelength (the distance between the wave fronts).

Measuring the time taken for 10 wave fronts to pass a point, and dividing by 10, should give a fairly accurate measure of the period. For even better accuracy, we could take repeated readings and then calculate a mean value from these. We can then calculate the frequency as $f = 1/T$.

To calculate the speed of a wave in a solid, one end of a long copper rod/tube could be hit by a hammer and the signal recorded by two microphones placed next to each end of the rod could be displayed on an oscilloscope.

The time difference between the signals is the time taken for the sound wave to travel along the rod, and by measuring the distance of the rod, you can calculate the speed of the wave.

For example, a 4 m copper rod shows two peaks on the oscilloscope 8.7×10^{-4} seconds apart. Therefore the speed of the sound wave in copper is:

$$speed = \frac{distance}{time}$$

$$v = \frac{s}{t} = \frac{4}{8.7 \times 10^{-4}} = 4598 \ m/s$$

Remember that in the equation above, s is the distance travelled.

WORKIT!

A guitarist plays an 'A' note with frequency of 440 Hz. Calculate the wavelength of this sound wave. (2 marks)

The speed of sound in air is usually about 330 m/s (1), so rearranging the wave equation $v = f\lambda$:

$\lambda = \frac{v}{f} = \frac{330}{440} = 0.75m = 75cm$ (1)

CHECKIT!

1 How can you work out the amplitude of a wave from a graph?

2 The frequency of the musical note 'middle C' is 261.6 Hz. Calculate the period of this wave.

3 A series of wave fronts in a ripple tank are generated with a period of 0.25 seconds, and the distance between the ripples is 1.2 cm. Calculate the speed of these water waves.

Reflection and refraction

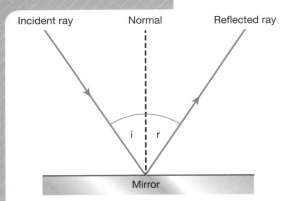

Incident ray   Normal   Reflected ray

i   r

Mirror

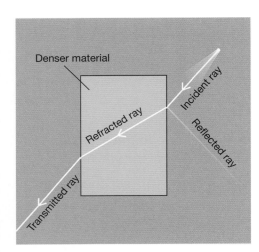

Denser material

Refracted ray

Incident ray

Reflected ray

Transmitted ray

A wave can be reflected at the boundary between two different materials. This means the wave bounces off the boundary at the same angle from the 'normal'.

The 'normal' is an imaginary line at a right angle (90°) to the boundary.

- angle of incidence (i) = angle of reflection (r)

A wave can be transmitted by a material. This means the material lets the wave through, and the wave (or part of it) comes out of the other side of the material.

A wave can be absorbed by a material. This means the material does not transmit or reflect the wave.

A wave can be **refracted** at the boundary between two different materials of different density. This means the wave changes direction at the boundary at a different angle from the 'normal'.

- If the transmitting material is denser than the first **medium**, the wave will slow down and bend towards the normal to the boundary.

- If the transmitting material is less dense than the first medium, the wave will speed up and bend away from the normal to the boundary.

- The angle of **refraction** of a wave transmitted through a material also depends on the **frequency** of the wave.

SNAPIT!

Pour some water in a glass and put the glass over a lamp until you see a reflection of the lamp on the surface of the water. Take a photo of the glass and the water from above. What is happening to the light from the lamp at the boundary between the air and the water?

Practical Skills

You will have investigated in class the reflection of light by different surfaces. Think about the apparatus you used. You might have used a light sensor to measure the light intensity before and after the reflection. This method would let us calculate the percentage of light reflected by each material. What were the possible sources of error? For example, some light might have dissipated as the travelling light ray spread out. This can be reduced by using lenses to focus the light rays more effectively.

Practical Skills

You might also have investigated in class the refraction of light by different substances. Think about how you could have increased the accuracy of your results. For example, by repeating the measurements of the angles of refraction for the same angles of incidence and then using these measurements to calculate the mean values.

STRETCH**IT!**

When a wave goes from a denser to less dense material, it refracts (bends) away from the 'normal'. When the refracted wave is at a right angle (90°) from the normal, the angle of incidence is called the critical angle. For any angle bigger than the critical angle, the wave will be reflected back into the denser material. This is called total internal reflection.

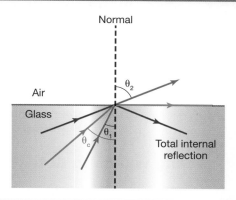

DO**IT!**

Put a pencil in a glass of water. Using the term refraction explain what you see.

CHECK**IT!**

1 What happens to a light ray incident on a mirror at 32° from the 'normal' to the mirror?

2 A wave travels from a less dense material to a more dense material, hitting the denser material at an angle more than 0° from the 'normal' to the boundary. What happens when the wave is transmitted by the denser material?

3 Jade looks at white light from a lamp through a red filter. The lamp appears to emit only red light to Jade. What has happened to the other frequencies of the light coming from the lamp?

Sound waves

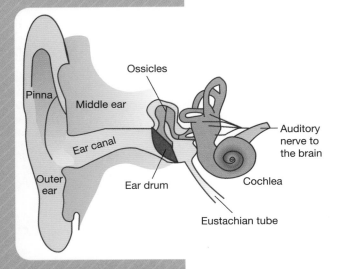

Sound waves can be reflected, absorbed and transmitted. When a sound wave is absorbed and transmitted by a solid object, the wave makes the solid vibrate.

Different solid objects absorb and transmit sound waves of different **frequencies**. So, solid objects will vibrate only when they absorb and transmit sound waves of specific frequencies.

The human ear has a solid membrane called the ear drum. It converts sound waves of frequencies between 20 Hz and 20 kHz into vibrations of the ear drum. These vibrations are then interpreted by the brain as sounds. This specific frequency range becomes more limited for people when they get older.

Using waves to detect and explore

Different types of waves are absorbed and reflected by solids and liquids in different ways. We can use these differences in **velocity**, reflection and absorption to detect and explore structures that we cannot observe directly, like the core of the Earth.

The frequency of ultrasound waves is beyond the human audible range, so humans cannot hear them. Ultrasound waves are partly reflected at a boundary between two different materials ('mediums' or 'media'). So, part of the ultrasound wave will come back to the detector from the first boundary, and the rest of the wave will continue to travel in the second material until it reaches another boundary between that and a third material. At this point, the wave is reflected again and will reach the detector at a later time than the first reflection. We can then use this time delay and the velocity of the ultrasound wave through the materials to show images of them. For example, manufacturers use ultrasound to test for cracks in materials.

DO IT!

Close the windows in your room when there is traffic on the road outside, or when someone is cutting the grass, or doing building work, so that you can still hear some noise from the outside. Then, place your hand on the glass pane. What do you feel?

Ultrasound waves can be used to detect cracks in rock.

Ultrasound scans use these properties of waves to show images of babies developing in the mother's womb.

Seismic waves (earthquakes) are used to study the structure and size of the Earth's core. There are two types of seismic waves:

- P-waves (primary waves) → **longitudinal**, travel at different speeds through solids and liquids, and are refracted at boundaries between different mediums

- S-waves (secondary waves) → **transverse**, cannot travel through liquids, and are refracted at boundaries between different mediums.

The study of seisimic waves allowed scientists to map the internal structure of the Earth and to discover parts of it that are not directly observable. It is possible to measure the depths of each of the Earth's layers using readings from seismic waves.

Echoes (reflected waves) of high-frequency sound waves are used to detect objects in deep water and to measure the depth of the water. This method of detection is called echo-sounding.

NAIL**IT!**

S-waves cause a lot more damage than p-waves. S-waves can devastate whole cities, for example, when a big earthquake happened in August 2016 to the town of Amatrice, in central Italy.

✓ CHECK**IT!**

H 1 What is the effect of a sound wave absorbed, or transmitted, by a solid object?

H 2 How can we detect cracks in solids using ultrasound waves?

H 3 How can we explore the size and composition of the Earth's core using seismic waves?

Electromagnetic waves

Electromagnetic waves transfer **energy** from a source to an absorber. For example, the infrared signal sent by the transmitter in a remote control sent to the receiver on your TV, or the ultraviolet radiation emitted by the Sun and absorbed by the skin, which gets tanned.

Electromagnetic waves are **transverse** waves. All electromagnetic waves travel at the same **velocity** in a vacuum (empty space) or in air.

Electromagnetic waves make up a continuous spectrum called the **electromagnetic spectrum**, where they are grouped according to their **wavelength** and **frequency**.

Long wavelength ————————————————————→ Short wavelength

Radio waves	Microwaves	Infrared	Visible light	Ultraviolet	X-rays	Gamma rays

Low frequency ————————————————————→ High frequency

The human eye can detect electromagnetic waves only within a limited range of frequencies, called **visible light**. However, we can detect the other waves of the electromagnetic spectrum indirectly using special instruments.

Properties of electromagnetic waves

Electromagnetic waves of different wavelengths are absorbed, transmitted, refracted or reflected in different ways depending on the materials they are travelling in. This affects things like the colour of objects (page 108).

Some effects happen because the waves have different velocities in different materials. For example, electromagnetic waves can be refracted at the boundary of two different materials. We can show how this happens using wave front diagrams, as shown below.

STRETCH IT!

How the wave bends depends on the densities of the different materials. If the wave starts at an angle more than 0° from the 'normal' (the bottom diagram), the wave bends toward the 'normal' (in a denser material, shown in the diagram) or away from the 'normal' (in a less dense material).

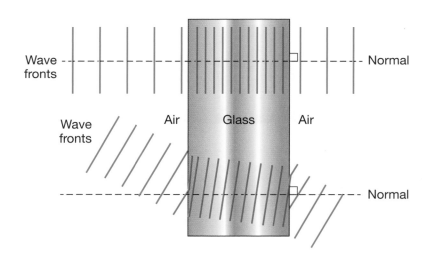

Refraction through a parallel plate

The wave slows down in the denser material (the glass in the diagram). So, the wave fronts get closer together in the denser material. The wave speeds up again in the less dense material (the air in the diagram). So, the wave fronts spread out again.

Oscillations in electrical circuits can generate radio waves, as shown in this diagram.

Oscillating charges in the transmitter circuit generate electomagnetic waves in the radio frequency range

Radio waves received by the receiver circuit cause charges to oscillate with the same frequency as the original signal

Radio waves travel from the transmitter to the receiver through air, or empty space

Dangers of absorbing electromagnetic radiation

The range of frequencies of electromagnetic waves in the electromagnetic spectrum can be generated by changes in atoms and in their nuclei. For example, γ-rays are generated by changes in the nuclei of atoms.

Absorbing electromagnetic waves can also result in changes in atoms and their nuclei.

The absorption of ultraviolet waves, X-rays and γ-rays are ionising and can damage human body tissue. These higher frequency EM waves carry more energy and can therefore penetrate the body further than lower frequency EM waves.

The effect of these hazards on body tissue depends on the type of radiation and the size of the dose. We measure radiation dose in sieverts (Sv), which is a measure of the risk of harm resulting from an exposure of the body to the radiation.

1000 millisieverts (mSv) = 1 sievert (Sv)

NAILIT!

Some of the hazards to human tissue can be:

• Ultraviolet waves → increase risk of skin cancer and cause skin to age prematurely.

• X-ray and γ-rays → **ionising** radiation that can cause mutation of genes and cancer.

WORKIT!

It is recommended that people working in radiation environments should not be exposed to more than 20 mSv per year. A medical physicist who works with γ-rays in a hospital is exposed to 0.08 mSv each day. Is the environment in which she works following the recommendations? The employee works 5 days a week. (2 marks)

There are 52 weeks in a year, so for a 5-day working week the medical physicist is exposed to
$0.08 \times 5 = 0.4$ mSv each week
and $0.4 \times 52 = 20.8$ mSv per year. (1)

The radiation dose the physicist is exposed to each year is more than the recommended dose. This shows that the hospital is not following the recommendations. (1)

SNAPIT!

Take a photo of the applications of electromagnetic waves diagram on the next page. Explain why each of the electromagnetic waves is suitable for the practical application. Use the photo to revise on the go.

Uses and applications of electromagnetic waves

Electromagnetic waves are used for a wide range of applications. Some examples are shown in this diagram.

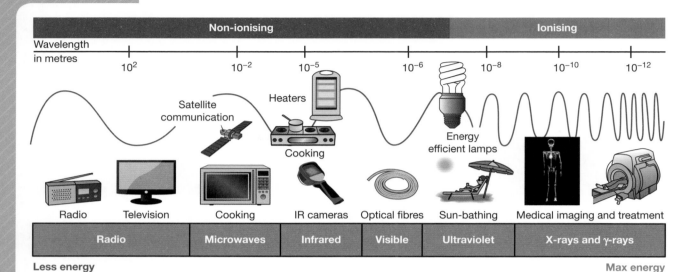

Practical Skills

You will have investigated in class how different surfaces absorb or radiate (emit or give out) infrared radiation. Think about the skills you needed. You probably focused on the method you used to collect accurate measurements (or data). For example, if you covered the sides of different beakers with sheets of different colours and/or materials, and then measured the temperature of hot water poured inside the beakers over time, a few things would have affected your results. Here are some ideas:

• Water can evaporate from the top of the beakers, so it is important to cover them with insulating material to reduce this effect.

• The thermometer/temperature probe should be completely immersed in the water and not touching the glass of the beaker, because you want to measure the temperature of the water.

• The beakers should be placed on insulating mats to reduce the effects of energy transfer by heating.

CHECKIT!

1 What do electromagnetic waves carry?

2 How are electromagnetic waves different from other waves, like sound or waves in water?

3 Why are some electromagnetic waves more dangerous than others?

Lenses

When light rays go through a lens, they change direction by **refraction** because of the shape of the lens.

There are two types of lens – **convex** and **concave** lenses. For both types of lens, when a light ray goes through the *centre* of the lens, it does not change direction (is not refracted).

Convex lenses

The symbol for a convex lens is ↕.

A convex lens bulges at the centre.

The image produced by a convex lens can be either real or virtual, and virtual images produced by a convex lens are magnified (bigger than the object).

In a convex lens, light rays that are parallel to each other come together (converge) at one point. This point is called the **principal focus** ('F' in the diagrams).

The distance between the lens and the principal focus is called the **focal length**.

We can look at the images of objects using convex lenses in three ways:

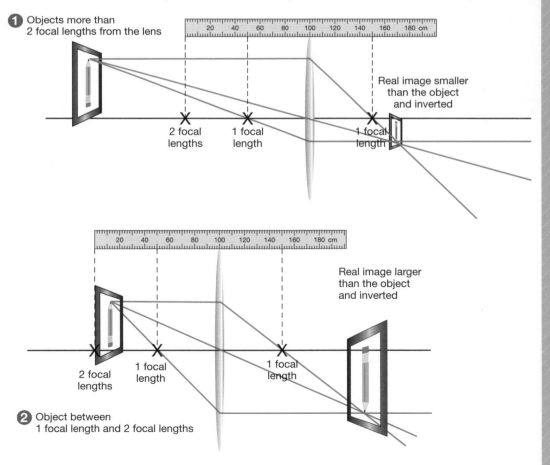

1 Objects more than 2 focal lengths from the lens

Real image smaller than the object and inverted

2 focal lengths   1 focal length   1 focal length

Real image larger than the object and inverted

2 focal lengths   1 focal length   1 focal length

2 Object between 1 focal length and 2 focal lengths

❸

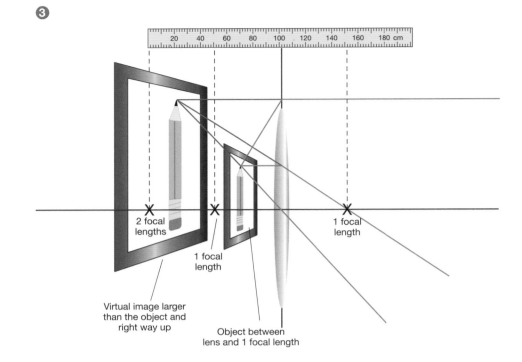

Virtual image larger than the object and right way up

Object between lens and 1 focal length

2 focal lengths

1 focal length

1 focal length

NAILIT!

To get the correct position of the image of the object in ray diagrams, just draw two light rays:

- a line parallel to the middle line, which goes through the principal focus **after** hitting the lens

- a line going from the top of the object and straight through the centre of the lens

- the point where these two light rays meet is where the image is formed.

DOIT!

Find a convex lens in your house and point it at some features outside your window. Then, put a white sheet of paper behind the lens and move it until a clear image of what your lens is pointing at is formed on the paper.

STRETCHIT!

A refractive telescope works by magnifying (using an 'ocular lens') the image that is formed (using an 'objective lens') inside the telescope. So, you are actually looking at a magnified version of an image of the object.

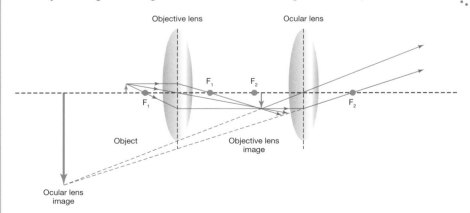

Concave lenses

The symbol for a concave lens is ⎞⎛.

A concave lens is thin at the centre.

The image produced by a concave lens is always virtual and it is diminished (smaller than the object).

In a concave lens, light rays that are parallel to each other spread out (diverge) from the principal focus.

This is why the image using a concave lens always forms *before* the lens and is a virtual image. In fact, we cannot project that image onto a screen.

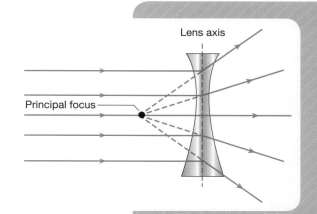

Magnification

We can calculate the magnification of a lens using the equation:

$$\textbf{Magnification} = \frac{\textbf{image height}}{\textbf{object height}}$$

As this is a ratio, magnification does not have a unit of measurement. However, the image height and object height should both be measured in the same units (e.g. mm or cm).

WORKIT!

Draw a ray diagram to find the image of the object through a convex lens. Then calculate the magnification. (2 marks)

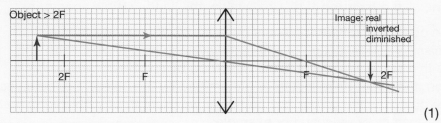

(1)

Each square on the graph paper is 1 mm. This means the object height is 5 mm and the image height is 4 mm, so:

$$\text{magnification} = \frac{\text{image height}}{\text{object height}} = \frac{4}{5} = 0.8 \ (1)$$

MATHS SKILLS

If the magnification is:

- *More* than 1, the image is bigger than the object

- *Equal* to 1, the image is the same size as the object

- *Less* than 1, the image is smaller than the object.

CHECKIT!

1 What are the main differences between convex and concave lenses?

2 How is an image formed using a concave lens?

3 If magnification is 1.2 and the object height is 0.6 cm, what is the image height?

Visible light

Light rays can be reflected off surfaces in two different ways, depending on the type of surface.

- Smooth surfaces reflect light rays in one direction. This is called **specular reflection**.

- Rough surfaces reflect light rays by scattering them in all directions. This is called **diffuse reflection**.

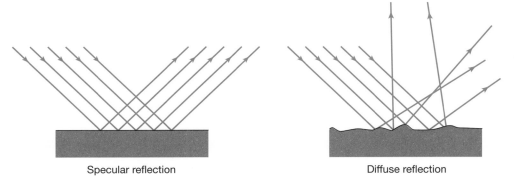

Specular reflection   Diffuse reflection

Colour

Visible light is the part of the **electromagnetic spectrum** our eye can detect. Visible light has **wavelengths** from about 380 to 700 nm. Our eyes see each narrow band of wavelengths as a different colour. White light contains all the **frequencies**, or wavelengths, in the visible spectrum.

We see objects of different colours because of differential absorption, transmission and reflection of different wavelengths of visible light. This means that *some* wavelengths are absorbed by an object, while *other* wavelengths might be reflected or transmitted by the object. So, our eyes will see the object as the colour (the particular wavelength of visible light) that the object transmits or reflects. For example:

- A blue object reflects the particular wavelength of light that our eyes see as blue, and it absorbs the other wavelengths.

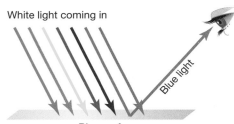

White light coming in

Blue light

Blue surface

- Strawberry squash looks red because it absorbs all the wavelengths of the visible spectrum between 380 and 620 nm, but it transmits red wavelengths (between 620 and 700 nm).

'nm' means 'nanometre', which is a unit of length equal to one billionth of a metre – this is very tiny!

Colour filters work by transmitting only particular wavelengths of visible light and absorbing the other wavelengths.

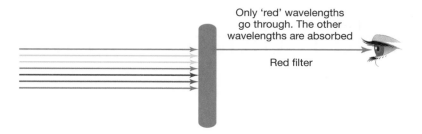

Only 'red' wavelengths go through. The other wavelengths are absorbed

Red filter

Objects that transmit light are either translucent or transparent (for example, strawberry squash is translucent).

Objects that do not transmit light are called opaque. They absorb all or almost all wavelengths, but they might reflect waves of a particular wavelength. For example, an object might look red in daylight because it strongly reflects red wavelengths. An object that:

- **Reflects all** (equally strongly) of the wavelengths of the visible spectrum will appear **white**.

- **Absorbs all** of the wavelengths of the visible spectrum will appear **black**.

SNAP**IT!**

Take a photo of a colourful object with your phone. Then, take the same photo again with a blue, red or green filter in front of the camera. Explain why the colours in your photo look different from the original photo.

CHECK**IT!**

1 What causes specular and diffuse reflection of light?

2 Why does a red brick look red to our eyes?

3 Jack is wearing a green jumper. What colour would Jack's jumper look if you saw it through first a red, then a green and finally a blue filter?

Emission and absorption of infrared radiation and black body radiation

All objects, whatever their temperature, emit and absorb infrared radiation.

The hotter the object, the more infrared radiation it emits in a particular time. The hotter the object:

- the higher the intensity of radiation it emits
- the shorter the **wavelengths** (and the higher the **frequencies**) of radiation it emits.

A **perfect black body** is an object that absorbs *all* of the electromagnetic radiation incident on it. A black body does not transmit or reflect any radiation.

As a good absorber is also a good emitter, a perfect black body is also the best emitter of radiation.

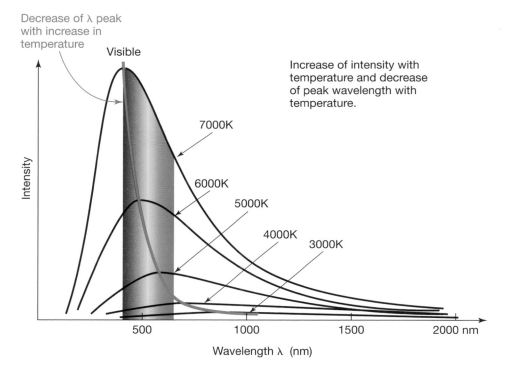

An object that does not change temperature absorbs the same amount of radiation that it emits in a given time. So, for an object at constant temperature:

rate of absorbed radiation = rate of emitted radiation

If an object absorbs radiation faster than it emits radiation, its temperature increases.

DO IT!

Make two cups of coffee, one with very hot milk and one with cold milk. Ensure that both cups have the same amount of liquid inside. Which cup cools down faster? Can you explain why?

H

NAIL IT!

The temperature of the object does not just depend on how fast or slowly it absorbs and emits radiation. It also depends on lots of other factors, like the amount of radiation it absorbs compared with the amount of radiation it emits.

For example, the temperature of an espresso coffee in a cup will decrease because it emits more radiation than it absorbs from the air around it. It also transfers energy to the air by heating through the walls of the cup.

STRETCH IT!

The temperature of the Earth also depends on the amount of radiation it reflects into space.

The diagram shows how the amounts of radiation absorbed, reflected and emitted by the atmosphere and the surface of the Earth are balanced.

- If there was a rapid increase in greenhouse gases, what would happen to the amount of radiation emitted by the Earth?

- What would this do to the Earth's temperature?

Solar radiation: 343 watts/m^2

Some of the solar radiation is reflected by the atmosphere and the Earth's surface

Outgoing solar radiation: 103 watts/m^2

Some of the infrared radiation passes through the atmosphere and out into space

Outgoing infrared radiation: 240 watts/m^2

Atmosphere

Greenhouse gases

Solar radiation passes through the atmosphere Incoming solar radiation: 240 watts/m^2

Some of the infrared radiation is absorbed and re-emitted by the greenhouse gas molecules.

About half of the solar radiation is absorbed by the Earth's surface Absorption of solar radiation: 168 watts/m^2

The Earth's surface emits infrared radiation (long wavelengths) to the atmosphere due to its temperature

Earth

NAIL IT!

Carbon dioxide, methane, nitrogen(II) oxide and fluorocarbons are all greenhouse gases.

CHECK IT!

1 What is a perfect black body?

H 2 What affects the temperature of an object?

H 3 What human activities could affect the temperature of the Earth's atmosphere? How are these activities affecting the radiation balance in the Earth's atmosphere?

1 **a** Use the two graphs to find the amplitude, period and wavelength of the wave. Draw and label on the graph these three properties of the wave.

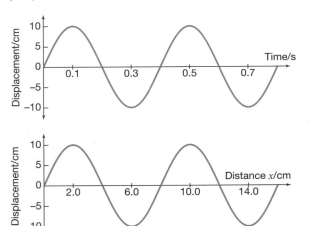

b Use the information you found in part **a** to calculate the speed of the wave.

2 Redraw the diagram below and write the parts of the electromagnetic spectrum in the correct order inside the grid.

3 Match the types of electromagnetic waves with their applications.

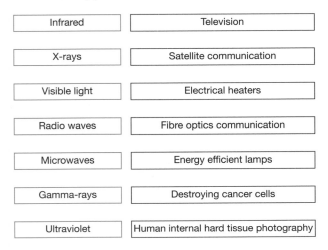

Infrared	Television
X-rays	Satellite communication
Visible light	Electrical heaters
Radio waves	Fibre optics communication
Microwaves	Energy efficient lamps
Gamma-rays	Destroying cancer cells
Ultraviolet	Human internal hard tissue photography

4 Complete the ray diagram to show how the red laser beam enters and exits the glass block.

5 **a** Laura hits a pan with a hammer 450 m away from Ollie. Ollie starts a stopwatch when he sees Laura hitting the pan, and stops it when he hears the sound of the bang. His stopwatch measures a time of 1.57 s. Calculate the speed of sound based on Ollie's recording, and compare it with the typical value of 340 m/s.

b Suggest what Ollie and Laura could do to improve their method.

Electromagnetism

Magnetism

Magnetic poles are the places on a magnet where magnetic forces are the strongest.

- Opposite poles attract each other.
- Same poles repel each other.

These forces of attraction and repulsion are examples of **non-contact forces**.

Opposite poles **attract**

Same poles **repel**

Magnetic fields

Permanent magnets generate their own **magnetic fields**. For example, a bar magnet as shown below.

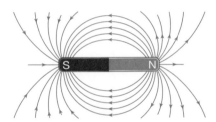

You can see the magnetic fields around this bar magnet

Induced magnets become magnets when they are placed in a magnetic field. For example, when an iron nail touches the pole of a bar magnet. When an induced magnet is removed from the magnetic field, it quickly loses most or all of its magnetism. Induced magnetism always causes a force of attraction.

A magnetic field is the area around a magnet where a magnetic force acts on another magnetic material.

Examples of magnetic materials are iron, steel, cobalt and nickel. The force between a magnet and a magnetic material is always a force of attraction.

To understand how a magnetic field affects magnetic materials, we can draw magnetic field lines around a magnet.

The strength of a magnetic field depends on the distance from the magnet. Magnetic field lines are concentrated at the poles and spread out the further they are from the magnet. This is why the magnetic field is at its strongest at the poles of the magnet, and weaker the further away from the magnet.

Magnetic field lines always point from the north pole to the south pole of a magnet. This is because, if you placed another north pole in the magnetic field, the direction of the force acting on it would be the same as the direction of the magnetic field at that point.

This also explains why like poles attract each other and unlike poles repel each other.

We can plot the pattern of magnetic field lines using small magnetic compasses, which contain a small bar magnet that is free to spin over a needle.

You can see how the compass needle change depending on their position in the magnetic field

The behaviour of the magnetic needle of a magnetic compass shows evidence that the Earth's core must be magnetic. The Earth's north geographic pole, is actually a south **magnetic pole**.

CHECKIT!

1 What is the difference between a permanent and an induced magnet?

2 How could you find the direction of the magnetic field lines of a bar magnet?

3 Explain why like poles repel each other, using the idea of magnetic field lines.

Motor effect

When a **current** flows through a **conducting** wire, a **magnetic field** is generated around the wire. Imagine gripping the wire in your right hand and pointing your thumb along the wire in the direction of the current. Your fingers curl in the same direction as the magnetic field lines.

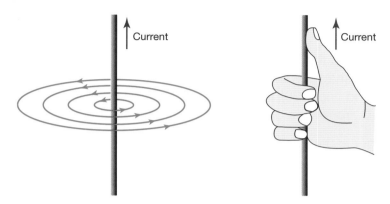

- The **bigger** the current, the **stronger** the magnetic field.

- The **further** the distance from the wire, the **weaker** the magnetic field.

The magnetic field can be made stronger by winding the wire into loops. The more loops there are, the *stronger* the magnetic field. Conducting wire wound into loops is called a **solenoid**.

- Inside a solenoid, the magnetic field is the same everywhere (uniform) and it is strong.

- Outside a solenoid, the magnetic field looks like the magnetic field around a bar magnet.

The magnetic field of the solenoid can be made stronger by wrapping the solenoid around an iron core. A solenoid with an iron core is called an **electromagnet**.

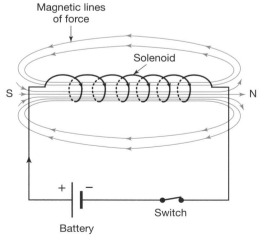

Field lines of the magnetic field through and around a current carrying solenoid

SNAPIT!

Curl the fingers of your left hand as if gripping the solenoid in the above diagram following the direction of the current through the coils of the solenoid pointing your thumb out. Take a photo of your hand. Your thumb should point in the direction of the magnetic field inside the solenoid.

Fleming's left-hand rule

When a conductor carrying a current is placed inside the magnetic field of a magnet, the conductor and the magnet exert a magnetic force on each other. This is called the **motor effect**.

We can find the direction of the force generated by the motor effect using **Fleming's left-hand rule**.

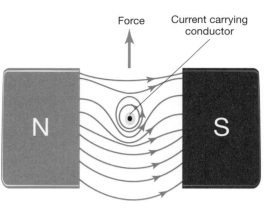

Catapult field

Put the thumb and first finger of your left hand in the shape of an L. Then put your second finger 90° from both your thumb and first finger (all three fingers are 90° from each other). Point each finger in this way:

1 First finger in the direction of the magnetic Field

2 SeCond finger in the direction of the Current

3 The thuMb gives the direction of Movement of the wire (the direction of the force exerted on it).

Left-hand rule

We can calculate the force on a conductor carrying a current at right angles (90°) to a magnetic field using the equation:

force = magnetic flux density × current × length

$$F = BIL$$

- F = force (unit: **newton**, N)
- B = magnetic flux density (unit: **tesla**, T)
- I = current (unit: **ampere**, or amp, A)
- L = length (unit: **metre**, m)

NAILIT!

This equation will be given to you, but make sure you know how to use it. As shown by the equation, increasing the magnetic flux density, the current, or the length of the wire will increase the force on the wire.

WORKIT!

Two permanent magnets are put onto a mass scale with unlike poles facing each other. A wire of length 4.0 cm is put between the magnets at 90° from the magnetic field. A current of 0.653 A is applied to the wire. The magnetic flux density is 0.02 T, and the direction of the field and current is such that the force produced on the wire is upward. What mass will the scale read if it was set to zero before the current was turned on? Explain your answer. (4 marks)

Circuit board wire loop

Triple-beam balance

Variable current source

Permanent magnet assembly

The length of the wire is 0.040 m.

$F = BIl$ ← Use the equation for the force on a wire carrying a current inside a magnetic field.

$= 0.02 \times 0.653 \times 0.040$

$= 5.2 \times 10^{-4} \text{ N}$ (1)

The mass scale measures mass. So, this force will be shown on the scale as the mass of an object of weight 5.2×10^{-4} N. (1) ←

And we can calculate the mass from $W = mg$ and rearrange it to get

$$m = \frac{W}{g} = \frac{5.2 \times 10^{-4}}{9.8} \quad (1)$$

Newton's third law tells us that an equal and opposite (downward) force will be applied by the wire on the pair of magnets.

$$= 5.3 \times 10^{-5} \text{ kg}$$

$$= 0.053 \text{ g} \quad (1)$$

Electric motors

When a coil of wire carries a current in a magnetic field, the coil of wire will rotate. This is how electric motors work:

1. The ends of the coil conductor are connected to the two sides of a 'split-ring commutator'.

2. Each side of the 'split-ring commutator' is connected to the opposite sides of the **dc power supply**.

3. The current in one side of the coil flows in the opposite direction to the current on the other side of the coil.

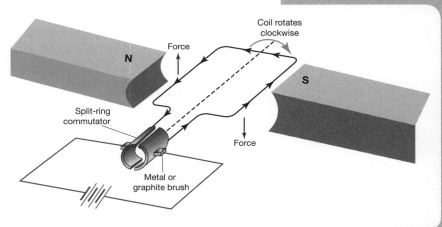

Coil rotates clockwise

Force

N

S

Split-ring commutator

Force

Metal or graphite brush

4. This causes the magnetic field to generate an upward force on one side of the coil and a downward force on the other side, which causes the coil to rotate.

5. When the coil has passed its vertical position, the connections on the 'split-ring commutator' will have swapped polarity, and the forces on the sides of the coil reverse, keeping the coil in rotation.

Loudspeakers

Loudspeakers and headphones use the motor effect to convert changes in the current (signals) in their electrical circuits into changes in the **pressure** of sound waves.

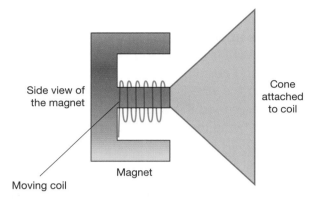

Side view of the magnet

Cone attached to coil

Magnet

Moving coil

1. The music device, for example, an MP3 player, sends an electrical signal with the same **frequency** as the music to the coil conductor.

2. The changes in the electrical current in the coil change the nearby magnetic field.

3. This changing magnetic field interacts with the magnetic field of the permanent magnet, moving the coil backward and forward with the same frequency as the music.

4. The cone attached to the coil is also moved backward and forward with the same frequency.

5. The cone compresses and expands the nearby air with the same frequency, so that sound waves travel through the air particles in the room to your ears.

SNAPIT!

Take a video of a loudspeaker playing some bass music. Use the motor effect to describe what you see happening to the cone of the speaker.

✓ CHECKIT!

1 The current through a wire in a magnetic field is decreased. How does the magnetic force on the wire change?

H2 How can you find the direction of the magnetic force on a wire carrying a current that is placed inside a magnetic field?

H3 A wire carrying 0.210 A experienced a force of 0.046 N when it was immersed perpendicularly in a magnetic field. If the wire is 0.751 m long, what is the magnetic flux density?

Electromagnetic induction

Induced potential difference

Two factors can induce a **potential difference (p.d.)** in an electrical **conductor**:

- when the conductor is moved inside a **magnetic field**, except for when it is moved parallel to the field lines

- when the magnetic field near the conductor is changed.

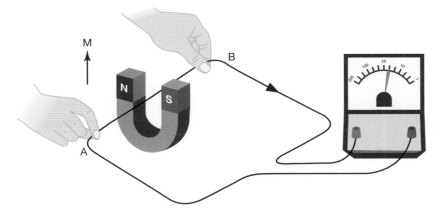

When the wire in the diagram is moved upward across the magnetic field of the **permanent magnet**, the galvanometer (ammeter) reads an electric **current** from A to B. This current is induced in the wire because the wire is part of a complete electrical circuit. This is called the **generator effect**.

On the previous page, you recalled that any electric current flowing through a conductor generates a magnetic field around the conductor. So, an induced current generates a magnetic field too. But this field will *oppose* the original change (the change in the magnetic field or the movement of the conductor).

The size of the induced p.d. or current can be increased by:

- increasing the speed of the relative movement between the conductor and the magnetic field

- strengthening the magnetic field

- adding more turns to a coil of wire.

The direction of the induced p.d. or current can be reversed by:

- changing the direction of movement of the conductor relative to the magnetic field

- changing the direction of the magnetic field.

Uses of the generator effect

A dynamo uses the generator effect to generate a **direct current**.

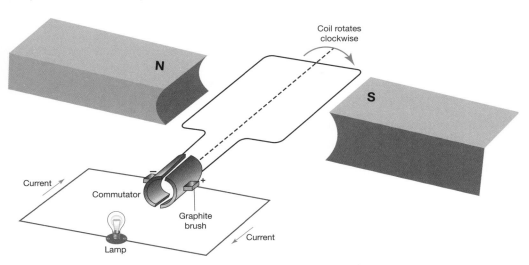

1. Each half of the 'split-ring commutator' is always in contact with the **right-hand** brush when its side of the coil is moving **downward** in the magnetic field.

2. Each half of the 'split-ring commutator' is always in contact with the **left-hand** brush when its side of the coil is moving **upward** in the magnetic field.

3. So the left-hand brush stays negative and the right-hand brush stays positive (in this diagram).

4. The direction of the magnetic field generated by the induced current opposes the rotation of the coil.

5. The induced p.d. is biggest when the coil is horizontal, and the induced p.d. drops to zero when the coil is vertical. This is shown in the diagram below.

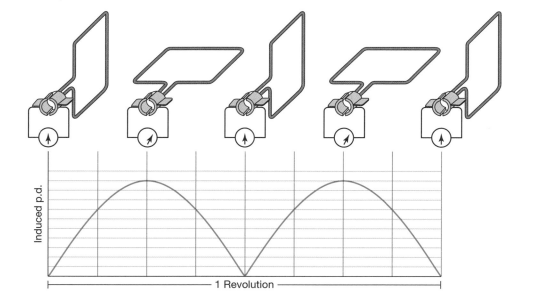

Alternators

(H)

An alternator uses the generator effect to generate an **alternating current**.

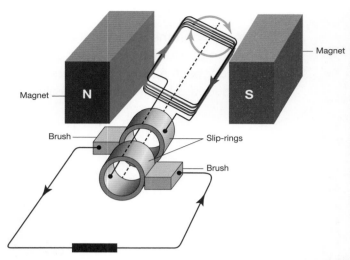

1. Each 'slip ring' is always in contact with the same brush throughout the rotation of the coil.

2. So, every half turn, the induced current through the coil and through the circuit completed by the brushes swaps direction.

3. The direction of the magnetic field generated by the induced current opposes the rotation of the coil.

4. The induced current is biggest (peaks) when the coil is horizontal, and the induced current drops to zero when the coil is vertical. It then peaks in the opposite direction when the coil is horizontal again (180° rotation).

Graph of output current from the ac generator

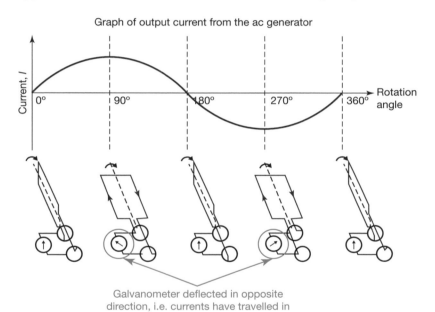

Galvanometer deflected in opposite direction, i.e. currents have travelled in different direction

You can better understand the differences between an alternator and a dynamo when you look at their graphs of induced current side by side.

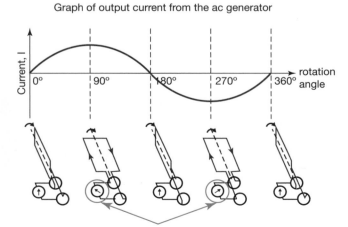

Graph of output current from the ac generator

Galvanometer deflected in opposite direction, i.e. currents have travelled in different direction

Graph of output current from the dc generator

Galvanometer deflected in same direction

DO IT!

Write an imaginary social media profile that could be used to describe an alternator, and another profile for a dynamo.

Microphones

A microphone works in the opposite way to a loudspeaker (which you looked at on page 118). A microphone uses the generator effect to convert the changes in air **pressure** generated by **sound waves** into changes in the induced current in electrical circuits.

Cross-section of dynamic microphone

Sound waves →

Wires carrying electrical audio signal
Magnet
Coil
Diaphragm

1 The moving coil is attached to the diaphragm.

2 A sound source (e.g. your voice) compresses and expands the air as sound waves, which makes the diaphragm move backward and forward.

3 As the diaphragm moves, the coil moves relative to the magnet with the same **frequency** as the sound waves.

4 This relative movement induces an electric current in the coil with the same frequency as the sound waves, and this signal can be carried to a sound amplifier and speakers.

CHECK**IT!**

1 How can a potential difference be induced in a conductor?

2 What are the differences and similarities between a dynamo and an alternator?

Transformers

Transformers work only with **alternating current** (ac).

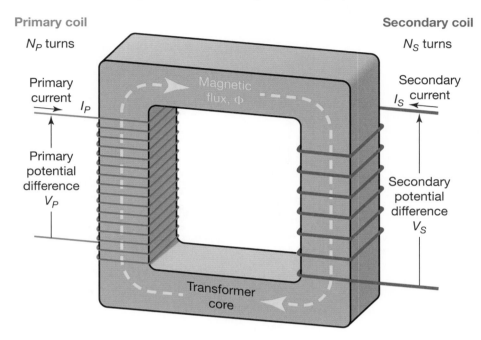

Primary coil
N_P turns

Primary current I_P

Primary potential difference V_P

Magnetic flux, Φ

Transformer core

Secondary coil
N_S turns

Secondary current I_S

Secondary potential difference V_S

1. An ac primary **current** I_p is applied across the primary coil.

2. This induces a changing **magnetic field** in the primary coil.

3. The changing magnetic field is channelled through the secondary coil by the iron core (iron is used because it can be easily magnetised).

4. The changing magnetic field inside the secondary coil induces an ac secondary current I_s in the secondary coil.

The ratio of the **potential difference** (p.d.) across the primary coil, V_p, and the p.d. across the secondary coil, V_s, depends on the ratio of the number of **turns** in the primary coil, n_p, and the number of turns in the secondary coil, n_s:

$$\frac{V_p}{V_s} = \frac{n_p}{n_s}$$

DO IT!

Draw a transformer that could increase a primary potential difference from 2 V to 6 V. What type of transformer is it?

There are two types of transformers:

- **Step-up** transformers (V_s is more than V_p)
- **Step-down** transformers (V_s is less than V_p)

A step-up transformer

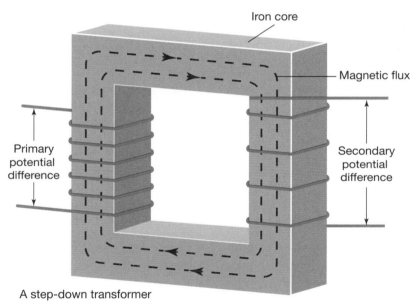

A step-down transformer

Efficiency and power in transformers

Modern transformers are nearly 100% efficient. This means the **power** input from the primary coil is nearly equal to the power output at the secondary coil. So, we can use the equation:

$$V_s \times I_s = V_p \times I_p$$

- $V_p \times I_p$ = power input (primary coil)
- $V_s \times I_s$ = power output (secondary coil)

MATH SKILLS

If you look at this equation, you should notice that in a **step-up** transformer, the p.d. (V_s) **increases**, but the current (I_s) **decreases**. The opposite happens for a step-down transformer.

The National Grid uses step-up transformers at power stations to increase V_s to very high potential differences and to decrease I_s to very small currents. This reduces the heating effects of the current flowing through the cables across the grid and makes transmitting power across the country very efficient.

WORKIT!

1 A transformer for a computer has an output p.d. $V_s = 15$ V. The primary p.d. from the mains is $V_p = 230$ V. If the primary coil has $n_p = 2230$ turns, how many turns n_s should the secondary coil have? (2 marks)

$$\frac{V_p}{V_s} = \frac{n_p}{n_s}$$

> This is a step-down transformer, so we can rearrange the equation.

to give:

$$n_s = n_p \frac{V_s}{V_p} \quad (1)$$

$$= 2230 \times \frac{15}{230} = 146 \quad (1)$$

2 The cable connected to the same computer in Question 1 has a current of 2 A flowing through it. What is the current in the cable going from the mains to the transformer box? (2 marks)

$$P_{in} = P_{out} = V_s \times I_s = 15 \times 2$$

> The transformer will be extremely efficient, so we can assume that the power input is equal to the power output.

$$= 30\,W \quad (1)$$

So, because $P_{in} = V_p \times I_p = 30\,W$, we can rearrange the equation to work out I_p:

$$I_p = \frac{P_{in}}{V_p} = \frac{P_{out}}{V_p} = \frac{30}{230}$$

$$= 0.130\,A \quad (1)$$

NAILIT!

These equations will be given to you. But make sure you know how to use and rearrange them.

✓ CHECKIT!

1 How do step-up and step-down transformers work?

2 The ratio $\frac{V_p}{V_s}$ for a transformer is 4.5. If $n_s = 300$ turns, what is n_p? Is this a step-up or a step-down transformer?

3 The ratio $\frac{n_p}{n_s}$ for a transformer is 0.33, and the primary coil p.d. V_p is 1.5 V. If the current in the secondary coil is $I_s = 0.250$ A, what is the power output?

1 Draw the magnetic field lines from the two magnets.

2 a Show on the diagram the direction of the current, *I*, the direction of the magnetic field, *B*, and the direction of movement of the wire, *F*.

b Suggest three changes to the system in the above system that would increase the force on the wire.

3 Complete the diagrams to show the missing poles, the direction of the magnetic fields and the direction of movement of the wire.

4 A copper wire of length 23 cm carrying a current of 0.43 A is immersed perpendicularly in a magnetic field of magnetic flux density 0.34 T. Calculate the force applied on the wire.

 a i Calculate the potential difference in the secondary coil.

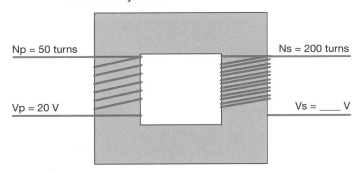

Np = 50 turns   Ns = 200 turns

Vp = 20 V   Vs = ____ V

ii Calculate the current in the secondary coil, knowing that I_p = 8 A.

b i Calculate the potential difference in the secondary coil.

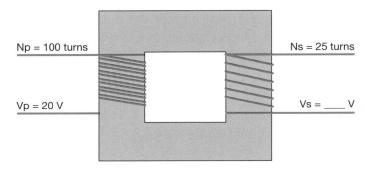

Np = 100 turns   Ns = 25 turns

Vp = 20 V   Vs = ____ V

ii Calculate the current in the secondary coil, knowing that I_p = 3 A.

Space physics

Our solar system

Our **solar system** is a small part of the Milky Way galaxy. A galaxy is a massive cluster of **stars** and their planets. The Milky Way galaxy is estimated to contain 100 billion stars.

Our solar system is made up of one star (the Sun), eight planets and the dwarf planets that orbit around the Sun.

NAILIT!

Remember that Pluto is a dwarf planet, *not* a planet.

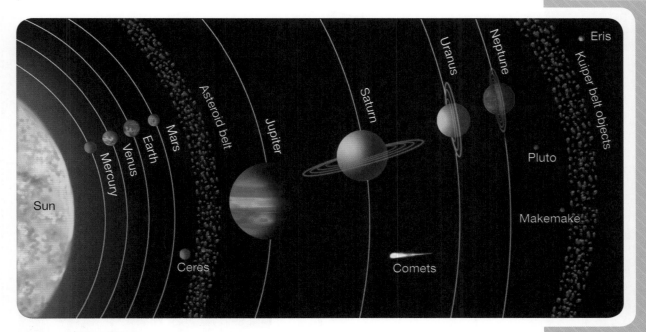

Objects that orbit around a planet are called satellites.

Artificial satellites are man-made devices that orbit the Earth and other planets to perform useful tasks, like communication. The Hubble Space Telescope is an artificial satellite that we use to look at stars.

Natural satellites, often just called moons, are naturally formed objects that orbit a planet. The Earth's only natural satellite is the Moon.

Big planets can have many moons. Jupiter has at least 67 known moons.

Planets and their natural and artificial satellites are kept in their orbits by the **forces** of **gravity** between the planets and the satellites (and between the Sun and the planets).

The Hubble Telescope

Our Moon

Orbital motion

Planetary orbits are almost circular, with the Sun in the centre.

In circular orbits, the force of gravity is always acting toward the centre of the orbit (the centre of the circle). So, because the direction of the planet or satellite keeps changing to keep it in a circle, this means that its **velocity** changes, but its **speed** does not change.

In stable orbits, if the speed of the orbiting object changes, then the radius of its orbit must change. For example, comets can have very stretched-out (elliptical or oval-shaped) orbits around the Sun. They **accelerate** to very high speeds when they get near the Sun (so their orbit has a smaller radius), then slow down when they get further away from the Sun (so their orbit has a bigger radius).

DOIT!

The International Space Station (shown in the picture on the right) is in orbit 400 km above the Earth, it is our largest artificial satellite and can even be seen with the naked eye. Look up online when it is visible from your home.

The International Space Station

CHECKIT!

1 What is the Milky Way?

2 What is our solar system made of?

3 Describe a circular orbit and a stable orbit.

Life cycle of a star

Recent theories about the life cycle of **stars** describe the birth, life and death of a star through different stages. The Sun is a main-sequence star with a diameter just under 1.4 million kilometres long.

This model of the life cycle of stars shows how stars of different sizes develop and die in different ways. In this model, the life cycle goes from top to bottom. It also shows the approximate diameters of the stars.

This model of the life cycle of stars shows how different sized stars develop and 'die' in different ways. The model also shows how lighter elements up to iron can be produced in the **fusion reactions** inside a star. Elements heavier than iron are produced in the massive explosions of very heavy stars. These explosions are called **supernovae**. As a supernova rapidly expands, it will spread out (distribute) the new elements formed throughout the **universe**.

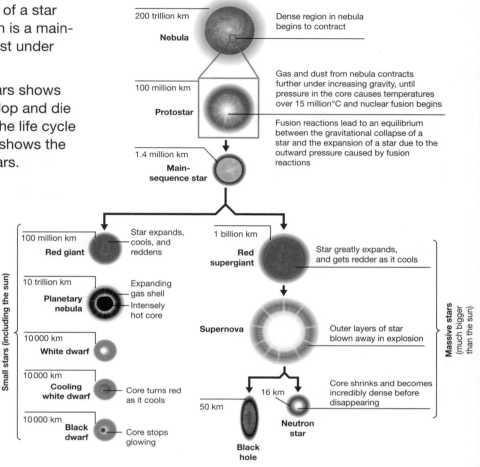

Nebula — 200 trillion km
Dense region in nebula begins to contract

Protostar — 100 million km
Gas and dust from nebula contracts further under increasing gravity, until pressure in the core causes temperatures over 15 million°C and nuclear fusion begins

Fusion reactions lead to an equilibrium between the gravitational collapse of a star and the expansion of a star due to the outward pressure caused by fusion reactions

Main-sequence star — 1.4 million km

Small stars (including the sun)

Red giant — 100 million km
Star expands, cools, and reddens

Planetary nebula — 10 trillion km
Expanding gas shell
Intensely hot core

White dwarf — 10 000 km

Cooling white dwarf — 10 000 km
Core turns red as it cools

Black dwarf — 10 000 km
Core stops glowing

Red supergiant — 1 billion km
Star greatly expands, and gets redder as it cools

Supernova
Outer layers of star blown away in explosion

Massive stars (much bigger than the sun)

Black hole — 50 km
Neutron star — 16 km
Core shrinks and becomes incredibly dense before disappearing

CHECKIT!

1 What is a nebula mainly made of?

2 What is the main factor that will determine how a star evolves from the main-sequence stage of its life?

3 How does the model of the life cycle of stars explain the formation of the elements in the universe?

Red-shift

The light from distant **galaxies** arrives on Earth with **wavelengths** shifted toward the red end of the **visible spectrum**. This means that the wavelengths of this light appear longer than they are.

This effect is called **red-shift**.

The further away and the faster the galaxies are moving, the bigger the increase in the observed wavelengths.

The red-shift is evidence that space (i.e. the universe) is expanding, because for this shift to take place the radiation must be travelling away from us in all directions. This movement increases the distance the radiation travels, 'stretching' the wavelengths so they appear longer (i.e. shifted towards the red end of the spectrum), the further the distance they have travelled.

This expansion of the universe is used to support the Big Bang theory. This is the theory that the whole universe (including space and time) began from a very small region that was incredibly hot and dense. Because of its enormous amount of **energy**, this tiny region expanded into our universe.

Big Bang

Galaxies are further apart as time goes on because the space in between them is expanding

SNAPIT!

Draw tiny spirals on a balloon to represent galaxies, then blow up the balloon. Take a photo when the balloon is quite small and another photo when it is quite big. What did you observe? This demonstration gives a simple picture of how space itself is expanding.

The observation that galaxies are receding (moving further away) from each other was first made by the physicist Edwin Hubble in 1929. Since 1998, scientists observing **supernovae** have noticed that distant galaxies are moving away from each other at an increasing rate (they are **accelerating** away from each other).

A supernova is the explosion of a star at the end of its lifecycle

This acceleration cannot be explained by the objects we can currently see in the universe. So, some scientists believe that an unexplained 'dark energy' is responsible for this increasing rate of expansion and are designing experiments to explain this acceleration. Scientists are also trying to detect an invisible form of matter called 'dark mass' which makes up most of the matter in the universe. This shows that there is still a lot to discover about our universe and how it works.

Building a theory

Scientists use observations like the red-shift of wavelengths of distant galaxies to build models and to suggest theories about the natural world. As scientists make more observations and repeat them to check that what they see is accurate, the theories are supported by stronger evidence. They analyse the observations to make better models. The Big Bang theory is one of the most widely accepted theories about the formation of the universe.

CHECKIT!

1 What is red-shift of light?

2 How does the red-shift from distant galaxies support the idea that the universe is expanding?

3 Explain how the expansion of the universe can be used to support the Big Bang theory.

1 Complete the list of planets in order of distance from the Sun.

_____

_____

Earth

Mars

_____

Saturn

_____

_____

2 Explain what prevents the gravitational collapse of a main-sequence star and why the star does not expand uncontrollably.

3 Copy and complete the gaps in the diagram below.

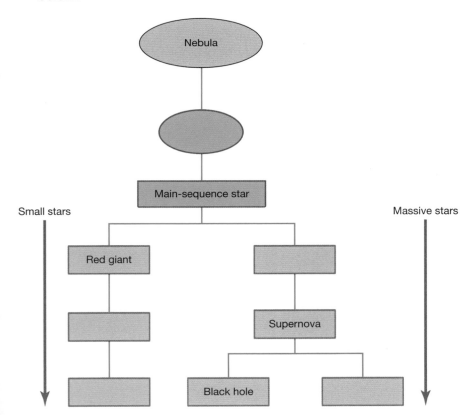

H 4 A satellite is in a circular orbit around the Earth. Explain how the velocity of the satellite changes.

5 Light from our Sun and from a distant galaxy are analysed with a spectrometer. The two spectra of light are shown in the image below.

Absorption lines from our Sun

Absorption lines from a distant galaxy

Explain why the absorption lines appear at different wavelengths for the two samples.

6 What does the theory of the Big Bang claim about the origins of the universe?

Glossary/Index

A

Acceleration Rate of change of velocity **84–6, 88**

Air resistance Frictional force due to air particles hitting a moving object. **71, 86**

Alternating current (ac) Current that changes in size and direction. **36, 121, 123**

Ammeter Instrument with virtually no electrical resistance used to measure electric currents. **27, 31**

Ampere Unit of electric current

Amplitude The intensity of a wave, usually measured as the distance between the centre of the oscillation and its peak/trough. **95**

Artificial satellites Man–made objects orbiting a planet. **127**

Astronomical model A model to explain how the universe was formed. **127–8**

Attractive forces Forces that cause two or more objects to attract each other (pull on each other). **40, 113–14**

B

Bar magnet A permanent magnet, usually shaped like a bar, or a rod. **113–14**

Battery A set of electrical cells connected in series to generate a potential difference. **27, 36**

Big bang model Model of the formation of the universe that states the universe began from a single point with a massive explosion that created all matter and space. **130–1**

Braking distance The distance a vehicle travels from the moment the brakes are applied until it stops completely. **90–1**

C

Cell An electrical component that generates a potential difference. **27**

Charge A physical quantity exerting a force that attracts other unlike charges and repels like charges. **29, 38, 40–1, 51**

Circuit A set of electrical components connected by wires to form one or more loops. **27–39, 103**

Circuit diagrams An electric circuit represented with drawn symbols and lines. **27–8, 31, 33, 34**

Component forces The effect of a force along a particular axis/direction. **69–70**

Component perpendicular The component (of a force) perpendicular to a surface, direction, or another physical quantity. **69–70**

Compression Squeezing **73, 95**

Concave lens Lenses that are thinner in the middle. The rays of light going through the lens spread out, i.e. they diverge. **105, 107**

Conduction The ability of a material to transmit (let through) electric currents. Often used for transmission of energy in the context of thermal conductivity. **19–20**

Conductor A material, or component, with high conductivity. **40, 119**

Conservation of energy Law of thermodynamics that states energy cannot be created nor destroyed, but it can only be redistributed in different parts of a system, or between systems. **19**

Contact forces Forces between two objects that act when they are touching each other (in contact). **66**

Convex lens Lens that is thicker in the middle. The light rays going through the lens get closer together (they converge). **105–6**

Coulomb

Coulomb Unit of electric charge.

Current Rate of flow of charge. **29–36, 117–22**

D

Dark energy Unobservable quantity thought to be responsible for the increasing acceleration in the expansion of the universe. **131**

Dark matter Physical quantity that is affected by gravitational forces but that cannot be observed directly, as it is not affected by electromagnetic radiation. **131**

dc power supply Electrical power supply that generates a dc potential difference. **36, 117**

Density Property of materials that shows the ratio between their mass and the volume occupied by that mass. **43–4, 79, 98–9**

Diaphragm The primary muscle used in the process of respiration. **122**

Diffuse reflection Reflection of light from a rough surface that reflects light at many angles. **108**

Diode Electrical component that lets current flow in one direction only. **28, 33**

Direct current (dc) Electric current of fixed value and direction. **36, 120**

Direct proportionality When the independent varial is doubled the dependent variable also doubles. **30, 32, 67, 75, 88**

Displacement The shortest way between the initial and the final position. In other words it is the distance with a direction. **71, 80, 85**

Dissipated energy Energy too spread out be used in a useful way. **10, 19**

Dynamo Generator that can generate a dc current. **120–21**

E

Earth wire Wire connected to the ground as safety for appliances. If there is a surge of current the earth wire is the path of least resistance for the charges to flow through, instead of the user. **36**

Elastic deformation When objects are stretched/compressed and return to their orignial shape when released. **73–5**

Electric field A force field generated by electric charges. **40–1**

Electrical signal Transmission of information coded in an electric pulse of current. **118**

Electrically charged An object carrying an electric charge. **40–1**

Electromagnet A magnet that can be switched on and off, as it is magnetic only when current flows through it. **115**

Electromagnetic spectrum The range of electromagnetic waves of different wavelengths and frequencies. **102, 104, 108**

Electromagnetic waves Transversal waves generated by oscillations of electric and magnetic fields that can travel through empty space. **95, 102–4**

Electron Subatomic particle carrying negative charge. **29, 40, 51**

Electrostatic repulsion A pushing force generated by electrostatic interactions, for example, two like charges close to each other will repel. **40, 89**

Energy Mathematical quantity associated to the configuration of a system. If a change in the system happens the energy is redistributed within the system. **10–26**

Energy stores A way to visualise where energy can be stored and measured in a system. They are not physical stores, like containers or boxes, but just a visual representation of a numerical value. **10–17, 23–4, 63, 71**

Extension The amount of length an object is extended (or compressed) from its original shape. **13–14, 73–5**

F

Fault A breakage in the circuit that can cause the live wire to be in contact with the outside casing. **36**

Fleming's left–hand rule A handy rule to see in with direction a conductor carrying a current will move when it is inside a magnetic field. **116**

Focal length The distance from the middle of a lense to the point where all parallel light rays will focus after going through a convex lens. **105**

Force–magnifiers Term referred to gears, as set of gears can be used to magnify the force applied to a gear connected to another gear. **77**

Forces Pushes or pulls applied between two or more objects. Forces are invisible and unobservable physical quantities, we cannot see forces, but we can measure their effects. **40–1, 66–94, 113, 116–17**

Frequency (waves) The number of waves passing through a point in 1 s (the unit of time). **96, 100**

Friction Force between two surfaces rubbing against each other. **10, 71**

Fuse Small wire with low melting point used as safety precaution in electrical appliances. If the current through the fuse becomes too high, the fuse melts and the circuit is broken. **27, 36**

Fusion reactions Nuclear fusion is the merging of light nuclei to create a heavier nucleus. The mass of the heavier nucleus is less than the mass of the two nuclei merging together, so the excess mass is released as energy. **64, 129**

G

Galaxy Cluster of billions of stars, planets and other objects, such as black holes. **127**

Galvanometer An instrument for detecting and measuring electric currents. Ammeters are a type of Galvanometers. **119**

Gas A state of matter where a substance has particles freely moving in all directions. **47–9**

Generator effect A potential difference, hence a current, can be generated by plunging a wire (or other conductor, like a coil of wire) into and out of a strong magnet and vice versa. **119–22**

Gravitational field A force field generated by a large mass, like a planet or a star. **67**

Gravitational field strength The value of the gravitational field at a particular place in the field. Near the surface of the earth the gravitational field strength is g = 9.8 N/kg. **12, 67**

Gravitational pull Gravitational force of attraction between two masses. **66–7, 69–72, 86, 89**

Gravity Force due to the interaction between two masses. **10, 12, 66–7, 89, 127–8**

Greenhouse gases Gases that cause the greenhouse effect, like carbon dioxide. **111, 128**

I

Indirectly proportional If a and b are indirectly proportional then $a \propto 1/b$. **30, 88**

Induced magnet A material that becomes a magnet when a current flows through it **113**

Inelastic deformation Stretching/compressing an object that will not return in its original shape after the extension/compression. **73, 75**

Inertia The resistance of an object (mass) to change its velocity. **87, 88**

Insulators Objects/materials that are poor conductors of electric currents. Often used for poor conductors of energy in the context of thermal conductivity. **20, 40**

Interaction pairs Pair of forces caused by the interaction between two objects. When two objects interact they will exert an equal and opposite force on each other. **89**

Internal energy The total kinetic energy and potential energy of all the particles (atoms and molecules) that make up a system. **45–6, 49**

Ionised An atom that has lost or gained one or more electrons in its outer electron shells. **40**

Ionising radiation Radiation capable of ionising atoms. **54–5, 103**

J

Joules Unit of energy. **18, 71**

K

Kilogram Unit of mass. **66**

Kinetic Term referred to moving objects. **12, 13, 47, 71, 90–1**

L

Lamp Electric component that glows when a current flows through it. **27, 32**

Latent heat The energy needed for a substance to change state. **45**

LED (Light-emitting diode) Electrical component that lets current flow in one direction only and emits light when current flows through it. **28, 33**

LDR (Light-dependent resistor) A resistor whose resistance depends on the intensity of light shining on it. **28, 33**

Limit of proportionality For an elastic material the limit of porportionality is reached when the material has been stretched/compressed so much that it will no longer return to its original shape. **13, 75**

Linear Arranged in a straight line. **32, 33, 75**

Live wire Wire in the electric plug that carries the alternating potential difference from the supply to the appliance. **36**

Longitudinal waves Waves whose oscillations are along the same direction (parallel) to the direction of travel of the wave. **95–7, 101**

M

Magnetic compasses Small bar magnets suspended and free to rotate, so the compass needle points in the direction of the Earth's magnetic field. **114**

Magnetic field A force field generated by a magnet. **113–19**

Magnetic materials Materials affected by a magnetic force, but that do not generate a magnetic field themselves. **113**

Magnetic poles The two sides of a magnet where the magnetic forces are the strongest. **113–14**

Mains electricity Potential difference and current from our household sockets generated at power stations and carried across the country through the National Grid. **36–9**

Mass Property of all matter. It is the measure of an object's resistance to acceleration when a net force is applied. **12–13, 43, 45, 66–7, 88**

Medium Material in which light and other EM waves can travel. **95–101**

Metres Unit of length **71**

Moment of force Turning effect of a force defined as the force x perpendicular distance of the force from the pivot. **76–7**

Momentum Mass x velocity of an object. **92–3**

Moon A natural satellite orbiting a planet. **127**

Motor effect The movement of a conductor (like a wire) caused by an electric current flowing in the conductor when it is in the presence of a magnetic field. **115–18**

N

Natural satellite A natural object orbiting a planet. **127**

Neutral wire It completes the circuit in an appliance plugged to the mains. **36**

Newton Unit of force.

Newton's first law Newton's law describing the tendency of objects to remain in their state of motion. **87**

Newton's second law Newton's law describing the relationship between the resultant force applied on an object, its mass and acceleration. **88**

Newton's third law Newton's law describing the relationship between two objects interacting with each other. **89**

Non–contact forces Forces between objects acting at a distance, i.e. without the need for them to touch each other. **40, 41, 66–7, 113**

Non-linear Arranged in a non–linear pattern, i.e. not in a straight line. **33, 75**

Non–ohmic A component that doesn't obey Ohm's law, i.e. its resistance will change with the potential difference applied across it. **32–3**

Non-renewable An energy resource that cannot be replenished. **23, 25**

O

Ohm Unit of electrical resistance.

Ohmic conductor A conductor whose resistance remains constant for constant temperature. **32, 33**

Orbit The path of on object moving around another object like a satellite orbiting the earth. **127–8**

Oscillation The vibrations of an object, or particles, generating a wave. **95, 103**

Output induced current Current output from a dynamo or generator. **119–21**

P

Parallel Two lines or planes that never touch. **31, 34–5**

Pascal Unit of pressure.

Perfect black body An object that absorbs all of the radiation incident on it. **110**

Period The time taken for a single wave to pass through a point. **96**

Permanent magnet A magnet that doesn't lose its magnetism and doesn't need a current to become a magnet. **113, 119**

Planet A massive object orbiting a star **127–8**

Polarity The property of having poles or being polar. **113–14, 117**

Potential difference (p.d.) The difference of electrical potential between two points. **27, 30–39, 119–20**

Potential stores Energy stores associated with the position of an object (gravity store), or the chemical composition of a substance (chemical store). **12–14, 71, 75**

Power The rate of transfer of energy, i.e. energy transferred in one second. **18, 21, 37–9, 124–5**

Pressure The force per unit area, i.e. the force applied on each square metre of surface. **47–9, 78–9**

Primary voltage Potential difference across the primary coil in a transformer. **123–5**

Principal focus The point where parallel light rays are brought to a focus in a convex lens. **105–7**

R

Radiation Emission of energy as electromagnetic waves or as moving subatomic particles. **51, 54–65, 103, 110–11**

Random With no particular pattern, of unpredictable outcome. **47, 58**

Rarefaction Regions of expanded air in sound waves. **95**

Ray diagram Drawing showing the path of light rays. **106, 107**

Red shift The observed increase in wavelength in the light from distant galaxies. **130–31**

Refraction Bending of light as it goes from a medium to another of different optical density. **98–9, 101, 102–3, 105–7**

Renewable An energy resource that can be replenished. **23–5**

Repulsive forces Pushing forces between two or more objects. **40, 89, 113, 114**

Resistance Ability to oppose something, e.g. resistance to movement, resistance to a flow of current. **27, 28, 30–35**

Resistor A component designed to control the current through a circuit by applying a resistance to it. **28, 31, 32–3, 35**

Resultant force The sum of all the forces acting on an object. **68–70, 87, 88, 92**

Ripple tank A device used to observe water waves generated in a tank. **97**

S

Scalar Physical quantity that does not have a direction. **66, 80**

Secondary voltage The potential difference induced in the secondary coil of a transformer. **123–5**

Series Components connected in the same loop with the source of potential difference. **31, 34–5**

Solar system A set of planets and other objects orbiting around a star, in our Solar sytem it the Sun. **127–8**

Solenoid A long coil of wire used as an electromagnet. **115**

Sound waves longitudinal waves generated by compressions and rarefactions of air. Also, in solids and liquids. **95, 97, 100–101, 118, 122**

Specific heat capacity The amount of energy required to raise the temperature of one kilogram of the substance by one degree Celsius. **15–17**

Specific latent heat The amount of energy required to change the state of one kilogram of the substance with no change in temperature. **45–6**

Specific latent heat of fusion Specific latent heat in the change of state from solid to liquid. **46**

Specific latent heat of vaporisation Specific latent heat in the change of state from liquid to gas. **46**

Specular reflection Reflection from a smooth surface in a single direction. **108**

Speed Distance travelled in the unit of time. **12, 80–83, 90, 96–7**

Split–ring commutator Device for reversing the current direction through every half turn in a motor. **117, 120**

Spring constant Property of elastic materials that determine how stiff and strong they are. **13, 73–5**

Standard form Way of writing down very large or very small numbers. **15**

Star A massive cluster of particles undergoing nuclear fusion in its core. **127, 129**

Step down Referred to a step down transformer, which reduced the output potential difference in the secondary coil. **39**

Step-down transformers A transformer that induced a lower potential difference in the secondary coil than the input potential difference across the primary coil. **39, 123–5**

Step up Refers to step up transformers which increase the potential difference at the secondary coil. **39**

Step-up transformers A transformer that induced a higher potential difference in the secondary coil than the input potential difference across the primary coil. **39, 123–5**

Store Referred to energy store, which is a part of the system where energy can be measured and stored. **10–14, 19, 21, 23–4**

Stroboscope A device used to make flashes of light matching the frequency of waves to observe them more easily. **97**

Supernova A star at the end of its life. Exploding star. **129, 131**

Switch A device that can break and close a circuit. **27, 29**

System An object or group of objects. **10–11, 15–22, 45**

T

Tangent Perpendicular to **83**

Tension Force due to the pulling of a rope, string, wire, etc. **66**

Tesla Unit of magnetic flux density.

Thermistor Electrical component whose resistance changes with temperature. **28, 33**

Thermal Relating to, or caused by, temperature. **15–17, 19–20**

Thinking distance The distance travelled by a vehicle while the driver reacts to a potential danger they spot before they apply the brakes. **90–1**

Transformer A device made of two coils and an iron core that can increase or decrease the output potential difference. **39, 123–5**

Transverse waves Waves whose oscillations are perpendicular to the direction of travel of the wave. **95–7, 101, 102**

Turning effect The effect of a force that causes objects to turn/rotate. **76–7**

U

Universe All existing matter and space considered as a whole. **130–31**

Useful That can be used for a specific purpose/job. **21, 38**

V

Vector A quantity having direction as well as magnitude. **66, 69–70**

Velocity Speed in a direction **69, 80–81, 84–6, 92**

Visible light Part of the EM spectrum detectable by the human eye. **102, 108–9**

Visible spectrum Part of the EM spectrum detectable by the human eye. **108–9**

Volt Unit of potential difference

Voltmeter Instrument used to measure the potential difference across two points. **27, 31**

Volume The space occupied by an object, or gas. **43–4, 47–8**

W

Watt Unit of power **18**

Wave front diagrams Drawings used to show how waves propagate through media. **102–3**

Wavelength Distance between two peaks, or two troughs, in a wave. **95, 97, 108–9, 130**

Work done Force x distance travelled in the direction of the force. **18, 49, 71–72, 74**

Answers

Energy

Energy stores and systems

1 First, choose the start and end point; second, find the energy stores at those points; third, show which stores empty and which stores fill up.

2 **a** Electrical working

   b Heating by particles

   c Mechanical working

   d Heating by particles

3 Example 1: A weightlifter lifting a weight transfers energy via mechanical working;
Example 2: A bonfire transfers energy via heating by radiation.

Changes in energy stores

1 301.6 J

2 1123 J

3 Cyclist A's E_k is 9 times higher than the E_k for cyclist B. This is because their speed is 3 times that of cyclist B, and $3^2 = 9$

Energy changes in systems – specific heat capacity

1 94 500 J

2 The thermal store will increase by 4200 J; as energy is conserved.

3 c

Power

1 (b) 850 W; because it transfers more energy per second to the water.

2 11 J

3 6930 J

Energy transfers in a system

1 Wear streamlined helmet and adjust body position to reduce air resistance; Lubrication between bike's chain and gears to reduce heating effects of friction; High pressure in tyres to reduce surface area of contact between the road and the tyres.

2 The infrared radiation from the heating elements in the toaster warms the surrounding air which rises; so not all the energy is transferred through heating by radiation to the toast.

3 Less fuel consumption; Tyres, brakes and other components do not get worn out as quickly.

Efficiency

1 Because in any change within a system some energy is dissipated to the surroundings.

2 Because the useful energy transferred is the numerator of the fraction and the input energy is the denominator; Since the useful energy transferred can never be greater than the input energy, the fraction can never return a value greater than 1.

3 Being only 25% efficient means that our body needs to transfer 4 times more energy from the chemical store to do the mechanical work needed during exercise, e.g. to lift a weight.

National and global energy resources

1 Renewable energy resources can be replaced (replenished); but non-renewable energy resources cannot be replaced and so will eventually run out if we keep using them.

2 Fossil fuels have high power output and are very reliable.

3 Accept any of the following: Large areas are needed to harness it; It has a low power output; It has a low conversion efficiency; It can only be harnessed during daylight hours.

Review It!

1 Renewable: water waves, biofuel, hydroelectricity, the Sun, geothermal, the tides.

Non-renewable: nuclear fuels, coal, oil, natural gas.

2 **a** *kinetic energy* = 0.5 × *mass* × (*speed*)²

$$E_k = \frac{1}{2}mv^2 \rightarrow m = 2\frac{E_k}{v^2}$$

   b *elastic potential energy* = 0.5 × *spring constant* × (*extension*)²

$$E_e = \frac{1}{2}ke^2 \rightarrow e = \sqrt{2\frac{E_e}{k}}$$

   c *g.p.e* = *mass* × *gravitational field strength* × *height*

$$E_p = mgh \rightarrow h = \frac{E_p}{mg}$$

3 $\Delta\theta$ is a temperature difference, and degrees Celsius and kelvin have the same magnitude; so using degrees Celsius or kelvin will affect the result of the calculation because the taking difference gives the same result; For example, the temperature increase between 2°C and 20°C is $\Delta\theta = 20 - 2 = 18$°C; which expressed in kelvin becomes $\Delta\theta = 293.15 - 275.15 = 18$ K.

4 **a** Lift B has greater power than lift A; because it can lift the same load the same height in less time; The rate of energy transferred is higher for lift B.

   b Energy transferred is

$$E_p = mgh \text{ and } P = \frac{E}{t} = \frac{mgh}{t}$$

$$h = \frac{Pt}{mg} = \frac{343 \times 15}{70 \times 9.8} = 7.5 \ m$$

So, each floor is $\frac{7.5}{3} = 2.5$ m high.

5 Aluminium has a higher thermal conductivity than plastic; so it will transfer energy by conduction to the ice cube at a higher rate than the plastic block; so the ice cube on the aluminium block will melt faster than the cube on the plastic block.

6 First we need to calculate the energy in the kinetic store when the car is at top speed.

$$E_k = \frac{1}{2}mv^2 = \frac{1}{2}0.520 \times 2.2^2 = 1.26 \ J$$

So, at top speed the toy car transfers 1.26 J to the kinetic store each second; This means a useful power output of 1.26 W; So, to find the efficiency of the toy car:

$$Efficiency = \frac{Useful \ power \ output}{Total \ power \ input}$$

$$= \frac{1.26}{1.5} = 0.84$$

We can multiply by 100 to find the percentage efficiency, i.e. 84%.

Electricity

Standard circuit diagram symbols

1 Ammeters have hardly any resistance; but voltmeters have very high resistance.

2 Their *I-V* characteristics are very similar and they both let current flow only in one direction; However, LEDs emit light, while diodes do not.

3 A diode in series with an LDR.

Electrical charge and current

1 An electrical current is the rate of flow of electrical charge.

2 Free electrons fill all the components of the circuit all the time, even when the circuit is open; So, when the circuit is closed all the free electrons will start drifting

in the same net direction at the same time.

3 31.4 C

Current, resistance and potential difference

1 $I = \frac{V}{R}$ **2** 1560 V **3** 20 W

Resistors

1 The current through an ohmic conductor (at constant temperature) is directly proportional to the potential difference across the ohmic conductor (resistor).

2 The resistance of the diode is very high for all negative values of p.d., then it suddenly decreases as the p.d. reaches a certain positive value; As the p.d. increases further the resistance drops by greater and greater amounts for equal increments in p.d.

3 A linear relationship between two variables follows a straight line in a graph of the two variables; whilst a non-linear relationship follows a curved pattern.

Series and parallel circuits

1 0.75 V

2 Because each component is individually connected to the power supply in its own loop.

3 V across R_1 = 6V and V across R_2 = 3V

Mains electricity

1 Because this is always at a potential of about 230 V, so if a fault occurs and the user touches the live wire or the metal casing of the kettle (if it is touching the live wire), this could electrocute the user.

2 In a DC the potential difference provided by the battery does not change in direction (sign) or value; In an AC the potential difference continually alternates in direction (sign) and changes value.

3 Such an appliance would draw less current when plugged to the mains in the USA; so it might not perform as well; For example, a mobile phone charger might take longer to charge your phone.

Electrical power, energy transfers in appliances and the National Grid

1 The power of an appliance depends on the potential difference across the device and the current through it.

2 When a car engine is working, the chemical store transfers some energy to the kinetic energy store associated with the car, through mechanical working; Some of this energy transferred will fill the thermal store of the surroundings by heating the engine and the air around it.

3 0.33 mA or 3.3×10^{-4} A

Static charge and electric fields

1 Negative charges (electrons) move and the positive charges (ions/protons) stay stationary.

Review It!

1

Light Dependent Resistor		It is a resistor that changes its resistance depending on how much light is shone on it.
Light Emitting Diode		It lets current flow through it in one direction only, but when current flows through it emits light.
Lamp		It has a very thin filament (wire), usually made of tungsten, which gets really hot when a current flows through it, so it glows and emits visible light.
Variable Resistor		It opposes the flow of current with a certain resistance and it can be set to different values of resistance within a specific range.
Battery		It is a collection of cells connected in series with each other.
Thermistor		It is a resistor that changes its resistance depending on its temperature.

2 a Electric current is the rate of flow of electrical charge, i.e. the amount of charge passing a point of a circuit in a second.

b If the ammeter had a resistance larger than zero, the current in the circuit would decrease; so the ammeter would not read the real value of current through the circuit.

3 $t = \frac{Q}{I}$

4 a An I-V graph would have I on the y-axis and V on the x-axis; so we would need to rearrange the equation to:

$$I = \frac{1}{R}V \quad \Leftrightarrow \quad y = mx + 0$$

2 As concentrations of opposite charges build on two objects close to each other, the electric field between the two objects increases; until the forces on the negative charges become strong enough to drag them away from the negatively charged object onto the positively charged object.

3 It moves away from the negatively charged sphere following the direction of the line between the centre of the sphere and the centre of the negative charge.

The gradient of this line graph would, therefore, be $m = \frac{1}{R}$.

b $I = \frac{V}{R} = \frac{9}{12000} = 7.5 \times 10^{-4}$ A

c Between 140–150 Lux of light intensity.

d First we find the current using

$$I = \frac{V}{R} = \frac{4.5}{2500} = 0.0018 \ A$$

The charge flowing through a point in a certain time can be calculated using:

$$Q = It = 0.0018 \times 90 = 0.162 \ C$$

Particle model

Density of materials

1 The mass per unit volume.

2 1.7×10^{-4} m^3

3 $\rho_{\text{fresh water}} = \dfrac{0.250}{0.000250} = 1000$ kg/m^3;

   $\rho_{\text{dead sea}} = \dfrac{0.250}{0.000202} = 1238$ kg/m^3;

   So a human body of density 985 kg/m^3 would float in both fluids; but better in the dead sea, as it is denser than fresh water.

Changes of state and internal energy

1 The specific latent heat of a material is the amount of energy needed to for 1 kg of that substance to change state (without a change in temperature); The specific heat capacity of a material is the amount of energy needed to for 1 kg of that substance to increase its temperature by 1°C.

2 Those flat sections would be longer, because it would take longer for the substance to change state.

3 2060.8 kJ

Particle model and pressure

1 The particles of a gas constantly move with random motion, i.e. in all directions and with a range of speeds (random velocity).

2 Because pumping more air in the tyre causes the number of air particles in the system to increase and may also cause the temperature to rise; pV is only constant for a *fixed* mass of gas at *constant* temperature.

3 $p_2 = \frac{1}{3} p_1$ so the difference between them will be $\frac{2}{3} p_1$.

Review It!

1 a kg/m^3

   b i Ethanol is less dense than olive oil; so it will float on top of it.

      ii The ratio $\dfrac{m_e}{m_o} = 0.97$

   c $r = \dfrac{m}{V} = \dfrac{0.437}{\pi r^2 h} = \dfrac{0.437}{\pi \times 0.012^2 \times 0.120}$

      $= 8050$ kg/m^3

2 a Latent heat of fusion is between solid and liquid; latent heat of vaporisation is between liquid and gas.

   b $E = mL = 0.185 \times 59000$

      $= 10915$ J

3

4 Increasing the temperature of the gas increases the average energy in the kinetic store; As the volume of the gas does not change, the increase in the kinetic store causes more collisions of particles per second and the force from each collision will also be greater due to the increased speed; and both effects produce an increase in the pressure of the gas.

5 The pressure on the piston is the same as the atmospheric pressure outside the syringe; so the pressure of the air inside the syringe must also be the same.

   When the temperature of the gas is higher (in hot water) the pressure of the air inside the syringe will increase; so the piston will rise until the volume of air increases enough to allow the gas pressure to rise to atmospheric pressure.

   When the temperature of the gas is low (icy water) the pressure of the air inside the syringe will decrease; and the piston will drop until the volume of air reduces sufficiently to allow the gas pressure to rise to atmospheric pressure.

6 a $p_1 V_1 = p_2 V_2 \Leftrightarrow p_2 = \dfrac{p_1 V_1}{V_2}$

      $= \dfrac{101325 \times 20}{55} = 36\,845$ Pa

   b We had to assume that the temperature remained constant.

Atomic structure

The structure of the atom

1 +2

2 92 protons and 146 neutrons

3 10 000 orders of magnitude

Developing a model of the atom

1 Positive charge fills the whole volume of the atom, with negatively charged particles (electrons) scattered inside the atom to balance its positive charge (the electrons resemble raisins inside a pudding).

2 In Rutherford's model the electrons can orbit the nucleus at any radius; but Bohr's model shows that only certain radii are allowed.

3 Because if the positive charge was spread out over a mass occupying the whole volume of the atom, it would not generate forces strong enough to cause an alpha particle to bounce off the atom with large angles; Therefore the mass and its positive charge must be concentrated in the centre of the atom.

Radioactive decay and nuclear radiation

1 Alpha and Beta particles and Gamma rays; Neutrons also accepted.

2 Neutrons because they are the most penetrating type of radiation; but they also interact with and can be absorbed by hydrogen-rich materials, like the water in our bodies, which can make our bodies radioactive and kill us.

3 Gamma radiation has no mass or charge, so it does not interact with other particles as strongly as alpha particles, which have a very high mass and charge; This means gamma radiation is not easily decelerated so it is more penetrating than alpha particles.

Nuclear equations

1 Its atomic number (number of protons).

2 $^1_0 n$

3 The atomic number would remain the same, but the mass number decreases by 1.

Half-life of radioactive elements

1 The isotope in the sample and the number of radioactive nuclei left in the sample.

2 The time taken for the number of nuclei of the radioactive isotope in a sample to halve/the time taken for the count rate (activity) from a sample of radioactive isotope to decrease to half its initial level.

3 73 days

Hazards and uses of radioactive emissions

1 Natural sources – rocks and cosmic rays from space; Man-made sources – testing of nuclear weapons and nuclear accidents.

2 Because isotopes with higher half-life will remain intensely radioactive for longer.

3 It has a relatively short half-life and emits gamma radiation which is less ionising and so less dangerous when the source is inside the body; as almost all the radiation will escape the body and not be absorbed by internal tissue.

Nuclear fission and fusion

1 Nuclear fission is when a heavy and unstable nucleus, like uranium or plutonium, splits into two smaller nuclei of roughly the same size.

2 Each nuclear fission normally releases 2 or 3 neutrons when the nucleus splits; These fission neutrons can go on to split other nuclei and very quickly start a chain reaction.

3 In this process some of the mass of the original nucleus is converted as energy transferred by radiation.

Review It!

1 **a** $^{23}_{11}Na \rightarrow$ 11 electrons, 11 protons and 12 neutrons

b $^{14}_{7}N \rightarrow$ 7 electrons, 7 protons and 7 neutrons

c $^{235}_{92}U \rightarrow$ 92 electrons, 92 protons and 143 neutrons

d $^{208}_{84}Po \rightarrow$ 84 electrons, 84 protons and 124 neutrons

e $^{9}_{4}Be \rightarrow$ 4 electrons, 4 protons and 5 neutrons

f $^{14}_{6}C \rightarrow$ 6 electrons, 6 protons and 8 neutrons

2 Bohr suggested that electrons orbited around the nucleus of atoms at specific distances, while in Rutherford's model electrons could orbit at any distance from the nucleus.

3 $^{1}_{0}n + ^{235}_{92}U \rightarrow ^{141}_{56}Ba + ^{92}_{36}Kr + 3^{1}_{0}n$ + Energy

4 **a** Half-life of element A = 2 days; and half-life of element B = 3.5 days.

b The count rate per minute drops to 6 after approximately 7 days, which is 3.5 half-lives.

c After two half-lives ¼ is left; The half-life of B is 3.5 days, so it takes two half-lives = 7 days to drop to ¼ the original value.

5 Radioactive contamination is the presence of radioactive atoms within other materials and irradiation is the exposure of an object to nuclear radiation.

6 **a** Some areas of England, Scotland, Wales, Southern France, Norway and the Netherlands.

b Some areas of Central and Northern Spain, Central France, Austria, Greece and some areas in Southern Finland.

c 3.0 to 5.0 mSv/year

Forces

Forces and their interactions

1 Power is an example of scalar quantity and momentum is an example of vector quantity.

2 Contact forces act between objects that are 'touching' each other and non-contact forces act at a distance.

3 The mass of an object is a scalar quantity and is the same anywhere in the universe, while the weight of an object is a force, i.e. a vector quantity, and it changes depending on the gravitational field (9.8 m/s² on Earth).

Resultant forces

1 The resultant force and it is the sum of all the forces acting on the object.

2 807 N upwards

H3 3.5 N; 3.5N

Work done and energy transfer

1 The force multiplied by the distance in the direction of the force.

2 530 J because work done equals energy transferred.

3 332 024 000 J

Forces and elasticity

1 Elastic deformation – the object returns to its original shape after deformation; Inelastic deformation – the shape of the object is permanently changed by the deformation.

2 70 N/m

3 0.0875 J; 0.0875 J

Moments, levers and gears

1 338100 Nm

2 Yes, because $F \times d = 2F \times \frac{1}{2}d$

3 When the effort (force) is on the smaller wheel, the larger wheel moves a smaller distance, but with a larger force , as $F \times d$ is conserved.

Pressure and pressure differences in fluids

1 It acts in all directions in a fluid and perpendicularly to at the surface of the fluid.

2 1013.25 N

H3 p_E = 5729 Pa and p_M = 935 Pa

Distance, displacement, speed and velocity

1 Distance and speed are scalar quantities and scalar quantities have no direction; displacement and velocity are vectors, which are different to scalar quantities because vectors have direction; So, displacement is the distance travelled in a given direction, and velocity is the speed in a given direction.

2 4.32 km

3 5.9 m/s

Distance-time relationship

1 The speed of the object.

2 Because the lower the gradient of a distance–time graph, the slower the object is travelling; and when an object slows down this means it is decelerating.

3 That is the reaction time of the driver.

Acceleration

1 Acceleration is a vector quantity.

2 1.1 m/s²

3 193 m

Newton's laws of motion

1 A resultant force needs to be applied on the object.

2 That the resultant force on an object is proportional to the mass of the object and its acceleration.

H3 Inertia is the tendency to stay at rest or constant motion; It cannot be measured; Inertial mass is the measure of how difficult it is to change the velocity of an object, and it can be calculated using the formula $m = F/a$; So inertial mass is a way of comparing and quantifying inertia.

Stopping distance

1 The velocity of the vehicle; its mass; road conditions; efficiency of vehicle's brakes; driver awareness.

2 A lot of friction on brakes makes them overheat; could lead to skidding and loss of control of vehicle, especially in wet or icy conditions; can cause bodies and other objects inside the vehicle to jolt forwards which may result in damage, especially if seatbelt not worn, e.g. thrown through a window.

3 21.7 m/s

Momentum

1 The mass of the object multiplied by its velocity.

2 This means that the total momentum of a system before and after an event (like a collision) is the same.

3 0.99 kg m/s

Review It!

1 a

b

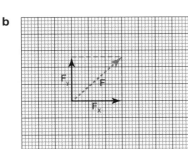

2 Due to Newton's 3rd law, the Earth and the Moon exert forces on each other equal in magnitude and opposite direction:

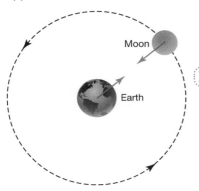

3 The yellow arrow represents the resultant force in this situation; Resultant force = 1784 N to the right.

4 Work done is W = Fs, so the distance travelled will be:

$$s = \frac{W}{F} = \frac{378652}{2 \times 523} = 362 \text{ m}$$

5 s = vt, so:

$$v = \frac{s}{t} = \frac{30}{3.78} = 7.9 \text{ m/s from}$$

stationary $v = \frac{30}{3.95} = 7.6$ m/s from the starting gun.

There is a difference of 0.17 s because of Usain Bolt's reaction time.

6 We need to calculate the resultant force first 950 N – 320 N = 630 N; Newton's 2nd law states that the resultant force is F = ma, so:

$$a = \frac{F}{m} = \frac{630}{81.5} = 7.7 \text{ m/s}^2$$

Waves

Transverse and longitudinal waves

1 Measure the distance between the middle line and a peak or trough on the wave graph.

2 0.0038 s

3 0.048 m/s

Reflection and refraction

1 The light ray will reflect off the mirror at an angle of 32° from the normal.

2 The light ray will partially be refracted inside the material at a smaller angle than the angle of incidence and partially reflected with the same angle as the angle of incidence.

3 All other frequencies apart from frequencies that appear red to the human eye have been absorbed by the red filter.

Sound waves

H1 The sound wave will cause the particles in the solid to vibrate more vigorously and increase the temperature of the solid slightly; The amplitude of the transmitted sound wave will be reduced if part of the sound energy is absorbed by the solid object.

H2 Ultrasound waves are partially reflected at a boundary between two different media; So part of the ultrasound wave will come back to the detector from hitting a crack in the material and the rest of the wave will continue to travel through the medium until it reaches the end of the material; At this point the wave is reflected again and will reach the detector later than the first reflection; The time delay and the velocity of the ultrasound wave in the medium can be used to calculate how deep/thick the cracks are.

H3 S-waves cannot travel through liquids, and by studying seismic waves scientists have noticed that some s-waves cannot be detected by instruments built on the opposite side of the Earth, which tells us that the Earth's core is at least partly liquid; Also, both s- and p-waves travel at different speeds in different mediums and they are both refracted at boundaries between mediums, so scientists have used information from seismic waves to detect boundaries within the Earth; indicating there is a solid mantle below the Earth's crust, the outer core is liquid and the inner core is solid; It is also possible to measure the depths of each of these layers at different places on Earth using readings from seismic waves.

Electromagnetic waves

1 Energy

2 They can travel through empty space.

3 EM waves of higher frequency, like gamma rays, carry more energy; so they can penetrate the body further and damage human tissue deeper inside the body.

Lenses

1 A convex lens bulges at the centre, and a concave lens is thinner at the centre; A convex lens converges light (bends it towards the centre) but a convex lens diverges light (bends it away from the centre); The image produced by a convex lens can be either real or virtual, but in a concave lens images are always virtual; Virtual images produced by a convex lens are magnified (bigger than the object), but virtual images produced by a concave lens are diminished (smaller than the object).

2 Parallel light rays hitting the lens spread out as if they were generated at the focal point; You cannot project that image onto a screen, but the image can be seen by the eye through the lens, which is why it is called a virtual image.

3 0.72 cm

Visible light

1 Smooth surfaces cause specular reflection (like in a mirror); because all the light is reflected in a single direction; rough surfaces cause diffuse reflection; because light is reflected in many different directions depending on the angle of incidence between the light and the surface at each point.

2 The red brick reflects red light; and absorbs all of the other frequencies of visible light.

3 Black; green; black.

Emission and absorption of infrared radiation and black body radiation

1 An object that absorbs 100% of all EM radiation and is the best emitter of radiation.

H2 The greater the difference between the amount of radiation it absorbs and the amount of radiation it emits, the higher the temperature.

H3 Releasing more greenhouse gases in the atmosphere through activities such as burning fossil fuels; This causes more of the radiation emitted by the Earth's surface to be absorbed by the atmosphere so the global average temperature is increasing (this is called global warming).

Review It!

1 a

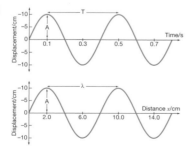

b $v = f\lambda = \dfrac{0.080 \text{ m}}{0.4 \text{ s}} = 0.2$ m/s

2

3

Infrared	Television
x-rays	Satellite communication
Visible light	Electrical heaters
Radio waves	Fibre optics communication
Microwaves	Energy efficient lamps
Gamma-rays	Destroying cancer cells
Ultraviolet	Human internal hard tissue photography

4

5 a Ollie's speed of sound is calculated as:
$$v = \frac{s}{t} = \frac{450 \text{ m}}{1.57 \text{ s}} = 287 \text{ m/s}$$
lower than 340 m/s (only 84%); It is low because Ollie's time measurement is too high. It is inaccurate because it includes two reaction times: one at the end minus the one at the beginning.

b To improve the readings and calculate a more accurate value of the speed of sound from this investigation, Ollie and Laura could repeat readings 10 or 15 times and calculate a mean time; They could also estimate Ollie's average reaction times when starting and stopping the stopwatch; They can then use those times to eliminate the error from each reading, or from the mean time recorded.

Electromagnetism

Magnetism

1 Permanent magnets generate their own magnetic fields, e.g. a bar magnet; They retain their magnetism; Permanent magnets can cause two types of force: attraction and repulsion; Induced magnets are materials that become magnets when they are placed in a magnetic field, but lose their magnetism when they are removed from the magnetic field; Induced magnets can attract, but not repel other magnets.

2 The direction of magnetic field lines from a magnet can be plotted found using small magnetic compasses; The arrow of the compass points towards the south pole of the magnet and away from the north pole, which is the same direction as the magnetic field.

3 Like poles repel because the magnetic field lines from them each pole are in opposite direction to each other, i.e. they are opposite forces; Magnetic field lines cannot cross so they band away from each other creating a repulsive force.

Motor effect

1 The force on the wire will decrease in direction proportion.

2 Use Fleming's left hand rule; Using your left hand, point the first finger in your direction of the field, your second finger in your direction of the current and your thumb will point in the direction of the force.

3 $F = BIL$ so $B = F/IL = 0.046/(0.21 \times 0.751) = 0.29$ T

Electromagnetic induction

1 When an electrical conductor is moved relative to a magnetic field a potential difference (p.d.) or when a magnetic field near an electrical conductor is changed, a potential difference (p.d.) is induced across the conductor.

2 Both use the generator effect to generate a p.d., but a dynamo induces a dc potential difference using a split-ring commutator and a generator uses slip rings to induce an ac p.d.

Transformers

1 The induced p.d. is directly proportional to the ratio between the number of turns in the primary and secondary coils; A step-down transformer induces a lower p.d. in the secondary coil, because the changing magnetic field induced by the primary coil cuts through less turns in the secondary coil; In a step-up transformer the secondary coil has more turns than the primary coil, so the p.d. induced is greater in the secondary coil than in the primary coil.

2 1350 turns; step down.

3 $(1.5 \times 0.25)/0.33 = 1.14$ W

Review It!

1

2 a

b Increase the current through the wire by adding more cells in series; increase the magnetic field by using stronger magnets or moving them closer together; increase the number of loops in the wire.

3

4 $F = BIl = 0.34 \times 0.43 \times 0.230$
$$= 0.034 \text{ N}$$

5 a i $\frac{V_p}{V_s} = \frac{n_p}{n_s} \rightarrow V_s = \frac{(V_p \times n_s)}{n_p}$
$$= \frac{(20 \times 200)}{50} = 80 \text{ V}$$

ii $V_s I_s = V_p I_p \rightarrow I_s = \frac{V_p I_p}{V_s}$
$$= \frac{(20 \times 8)}{80} = 2 \text{ A}$$

b i $\frac{V_p}{V_s} = \frac{n_p}{n_s} \rightarrow V_s = \frac{(V_p \times n_s)}{n_p}$
$$= \frac{(20 \times 100)}{25} = 5 \text{ V}$$

ii $V_s I_s = V_p I_p \rightarrow I_s = \frac{V_p I_p}{V_s}$
$$= \frac{20 \times 3}{5} = 12 \text{ A}$$

Space physics

Our solar system

1 The Milky Way is our galaxy.

2 The Sun, the eight planets orbiting around it and their moons, as well as asteroids from the asteroid belt, comets and dwarf planets.

3 In a circular orbit the radius of the orbit and the speed of the object do not change, which is a stable orbit; However, sometimes both the radius and speed of the object change regularly to trace out an ellipse, and this is a also stable orbit; So not all stable orbits are circular, some are elliptical.

Life cycle of a star

1 Gas and dust particles.

2 The size of the star in its main sequence stage.

3 When the star is in its main sequence stage, the lighter elements between helium and iron in the periodic table are formed by nuclear fusion in the core of the star; When the star dies as a supernova, elements larger than iron are formed and scattered across the universe.

Red-shift

1 We see the light from distant galaxies with wavelengths shifted towards the red end of the visible spectrum; This means that the wavelengths of this light appear longer than they are.

2 The red-shift is evidence that space (i.e. the universe) is expanding, because for this shift to take place the radiation must be travelling away from us in all directions; This movement increases the distance the radiation travels, 'stretching' the wavelengths so they appear longer (i.e. shifted towards the red end of the spectrum), the further the distance they have travelled.

3 If the universe is expanding, this is evidence that all galaxies and space itself started from a single point and expanded with incredible energy (the Big Bang).

Review It!

1 Mercury, Venus, Earth, Mars, Jupiter, Saturn, Uranus, Neptune.

2 The energy released in nuclear fusion reactions in the core of the star create a force in the opposite direction to gravity, and in the main sequence these two forces are in equilibrium; This prevents the gravitational collapse of the star.

3

```
            Nebula
              |
           Protostar
              |
       Main sequence star
Small stars    |    Massive stars
   |           |         |
Red giant           Red super giant
   |                     |
White dwarf          Supernova
   |                     |
Black dwarf    Black hole    Neutron star
```

H4 The force of gravity of the Earth on the satellite always pulls the satellite towards the centre of the Earth; so the speed of the satellite remains the same (as the satellite orbits around the Earth in a circle); but the direction of the velocity constantly changes (as the acceleration is towards the centre of the Earth).

5 Light from the distant galaxy is shifted towards the red end of the spectrum (red-shift); A possible explanation for this is that the distant galaxy is moving away (receding) from our galaxy (the Milky Way).

6 The Big Bang theory claims that everything in the universe (even space and time) started from an incredibly small region that was very hot and dense; This energy caused this point to expand into everything we observe in the visible universe today.

Energy stores and systems

(1) Complete the gaps with the following words. The words can only be used once. (3 marks, ★★★)

A system is an object, or group of objects. The .... in a system is a numerical

.... that tells us whether certain .... in the system could, or could

not, happen. The total .... of energy in a system is always the ....

no matter what changes happen in the system, but the energy available can be ....

in different parts of this system.

amount	form	different	energy	changes
same	redistributed	kinetic	decreases	value

(2) Match the following energy stores to where they are found. Two have been done for you. (3 marks, ★★)

1 Gravitational potential	**a** Fuel
2 Kinetic	**b** A position in the gravitational field
3 Thermal	**c** In a stretched or compressed spring
4 Nuclear	**d** In a warm object
5 Magnetic	**e** In two separated magnets that attract/repel
6 Elastic potential	**f** In two separated charges that attract/repel
7 Electrostatic	**g** Large unstable nuclei such as plutonium and uranium
8 Chemical	**h** In a moving object

(3) Complete the flowchart below for someone making a cup of tea at a campsite with a saucepan and butane burner. (5 marks, ★★)

2 By ....

4 .... store

Hot water in pan

Butane and oxygen

1 .... store

Pan and air surrounding pan

3 By ....   5 .... store

DO IT!

Think about different situations and the changes in the energy stores that take place. Can you identify the useful energy stores or pathways? For example, a boy flicking an elastic band, girl climbing up some stairs, sky diver on his descent.

NAIL IT!

Use a mnemonic to learn the types of energy store: **T**hermal, **N**uclear, **E**lectrostatic, **C**hemical, **G**ravitational potential, **E**lastic potential, **M**agnetic. The first letter of the mnemonic is the first letter of each energy store: **T**homas **N**ever **E**ats **C**arrots **G**ranny **E**ats **M**any.

Changes in energy stores: kinetic energy

(1) a **Write the equation used to calculate the kinetic energy of a moving object.** (1 mark, ★★)

....

b **Write the unit for the energy in a kinetic store.** (1 mark, ★★)

....

(2) **A car of mass 1000 kg is moving at 10 m/s. Calculate the car's energy in the kinetic store.** (2 marks, ★★★)

....

....

WORKIT!

How to tackle a question where you would normally rearrange the equation at the beginning.

Calculate the speed of a 6000 kg bus with 3.7 MJ of energy in the kinetic store. (4 marks, ★★★)

Step 1 $E_k = 0.5 \times m \times v^2$ ← Write the formula but don't try to rearrange. Write 0.5 instead of 1/2.

Step 2   Substitute in the values you are given.

     $3\,700\,000 = 0.5 \times 6000 \times v^2$ (1) ← Leave v^2 alone!

Step 3   Multiply out right-hand terms 0.5 and 6000.

     $3\,700\,000 = 3000 \times v^2$ (1) ← To get v^2 on its own divide both sides by 3000.

Step 4 $\dfrac{3\,700\,000}{3000} = \dfrac{3000}{3000} \times v^2$

Step 5   Swap v^2 to the left-hand side and take the square root of both sides.
     Remember → $\sqrt{v^2} = v → v = \sqrt{1233} = 35\,\text{m/s}$ (1)

The bus is going at 35 m/s which is approximately 70 mph. It should slow down! (1)

For those who are good at rearranging equations: $v = \sqrt{\dfrac{2 \times E_k}{m}} = \sqrt{\dfrac{2 \times 3\,700\,000}{3000}} = 35\,\text{m/s}$

③ **A train is travelling at a speed of 10 m/s and has 0.8 MJ of energy in the kinetic store. Calculate the train's mass.** (4 marks, ★★★★)

....

....

....

....

NAILIT!

Don't forget that the unit of kinetic energy is joules or J. Remember that all the different energy stores and work done have the unit joules or J. It doesn't matter whether it is nuclear or chemical. Energy stores are always measured in joules or J.

Changes in energy stores: elastic potential energy

(1) **State the elastic potential energy equation.** (1 mark, ★★★)

....

....

(2) **A spring has a spring constant $k = 10\,\text{N/m}$.**

A force is applied to stretch the spring. The spring's length increases from 5 cm to 25 cm.

Calculate the energy in the elastic potential store of the spring. (4 marks, ★★★★)

Metre rule

Spring

Slotted mass

....

....

....

(3) **A force of 2.5 N is applied to a spring. The spring's length increases from 10 cm to 20 cm.**

Calculate the spring constant of the spring. Express your answer in N/m. (4 marks, ★★★)

....

....

....

....

(4) **A fisherman has a fish on the end of his rod, and is trying to reel it in.**

His fishing rod line has 20 J of energy in the elastic potential store. The spring constant of the line is 10 kN/m.

Calculate the extension of the line in cm. (4 marks, ★★★★★)

....

....

....

NAILIT!

In calculation questions, always write the equation first. Then substitute in the values from the question. You might get some marks just for showing you know the equation and can substitute in the correct values.

NAILIT!

Formulas for kinetic energy and elastic potential energy both include the fraction $\frac{1}{2}$ in the formula. Remember to enter it as 0.5 on a calculator when trying to work out a problem.

Changes in energy stores: gravitational potential energy

(1) State the gravitational potential energy equation. (1 mark, ★★★)

....

....

....

DO IT!

Memorise the gravitational potential energy equation. Write it out over and over again.

Use (g = 10 N/kg) for all questions.

(2) Calculate the (energy) gain in the gravitational potential store of a power drill when a power drill of 4 kg is lifted upwards 4 m by a man climbing a ladder. (2 marks, ★★★)

....

....

....

NAILIT!

Remember that weight is a force and
weight = mass × gravitational field strength.
Do you notice any similarity between the formula for work done and gravitational potential energy?

(3) Calculate the (energy) gain in the gravitational potential store when a mass of 40 kg is lifted upwards 500 cm by a forklift. (2 marks, ★★★)

....

....

....

(4) Calculate the height fallen by a ball of mass 300 g if the energy in the gravitational store decreases by 90 J. (4 marks, ★★★★)

....

....

....

....

Energy changes in systems: specific heat capacity

Specific heat capacities to be used in questions:

Water: 4200 J/kg °C   Ethanol: 2400 J/kg °C

Rubber: 2000 J/kg °C   Air: 1000 J/kg °C

Copper: 390 J/kg °C

(1) **a Write a definition for specific heat capacity.** (1 mark, ★★)

....

....

b State the equation for specific heat capacity. (1 mark, ★★)

....

c Write the unit for specific heat capacity. (1 mark, ★★)

....

(2) **Two objects of the same mass are heated up on a hotplate for the same amount of time.**

One is made of copper, the other of steel.

The copper object rises in temperature from 25 °C to 35 °C.

The temperature of the iron object increases only from 25 °C to 30 °C.

Using ideas about specific heat capacity, explain why this happens. (3 marks, ★★★★)

> **NAILIT!**
>
> Remember specific heat capacity is a measure of how much energy is required to raise the temperature of 1 kg of a substance by 1 °C. Metals require less energy to change their temperature than non-metals. Use this to consider why metals feel colder than non-metals.

....

....

....

(3) **A teacher uses a Bunsen burner to heat some ethanol in a beaker.**

The energy supplied by the burner is 1.5 kJ.

The temperature increases from 25 °C to 35 °C.

Find the mass of ethanol in kg that was heated.

(4 marks, ★★★★)

> **DOIT!**
>
> Think about why a fruit pie feels quite cool on the outside but when you bite into the filling it burns your tongue. Try to explain why this happens. It has something to do with specific heat capacity.

....

....

....

Power

(1) **Bill and Ted went to the gym. They argued about who was the most powerful. They decided on three tests in the gym to see who was correct. First, they bench-pressed 30 kg for 60 seconds. Next they timed how many step-ups they could do in 60 seconds. Finally, they did kettle bell raises for 60 seconds. Their results are shown in the table.**

Activity	Bill	Ted
Bench press	50 repetitions in 60 s Uses 7.5 kJ in total Power	42 repetitions in 60 s Uses 6.3 kJ in total Power ....
Step-ups	89 repetitions in 60 s Uses 17.8 kJ in total Power	100 repetitions in 60 s Uses 20 kJ in total Power ....
Kettle bell raises	60 raises in 60 s Uses 7.2 kJ in total Power	67 raises in 60 s Uses 8.04 kJ in total Power ....

power = energy transferred ÷ time

a Calculate the power of each man for each activity and add to the table above. (6 marks, ★★★)

b Who was the most powerful overall? (2 marks, ★★★)

....

(2) A television has a power rating of 50 watts.

It is switched on for $7\frac{1}{2}$ hours.

Calculate the energy transferred in this time. (2 marks, ★★★)

....

....

(3) A forklift works at 100 kW of power.

The forklift requires 2200 kJ of energy to lift a heavy crate onto a higher loading platform.

Calculate the time taken for the forklift to load the crate onto the platform. (3 marks, ★★★★)

....

....

....

DO IT!

Make an effort to learn what the different metric prefixes mean. They are used a lot in power and energy questions. Make sure you know:

1 kW = 1 kilowatt = 1000 watts and 1 MW = 1 megawatt = 1 000 000 watts.

If you are confident in the use of standard form then use the following notation: 1 kW = 1×10^3 W and 1 MW = 1×10^6 W

Energy transfers in a system

(1) **State the conservation of energy law.** (2 marks, ★★★)

....

....

(2) **Look at the table.**

Complete the table by giving examples of devices where electricity can be transferred into each of the energy stores. (3 marks, ★★★)

Electricity changes into:	Example
Gravitational potential store	
Vibrational store	
Thermal store	

(3) **For each of the following statements, write down the changes in energy stores that take place.** (4 marks, ★★★★)

a **A person base-jumping off the Eiffel Tower** ....

b **A gas fire** ....

c **Shooting a stone from a catapult** ....

d **Boiling water in an electric kettle** ....

WORKIT!

Describe the changes in the way energy is stored if a rocket is fired. Explain the journey until it runs out of fuel. (3 marks, ★★★)

> Remember to break questions into short sentences. This will make your question easier to mark for the examiner.

Before the rocket is launched the chemical store is full. (1)

At the instant the fuel is lit the chemical store begins to empty and kinetic and thermal stores fill. (1)

As the rocket goes higher its gravitational store increases. The kinetic store will also keep increasing until the rocket runs out of fuel. If the fuel is burned at the same rate, the thermal store will remain fairly constant, but some of the thermal energy store will be dissipated to the surroundings. (1)

DOIT!

Practise the mnemonic you have learned. Can you remember what every letter stands for? **T**homas **N**ever **E**ats **C**arrots **G**ranny **E**ats **M**any.

NAILIT!

Do not confuse energy resources with energy stores.

Energy resources are: nuclear, coal, gas, oil, geothermal, tidal, wind, wave, biofuels, and hydroelectric.

Think of your own mnemonic to learn the ways of generating energy.

Efficiency

① **a** **State the efficiency equation.** (1 mark, ★★★)

....

b **State the two ways of stating a value of efficiency.** (2 marks, ★★★★)

....

....

② **Complete the table below. The first example has been done for you.** (3 marks, ★★★)

Device or situation	Initial energy store	Final energy store
Catapult	Elastic	Kinetic
A go kart freewheeling down a hill		
A car going uphill		
A growing plant		

③ **An MP3 changes 500 joules of energy via electrical work to 360 joules of useful energy stores. How efficient is it?** (2 marks, ★★★★)

....

....

....

④ **What is the efficiency of a van that requires 5000 joules of energy from its chemical store to transfer 900 joules to its kinetic store?** (2 marks, ★★★★)

....

....

....

NAILIT!

The efficiency of an energy transfer will never be 100% efficient in practice. In a laboratory or practical situation some energy is always dissipated, increasing the thermal store of the air around us.

National and global energy resources

(1) **The table below lists some renewable and non-renewable sources of energy.**

Source	Renewable?	Requires burning
Geothermal Power	Yes	No
Coal		
Biofuels	Yes/No	Yes
Oil		
Uranium		
Wave Power		
Solar Farms		
Wind Power		
Hydroelectricity		

Complete the table above to show whether each source:

a **Is renewable.** (4 marks, ★★)

b **Needs to be burned.** (1 mark, ★★★)

(2) **Why are biofuels identified as both renewable and non-renewable?** (1 mark, ★★★★)

....

....

DO IT!

Make your own flashcards on each way of generating energy. Remember to include advantages, disadvantages and show a basic understanding of how each method works.

NAILIT!

Make sure you can explain the advantages and disadvantages of different ways of generating energy. Remember to go into detail. Don't say 'wind energy is free'. Say 'once the initial investment and maintenance is covered, it is free'. Don't say 'tidal energy doesn't cause pollution'. Say 'tidal energy does not emit greenhouse gases, so it doesn't contribute to climate change'.

3 **The graph below shows how the power output from a wind turbine changes with wind speed.**

Wind turbine output vs. Wind speed

a **At what wind speed is the power at a maximum?** (2 marks, ★★★)

....

....

b **If this maximum power output was constant, how many of these wind turbines would be needed to provide a total power output of 10 MW?** (2 marks, ★★★)

....

....

c **Why is it unlikely that a wind farm would produce a constant power output?** (1 mark, ★★★)

....

....

4 **State one advantage and one disadvantage that wind power has compared to power from burning fossil fuel.** (2 marks, ★★★)

....

....

....

Standard circuit diagram symbols

① **Name and draw a component in the box that matches the description.** (4 marks, ★★★★)

1 Used to measure current	(**A**)	Ammeter
2 Changes resistance with light intensity		
3 Only lets current flow in one direction		
4 Can be used to vary resistance		
5 A safety component that melts when the current gets too high.		

② **A student wants to get the *I–V* characteristic for a filament lamp.**

a **Draw a circuit diagram to show the components they would use.** (2 marks, ★★★★★)

b **Explain the method they would use to carry out the experiment.** (6 marks, ★★★★★)

....

....

....

....

....

....

NAILIT!

Remember that a cell and a battery are both power supplies, but a battery is two or more cells joined together.

DOIT!

The only way to learn the circuit symbols is to keep drawing and redrawing them. Use a ruler and a 5p or 1p coin to draw ammeters, voltmeters, light dependent resistors and diodes.

Electrical charge and current

(1) **State the equation linking charge, current and time.** (1 mark, ★★)

....

(2) **Complete the following sentences.** (6 marks, ★★★)

.... is the name given to the flow of negatively .... particles around a closed circuit. These particles are called .... Because of their charge they are attracted to the .... terminal of a cell or .... In books we refer to the opposite direction and call this .... current flow. This is where the current flows from the positive to negative terminal of the power supply.

conventional	charged	electrons	positive	current
energy	alternating	protons	negative	battery

(3) **Use the formula that links charge, current and time to complete the table.** (4 marks, ★★★)

Charge (C)	Current (A)	Time (s)
10	10	1
40	2	
10	2	
100		500
	6	150

DOIT!

Make a mnemonic to learn difficult symbols such as Q for charge. An example is: the **Q**ueen is in **C**harge. Remember if you make your own, you will remember them much more easily.

WORKIT!

A reading light is switched on for 1 hour. It works on a current of 0.25 A. How much charge flowed in 1 hour? (2 marks, ★★)

Choose the right equation.

Charge flow = current × time = or Q = It

1 hour = 60 × 60 = 3600 s

You have to convert hours to seconds.

Q = It

= 0.25 A × 3600 (1)

= 900 C (1)

Substitute the values in the equation.

(4) **In an electrolysis experiment a current of 6 A was passed through some copper sulfate solution. During this time a charge of 1800 C flowed through the copper sulfate solution.**

Calculate how long the current flowed through the copper sulfate in seconds and in minutes. (3 mark, ★★★)

....

....

....

....

NAILIT!

Topic link: you will have learned about electrolysis in chemistry.

NAILIT!

Success in the electricity topic hinges on learning all the circuit symbols and then learning the formulas, symbols and units. Keep testing yourself over and over again. Repetition is the key.

For example:
What does Q stand for?
What is the unit for Q?
What does I stand for?
What is the unit for I?
What does V stand for? etc.

Current, resistance and potential difference and resistors

① a **State the equation linking potential difference, current and resistance.** (1 mark, ★★)

....

b **What is this equation called?** (1 mark, ★★)

....

c **What condition needs to be present for it to work?** (1 mark, ★)

....

② **The diagram below shows part of an electric circuit.** (4 marks, ★★★★)

Complete the circuit diagram by adding:

a **A variable resistor in series with the battery.**

b **A fixed resistor in series with the battery.**

c **A voltmeter that measures the potential difference across the fixed resistor.**

d **An ammeter in series that measures the total current in the series circuit.**

③ **Explain how the experimental set-up in the question above could be used to find the resistance of the fixed resistor.** (6 marks, ★★★★)

Include the following: how equipment is used, which measurements are taken, and how results are analysed to plot a graph.

....

....

....

....

....

....

④ **The resistance vs temperature graph for one type of electrical component is drawn below.**

a **What component would have this relationship?** (1 mark, ★★)

....

b **Complete the diagram to show a circuit that can be used to make a results table of resistance vs temperature for the device.** (4 marks, ★★★★)

NAILIT!

Use the correct circuit symbol for each component that you add to the diagram.

NAILIT!

Knowing the *I–V* characteristics for the following components is essential: wire, resistor, filament lamp and diode.

Make sure that you know how to get the data from an experiment and then how you would plot a graph of *I–V* to observe whether the component always follows Ohm's law.

Which of those four components are ohmic and which are non-ohmic?

c i **What other measuring device would you need to gather the data for the graph, and how would you control the temperature?** (2 marks, ★★★)

....

....

ii **Use the graph to find out the resistance of the device at 10°C.** (2 marks, ★★★)

....

....

iii **How could the device be used in a practical application?** (1 mark, ★★★)

....

(5) **Calculate the total resistance in the following resistor combination.** (2 marks, ★★★)

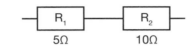

R_1 — 5Ω R_2 — 10Ω

....

....

(6) **In the following circuit $V_1 = 5V$ and $A_1 = 1A$. Complete the missing values.** (2 marks, ★★★)

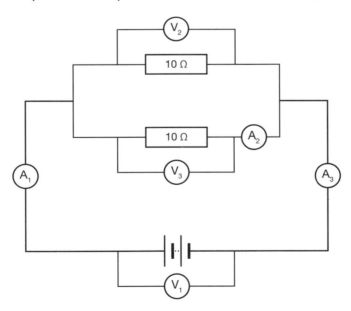

$A_2 = $ .... $A_3 = $ .... $V_2 = $ .... $V_3 = $ ....

DO IT!

Practise sketching the *I–V* graph for a component that follows Ohm's law. Annotate how you would work out the resistance of the component if the graph is a straight line.

Remember that if you put potential difference on the *x*-axis and current on the *y*-axis, then the gradient will not be the resistance.

It will be the reciprocal of the resistance or $\dfrac{1}{\text{resistance}}$

Series and parallel circuits

① **Complete the sentences with the words below. Each word can be used only once.**
(5 marks, ★★★)

In a series circuit, current is the .... throughout the circuit and potential difference
.... across the components. In a parallel circuit, ... is the same across each
branch of the circuit and current splits through the parallel branches. An ammeter must be
connected in .... to work correctly. A voltmeter must be connected in .... to
work correctly.

series	splits	potential difference	resistance	current
parallel	same	energy	circuit	battery

② **Draw series circuits in the three boxes below with the following instructions. A complete circuit that contains:**

a **One bulb, one cell and a switch.** (2 marks, ★★)

b **Two cells (connected together correctly) and three bulbs. Connect an ammeter to measure the circuit current.** (3 marks, ★★★)

c **A battery, thermistor and bulb. Connect a voltmeter to measure the potential difference of the thermistor.** (4 marks, ★★★★)

a	b	c

③ **Draw parallel circuits in the boxes below with the following instructions. A complete circuit that contains:**

a **One battery, two bulbs in parallel and a switch that switches off both bulbs.** (2 marks, ★★)

b **One battery, three bulbs in parallel and a switch that only switches off one bulb.** (2 marks, ★★★★)

c **A battery, bulb and thermistor in series and a bulb connected in parallel with the thermistor.** (2 marks, ★★★★)

a	b	c

NAILIT!

Knowing how to draw parallel and series circuits is really important. Make sure you practise drawing them. Remember:

A **series** circuit means one loop only. **Ammeters** are always connected in **series**.

A **parallel** circuit means more than one loop. **Voltmeters** are always connected in **parallel**.

(4) **Explain why all the lights in a house can be switched off separately in different rooms.** (2 marks, ★★★)

....

....

....

NAILIT!

Learn these rules: **current is the same in a series circuit** and **potential difference splits in a series circuit**.

Then for a parallel circuit it is just the opposite: **potential difference is the same** (across each branch) **in a parallel circuit** and **current splits in a parallel circuit**.

Mains electricity: direct and alternating potential difference (dc/ac)

1. a **What do the terms dc and ac stand for?** (2 marks, ★★★)

   ....

   b **Describe the difference between ac and dc.** (2 marks, ★★★)

   ....

   ....

2. **Explain why we have to use ac for domestic supply.** (4 marks, ★★★★)

   ....

   ....

   ....

3. **What type of potential difference is being supplied in the diagram to the right? What is the potential difference's value if each square represents 2V?** (2 marks, ★★★★)

   ....

   ....

   ....

4. **An ac source is connected to an oscilloscope. The waveform of the alternating potential difference from the source is displayed on the oscilloscope screen to the right.**

   The Y-gain setting of the oscilloscope is 5V/square. Determine the amplitude of the alternating potential difference. (2 marks, ★★★★★)

   ....

   ....

   ....

DO IT!

Learn the definitions for ac and dc, and explain the difference using a diagram. In one of them the current travels in one direction. In the other the current changes direction 50 times every second. Which is which?

NAILIT!

Small portable devices generally run on dc, for example, laptops, torches, and mobile phones.

Larger domestic appliances or heaters usually run on ac, for example fridges, ovens, freezers, and toasters.

Mains electricity

(1) Complete the gaps using the words below. (3 marks, ★★)

The .... supplied to our homes is called .... electricity and it is an .... current supply. This type of current .... direction many times per second. In fact the current goes forwards and back .... times per second. This means it has a .... of 50 Hz.

frequency	changes	fifty	alternating	mains	one-hundred
electricity	direct	wavelength	charge	domestic	

(2) Complete the labels on the following diagram of the plug. (4 marks, ★★★)

Cable grip

a ....

b ....

c ....

d ....

DO IT!

Practise drawing the inside of a plug and make an effort to remember the colour and main job of each cable.

(3) Explain the role of the following in mains electricity and give the typical potential difference values for them when the circuit is working correctly.

a **Earth wire** (1 mark, ★★★) ....

....

b **Live wire** (1 mark, ★★★) ....

....

c **Neutral wire** (1 mark, ★★★) ....

....

(4) a **Explain why a live wire may be dangerous even if a switch in the live circuit is open.** (2 marks, ★★★)

....

....

b **Explain why it is not necessary to connect an earth wire to a device that has a plastic casing.** (2 marks, ★★★)

NAILIT!

Sockets and the cases of plugs are generally made out of hard plastic. Plastic is used because it is a very good electrical insulator and can be moulded to completely surround the cables.

....

....

Electric power (with electrical devices)

(1) **State three formulas for calculating power.** (3 marks, ★★★)

....

....

....

(2) **A 20 V battery supplies 2 A through a resistor. Calculate the power dissipated in the resistor.** (3 marks, ★★)

....

....

....

(3) **A torch has a current of 0.1 A and has a resistance of 100 Ω. What is its power rating?** (2 marks, ★★★)

....

....

(4) **A 10 kW electric fire consumes 36 MJ of energy.**

How long is it on for in seconds and hours? (3 marks, ★★★★)

....

....

....

WORKIT!

A 25 kW shower is turned on for 3 minutes. Calculate the energy transferred in MJ to the water, assuming there is no dissipation of energy to the pipes or to the air in the room. (3 marks, ★★)

Energy transferred = power × time = P × t ◄──── Choose the correct equation.

25 kW = 25 000 W ◄──────── Remember to check for units and prefixes that require attention.

3 minutes = 180 s (1)

P × t = 25 000 W × 180 s ◄──── Substitute in the values.

　　　= 4 500 000 J (1)

To convert to MJ divide by 1 000 000 → $\dfrac{4\,500\,000}{(1\,000\,000)}$ = 4.5 MJ (1)

Energy transfers in appliances

(1) State two formulas for calculating energy. (2 marks, ★★)

....

....

(2) Complete the following sentences. Each word can only be used once. (3 marks, ★★★)

Everyday electrical .... are designed to bring about .... transfers. The
.... of energy an appliance .... depends on how .... the appliance is
switched on for and the .... of the appliance.

Amount	transfers	long	energy	charge
appliances	power	heat	symbols	size

(3) a A 20 V internet digital radio is switched on and a charge of 500 C flows. How much energy is transferred? (2 marks, ★★★)

....

....

b The radio above had a constant current of 2 A. How long was the radio switched on for? (2 marks, ★★★)

....

....

(4) An electric toothbrush operates at 12 V and draws a current of 2 A. It is used for 2 minutes. Calculate:

a The toothbrush's resistance. (3 marks, ★★)

....

....

b The charge flowing through the toothbrush in 2 minutes. (3 marks, ★★★)

....

....

c The energy supplied to the toothbrush in 2 minutes. (3 marks, ★★★)

....

....

....

NAILIT!

Remember the unit for energy is the joule, and the unit for power is the watt.

1 watt is also equivalent to 1 joule/second. This is because:

$$\text{Power} = \frac{\text{energy}}{\text{time}} = \frac{E}{t}$$

So sometimes you might see J/s instead of W. These two units are interchangeable.

The National Grid

(1) **Label a to f in the diagram below with the following words.** (3 marks ★★)

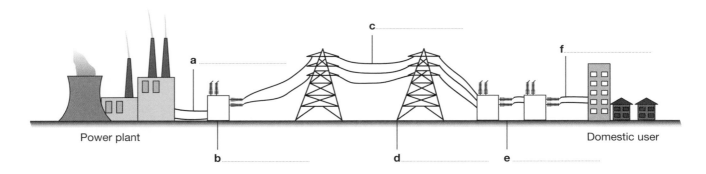

Power plant

Domestic user

230 V	60 Hz	675 kV	2.3 kV	pylon
step-up transformer	step-down transformer	step-up transducer	underground cables	step-down transducer

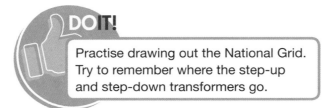

DO IT!

Practise drawing out the National Grid. Try to remember where the step-up and step-down transformers go.

NAILIT!

You don't need to remember the exact values of potential difference except for domestic supply which is 230 V at 50 Hz.

(2) **Explain how increasing the potential difference in power transmission reduces power losses. You could refer to the equations $P = I^2 R$ or $P = VI$.** (3 marks, ★★★★)

....

....

....

....

③ A student tries to make a model of the National Grid, it looks like the circuit below.

3 V
supply

2 metres of power line

Power station
end

Village end

a Explain why the bulb is very dim when the circuit is set up like this. (1 mark, ★★★)

....

....

b He improves the design and sets up a circuit like the one below. Why is the bulb now bright? Explain the roles of transformers A and B in the circuit. (4 marks, ★★★★)

3 V
supply

Transformer
A

Transformer
B

....

....

....

....

....

NAILIT!

Remember that to transfer electrical energy over long distances we need to step-up the potential difference to a higher value. The **power** is constant and we can use the power formula $P = IV$ to explain that if **voltage** goes up, current goes down. If we then put a really small current into another formula for power, $P = I^2 R$. The power losses through heating of the cable are much smaller. Think about it. Try squaring a really small number (a number less than 1) using your calculator and see what happens.

Static charge and electric fields (1)

(1) **The picture shows an investigation of static electricity. A girl rubs a balloon on her head so the balloon gains a negative charge. She then holds the balloon close to her head, and her hair rises.**

a **Explain, in terms of moving charges, how the balloon becomes negatively charged.** (2 marks, ★★★)

....

....

b **Explain why the girl's hair rises.** (2 marks, ★★★)

....

....

c **Later the balloon is placed against a wall and it stays 'stuck' to the wall. Explain why.** (2 marks, ★★★)

....

....

d **Explain why the balloon won't stay there for as long if the air is damp.** (1 mark, ★★★★)

....

NAILIT!

Success in statics questions is mostly about using the following key words with confidence: electrons, friction, insulator, conductor, earth, positive, negative, like, unlike, repel, attract, discharge, and so on.

Remember that in the question it is always something to do with the movement of electrons from one place to another!

> Write the answer in short sentences and focus on using key words.

WORKIT!

Explain why the powder paint that leaves a spray paint machine spreads out.

How can static electricity be used to make the paint stick to a car body? (3 marks, ★★)

Friction between the paint and plastic paint nozzle transfers electrons from paint to paint nozzle. The paint powder is now positively charged. (1)

The positively charged paint repels itself as like charges repel. The paint spreads out evenly. (1)

The car is connected to an earth cable so compared to the paint is negatively charged. The positive paint is attracted to the negatively charged car. (1)

Static charge and electric fields (2)

(1) **Complete the following sentences. Each word can only be used once.** (3 marks, ★★★)

A .... object creates an .... field around itself. For example, a car can become

charged because of .... removing electrons from it and .... them to dust

particles as the car is moving through .... This would leave the car with a ....

electric field.

charged	friction	electric	uncharged	transferring
positive	air	force	conduction	negative

(2) **a Draw a diagram of the electric field pattern around the proton below.** (2 marks, ★★)

(P)

b Another proton is brought towards the first proton. Sketch the field lines. (3 marks, ★★★★)

(P) (P)

(3) **Use ideas about fields to explain how a lightning rod works.** (3 marks, ★★★★)

....

....

....

DOIT!

Practise drawing field lines for these situations:

- positively or negatively charged objects on their own
- two positively charged objects
- two negatively charged objects
- two objects with opposite charges.

NAILIT!

- Electric field lines always go from positive to negative.
- Field lines never cross.
- The further apart the field lines, the weaker the field.
- The closer together the field lines, the stronger the field.

Particle model of matter and density of materials

(1) Complete the sentences. Some of the words can be used more than once. (6 marks, ★★★)

The formula for density is .... divided by .... and the standard SI unit is

.... Sometimes the values are very large so .... are used instead. A density of

.... kg/m³ is equal to the density of .... g/cm³. This is also the density of water.

1000	kg/m³	force	1	g/cm³
area	newtons	mass	1 000 000	volume

(2) A metal block has a volume of 0.005 m³ and mass of 56.5 kg.

   a Calculate the density of the metal block in kg/m³. (2 marks, ★★★)

   ....

   b Convert the density to g/cm³. (1 mark, ★★★★)

   ....

(3) A large wooden block has a volume 8000 cm³ and density of 600 kg/m³.

Calculate the mass of the wooden block in kg. (3 marks, ★★★★)

....

....

Measuring cylinder

Water

Stone

(4) A small stone of mass is 18 g is lowered into a measuring cylinder.

The water level increases from 20.0 to 27.5 ml.

Calculate the density of the stone in g/cm³. (4 marks, ★★★★)

....

....

DO IT!

Make an effort to learn the symbol and units for density. The symbol is ρ and is pronounced 'rho' and it is from the Greek alphabet. The units for density are generally g/cm³ or kg/m³. Make sure you can convert between the two.

NAIL IT!

Don't get confused with conversions between m³ → mm³ and m³ → cm³ and vice versa.

Remember 1 m = 100 cm   or   1 m = 1000 mm

$1 m^3 = 1 m \times 1 m \times 1 m = 1 m^3$

$1 m^3 = 100 cm \times 100 cm \times 100 cm = 1\,000\,000 cm^3$ (or $10^6 cm^3$)

$1 m^3 = 1000 mm \times 1000 mm \times 1000 mm = 1\,000\,000\,000 mm^3$ (or $10^9 mm^3$)

Changes of state and internal energy

(1) **Marbles in a box are a good model to represent the molecules in a solid, liquid and a gas. Explain which box best represents each state of matter and briefly explain why.** (6 marks, ★★★★)

A B C

A ....

B ....

C ....

(2) **Explain why the temperature of a window increases when water condenses onto its surface.** (3 marks, ★★★★)

....

....

(3) **What term describes the type of change when ice melts and becomes water? Tick one box.** (1 mark, ★★)

Physical	
Chemical	
Sublimation	
Radiation	

WORKIT!

If alcohol is dropped onto the back of your hand, why does it make your hand feel cool? (4 marks, ★★★★)

Your hand is warm (higher thermal store) and the alcohol has a lower temperature (lower thermal store). A difference in temperature between two touching objects causes the hotter object's thermal store to go down and the colder object's thermal store to go up. (1)

The thermal store of the hand goes down (reducing the temperature) and the thermal store of the alcohol goes up (increasing the temperature). (1)

The increase in the thermal store of the alcohol causes the alcohol to evaporate (alcohol has a fairly low boiling point, so it evaporates at a lower temperatures than water, for example). (1)

Evaporation of alcohol causes a reduction of the energy store in your hand, decreasing the internal energy of your hand. This makes your hand feel cool. (1)

NAILIT!

Practise drawing the diagrams for liquids, solids and gases. Remember to do the following:

- Draw particles as circles and make them all approximately the same size.
- The particles in solids are ordered in straight rows and are touching on all sides. The gaps between them are very small.
- The particles in liquids are still touching but are not as organised and look a little chaotic. They still fill the container and no gaps are bigger than the particles themselves.
- For gases draw very few atoms that are far apart.

Changes of temperature and specific latent heat

(1) **State the formula for specific latent heat.** (1 mark, ★★)

....

....

(2) **The following diagram represents energy supplied in kJ by a heater to increase the temperature of water from below 0°C to above 100°C.**

> **NAILIT!**
>
> Don't confuse specific heat capacity (S.H.C) with specific latent heat (S.L.H). Specific heat capacity is the energy required to increase the temperature of a kilogram of a substance by 1°C. Specific latent heat is the energy required to melt, or turn to gas 1 kg of a substance without changing the temperature.

What happens to the energy of the particles of the solid/liquid in each state-change as more energy is supplied by heating? (6 marks, ★★★★)

....

....

....

....

....

....

(3) **Calculate the energy in kJ required to melt 100 g of ice. The specific latent heat of fusion for ice is 334 000 J/kg.** (3 marks, ★★★★)

....

....

....

> **DOIT!**
>
> Learn the units for S.H.C and S.L.H. One is J/kg the other J/g°C. Make sure you can remember which is which.

Particle motion in gases (1)

(1) **Complete the gaps with the words below.** (6 marks, ★★★)

The molecules of gas are in constant .... motion. The average .... energy of the .... is proportional to temperature on the .... scale. Changing the temperature of a gas in a container of fixed volume will change the .... exerted on the sides of the ....

kinetic	random	Celsius	container	kelvin
ordered	gravitational potential		particles	pressure

(2) **This diagram shows a sealed box filled with oxygen molecules.**

Describe the motion of the molecules. (2 marks, ★★)

....

....

....

(3) **Define internal energy.** (2 marks, ★★★)

....

....

....

WORKIT!

This diagram shows the kinetic energy of the different gas molecules in a sealed container.

Some of the gas condenses on a cool side of the container.

Referring to the graph explain why the temperature of the remaining gas would initially increase. (4 marks, ★★)

The slower moving molecules would condense onto the surface more readily, as they would require less energy to change from a gas into a liquid. (1)

Molecules with higher kinetic energy (E_k) would remain. (1)

The kinetic energy, or E_k of molecules, is proportional to temperature (in Kelvins). (1)

As more higher speed molecules remain, the average temperature will go up. (1)

DOIT!

Remember that when doing these calculations, unless you are calculating a temperature change, it is always necessary to convert degrees Celsius (°C) into kelvin (K).

A helpful rhyme to learn the conversion is 'K is C plus 273' for K = °C + 273.

Particle motion in gases (2)

(1) **State the equation that links pressure and volume in gases.** (1 mark, ★★★)

....

(2) **The initial temperature of a gas trapped in a container is –23°C. The container is heated and the final temperature of the gas is 477 °C.**

   a **Calculate the temperature change in °C and then state it in kelvins.** (2 marks, ★★★)

     ....

     ....

   b **What is the change in kinetic energy of the particles in the gas?** (2 marks, ★★★★)

     ....

     ....

(3) **A gas has an initial volume of 120 cm³ at a pressure of 75 kPa.**

   Assume that the temperature remains constant.

   Calculate the final volume of this gas if pressure is increased to 225 kPa. (3 marks, ★★★★)

....

....

....

(H)(4) **When a bicycle pump is used to pump up a tyre, the pump starts to feel warm. Explain why this happens.** (3 marks, ★★★★)

....

....

....

NAILIT!

Work done = energy transferred

If we do work on a gas it increases the internal energy of the gas molecules, and this leads to an increase in temperature (remember, E_k is proportional to temperature).

DOIT!

Make sure you learn the units for pressure. The standard unit is the pascal, abbreviated to Pa, which is equivalent to N/m².

The structure of the atom (1)

① **Complete the following sentences.** (3 marks, ★★)

a The atom is composed of three subatomic particles: ...., ... and

....

b The centre of the atom is called the .... and contains .... and

....

c An atom contains the same number of .... and .... and has a

.... charge.

② **The diagram shows a simplified helium atom. Insert on the diagram the missing names of the subatomic particles.** (3 marks, ★★)

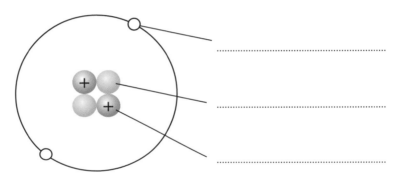

....

....

....

③ **Complete the table below.** (4 marks, ★★)

Particle	Symbol	Relative mass	Charge
Proton	p		+1
Neutron	n	1	
Electron	e⁻		

NAILIT!

Ideas about the atom have evolved over the centuries. Make sure that you understand the basics of each model.

④ **Describe our current understanding of the nuclear model of the atom. Make particular reference to the following: radius, size of atom, electron arrangement and mass of atom.** (6 marks, ★★★★)

....

....

....

....

....

The structure of the atom (2)

1 **State how many protons, neutrons and electrons there are in the atoms below.** (6 marks, ★★★)

Protons ....

Neutrons ....

Electrons ....

Protons ....

Neutrons ....

Electrons ....

2 **Complete the sentences below. Some words may be used twice.** (6 marks, ★★★)

An .... is an atom with the same number of .... and a different number

of ....

.... have the same chemical properties as the atom. If the .... number

is altered, the .... changes.

isotope	electrons	protons	different	neutrons	isotopes
electron	ion	ions	atomic	element	

 NAILIT!

Atoms are neutral. This means they have the same number of protons and electrons. If they lose or gain electrons we call this ionisation. Remember that atoms cannot lose or gain protons or neutrons as easily. A change in the number of protons and neutrons is a nuclear process.

 DOIT!

Make an effort to learn the relative mass and charge of each part of the atom: protons, neutrons and electrons.

③ **Circle true (T) or false (F) for the following statements.** (4 marks, ★★★★)

a To form an ion you have to remove a proton from an atom.   T   F

b An ion can be formed by gaining or removing an electron.   T   F

c Metal atoms lose electron(s) to form positively charged ions.   T   F

d Non-metal atoms lose electrons to form negatively charged ions.   T   F

WORKIT!

These chlorine atoms have different mass numbers.

a How can this be explained? (2 marks, ★)

The mass number is different but the atomic number is the same. (1)

This can only mean one thing. They are isotopes of chlorine. (1)

b Why is the mass number of chlorine commonly stated as 35.5? (3 marks, ★★)

In nature there are three different naturally occurring isotopes of chlorine. (1)

The isotopes have different mass numbers, 35.5 is the weighted average. (1)

This does not mean that any of the isotopes have 35.5 protons and neutrons. (1)

Developing a model of the atom

(1) In the early part of the 20th century, scientists thought that the atom was like a 'plum pudding'. They used this model to explain the internal structure of the atom.

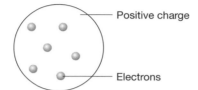

Plum pudding model

Positive charge

Electrons

Describe the main features of the plum pudding model that were put forward to explain the internal structure of the atom. (3 marks, ★★★★)

....

....

....

(2) An experiment, designed to investigate the 'plum pudding' model, involved firing alpha particles at thin gold foil leaf.

The diagram shows the main paths, A, B and C, of several thousand alpha particles. The results are expressed as percentages.

Explain what each of the paths A, B and C tells us about the atom. Your ideas should reference why the plum pudding model was wrong. (6 marks, ★★★★★)

Path A: Very small deflection of 0 to 4 degrees was taken by approximately 62% of the alpha particles

Path B: Small to medium sized deflection of 4 to 30 degrees were taken by approximately 38%

Path C: Large deflection of more than 120 degrees or backscattering was taken by only 0.01% of the alpha particles

Gold nucleus

....

....

....

....

....

....

....

....

....

....

....

Radioactive decay and nuclear radiation

(1) **Fill in the missing words in the paragraph below, using words from the box.** (6 marks, ★★★)

Some atomic nuclei are .... The nucleus gives out .... as it changes to

become more stable. This is a .... process called radioactive ....

Activity is the rate at which a source of .... nuclei decays. Activity is measured in

.... (Bq).

decay	becquerel(s)	stable	random	radioactive
waste	radiation	unstable	fusion	fission

(2) **Complete the table below about alpha, beta and gamma radiation.** (3 marks, ★★★)

Radiation type	What it is made of?	What stops it?	Ionising effect
Alpha			Highly ionising
Beta		A few millimetres of aluminium	
Gamma	High energy EM wave		

(3) **The following diagram shows how beta radiation can be used to make sure paper is made with a fairly constant thickness.**

a **Why is beta suitable for this task, and not alpha or gamma?** (2 marks, ★★★)

....

....

....

Rollers
Source of beta radiation
Paper pulp
Sheet of paper
Detector
Signal sent to computer which controls the rollers
Feedback to rollers

b **How does feedback ensure that paper is of uniform thickness?** (2 marks, ★★★)

....

....

NAILIT!

The unit for activity is the becquerel. The becquerel is equivalent to 1 disintegration, or decay of one nucleus, per second. Activity cannot be detected directly but can be estimated with a Geiger–Muller tube, which measures count-rate. Count-rate can also be stated as 'number of counts per minute, hour, day or year'. Whereas activity is always in Bq – nuclear disintegrations **per second**. Count-rate and activity are not always the same because the Geiger–Muller tube has a dead time in which it doesn't detect some nuclear disintegrations.

DOIT!

Alpha (α), beta (β) and gamma (γ) are the three kinds of radiation. For each one make sure you learn:

- What is it composed of?
- What stops it?
- How heavily ionising is it?
- Is it affected by magnetic fields?

Nuclear equations

1 **Uranium-238 eventually decays to the stable isotope lead-208.**

All the steps in this process can be shown on a diagram. This is called a decay chain and the process takes several billion years. An example is shown below:

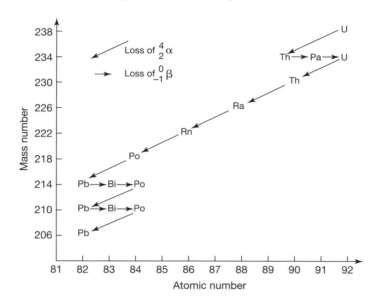

Use the mass number and atomic number references in the above decay chain to complete the following nuclear decay equations. Complete the mass and atomic number for each particle.

a $^{214}_{82}Pb \rightarrow \boxed{}Bi + \boxed{}_{-1}e$ (2 marks, ★★★)

b $^{214}_{84}Po \rightarrow \boxed{}Pb + \boxed{}He$ (2 marks, ★★★★)

H c $^{230}_{90}Th \rightarrow$ (4 marks, ★★★★★)

NAILIT!

Changes take place in the atomic and mass numbers during alpha (α) and beta (β) decay, but not during gamma (γ) decay. In nuclear equations, make sure that the atomic numbers and mass numbers balance on each side of the equation.

DO IT!

You do not need to remember specific nuclear equations but you do need to be able to balance the mass and atomic numbers for nuclear equations for alpha (α) and beta (β) decays.

Complete the following example and state if it is an example of beta (β) or alpha (α) decay.

$$^{238}_{92}U \rightarrow \boxed{}Th + \boxed{}\boxed{}$$

To check your atomic and mass numbers refer back to graph of mass number vs atomic number.

Half-life of radioactive elements

1. **Write a definition for the term half-life.** (2 marks, ★★★)

....

....

....

DO IT!

Learn the definition for half-life from memory. It often comes up in exams

2. **A body was found in a bog in rural Ireland.**

   A sample of bone from the body was analysed using radio-carbon dating techniques.

   Once a living thing dies, the carbon-14 in its body decays. Carbon-14 has a half-life of 5700 years.

   Consequently, archaeologists can use any material containing carbon to determine the age, such as bone, wood or leather.

   a **If a bone contained $\frac{1}{4}$ of the expected carbon-14, how old would it be?** (3 marks, ★★★★)

   ....

   ....

   ....

   b **If a bone contained $\frac{1}{16}$ of the expected carbon-14, how old would it be?** (3 marks, ★★★★)

   ....

   ....

   c **Draw a sketch of the graph of the half-life. Assume an initial count-rate of 4000 cpm.**
   (4 marks, ★★★★)

NAILIT!

If you are a Higher Tier student remember that you need to be able to express the net decline of radioactive isotopes as a **ratio**.

Hazards and uses of radioactive emissions (1)

1 **There are two main ways in which people can be exposed to radiation.**

State the two ways they can happen and the effects of radiation on body tissue.
(6 marks, ★★★★)

....

....

....

....

2 a **What protective measures can be taken to protect those who regularly come into contact with radioactive sources?** (5 marks, ★★★★)

....

....

....

....

....

b **Why is it important for findings on the effects of radiation on humans to be published?**
(2 marks, ★★★★)

....

....

3 **This pie chart shows the main sources of background radiation in the UK. Each source contributes to the average yearly radiation dose.**

a **What is meant by background radiation?**
(1 mark, ★★)

....

....

Sources of background radiation

b **Suggest why an astronaut is likely to get a higher dose of background radiation than the average person.** (2 marks, ★★★)

....

....

....

DO IT!

Some background radiation is artificial but most is natural. Make sure you know three examples of each.

Hazards and uses of radioactive emissions (2)

(1) **The table below shows the different half-lives and type of decay for several radioactive isotopes.**

Radioactive isotope	Decay type	Half-life
Radium-226	Alpha	1600 years
Bismuth-214	Beta	20 minutes
Lead-210	Beta	22 years
Polonium-210	Alpha	138 days
Bismuth-210	Alpha, beta and gamma	5 days
Radon-222	Alpha	3.8 days

The initial count-rate of a sample of rock containing bismuth-214 is 4000 counts/minute. How many counts/minute would be detected 1 hour later? (2 marks, ★★★)

....

....

(2) **Radium-226 decays into radon-222 via alpha decay. A rock is found that once had a large deposit entirely made of radium-226. Now an eighth of the deposit is the original radium-226 but seven eighths of this part of the rock is filled with radon-222 gas.**

a **How many half-lives have passed?** (2 marks, ★★★★)

....

....

b **How long has passed since all of the original radium-226 was present?** (2 marks, ★★★)

....

....

DO IT!

Radioactive isotopes have many applications in our day-to-day lives: smoke alarms, treating cancer, destroying bacteria, detecting metal or paper thickness, as tracers and dating. Study these examples and make flashcards to help you remember.

NAILIT!

Radioactive isotopes can be alpha (α), beta (β) or gamma (γ) emitters. They emit this radiation to make their nuclei more stable. Half-lives can range from a fraction of a second to billions of years.

H③ Lead-210 decays via beta decay to bismuth-210. It has a half-life of 22 years.

A sample is found that originally consisted completely of lead-210.

Now it exists with one lead-210 atom for every seven bismuth-210 atoms.

a **How many half-lives have passed?** (2 marks, ★★★★★)

....

....

b **How old is the sample?** (1 mark, ★★★)

....

WORKIT!

A safe level of radon-222 gas is 20 Bq. A house's basement contains trapped radon-222 gas which has an activity of 320 Bq. Building changes are made and radiation levels are checked by physicists. If no radon enters or leaves the basement, how long would it take the trapped radon-222 to reach safe levels? (3 marks, ★★)

The original activity is 320 Bq and the safe activity is 20 Bq. (1)

320 → 160 → 80 → 40 → 20 ◄—— How many times do you have to halve 320 to reach 20?

It had to be halved 4 times. (1)

This means 4 half-lives have elapsed.

4 half-lives = 4 × 3.8 days

= 15.2 days (1)

Hazards and uses of radioactive emissions (3)

Radioactive isotope	Decay type	Half-life
Technetium-99	Gamma	6 hours
Xenon-133	Gamma	5 days
Strontium-90	Beta	28 years
Americium-241	Alpha	433 years
Protactinium-234	Beta	80 seconds

Answer questions 1 and 2 using the table above, and make reference to half-life and decay type in your answers.

(1) **Which type of radioactive isotope is used to investigate whether a person's liver is functioning correctly? Why is this type chosen?** (3 marks, ★★★★)

....

....

....

(2) a **Cobalt-60 is the most commonly used isotope to treat brain tumours. If it wasn't available, which type of radioactive isotope from the table would be the most suitable to kill cancer cells? Explain why.** (3 marks, ★★★★)

....

....

....

b **Cobalt-60 has a half-life of over 5 years. Why is this an advantage over the radioactive isotope you chose in part a?** (1 mark, ★★★)

....

(3) **Explain why the use of radiation to destroy cancerous cells is classed as a 'high risk method' for the treatment of cancer. What are the risks of chemotherapy and radiotherapy?** (4 marks, ★★★)

....

....

....

....

Nuclear fission and fusion

① The diagram to the right shows what can happen when the nucleus of a uranium-235 atom absorbs a neutron.

What name is given to the process shown in the diagram? (1 mark, ★★)

....

Neutron

U−235

Te−137

Zr−97

2 neutrons + energy

② **How do the mass number and atomic number of an atom change when its nucleus absorbs a neutron?**
(2 marks, ★★★)

....

....

③ **Explain why control rods are used in a nuclear fission reactor.** (3 marks, ★★★)

....

....

④ a **Explain what fusion is.** (2 marks, ★★★)

....

....

b **Compare the similarities and differences between fission and fusion.** (6 marks, ★★★★)

....

....

....

....

....

DO IT!

Make an effort to learn the roles of the moderator, coolant and control rods in a nuclear reactor. The moderator slows down the neutrons so they can be absorbed by the uranium nuclei. The coolant transfers heat energy to the heat exchanger from the reactor core. The control rods absorb excess neutrons and can be used to control the rate of the chain reaction and keep it at steady energy output.

NAILIT!

Naturally occurring uranium is mostly uranium-238 (non-fissionable) and contains 1% uranium-235 (fissionable). Uranium must be 'enriched' to increase the percentage of uranium-235 from 1% to 3%. Then it can be used in nuclear reactors. This is known as **enrichment** and is a technically difficult and costly process.

Forces and their interactions

(1) **Tick which of the following quantities is a vector.** (1 mark, ★★★)

Speed	
Distance	

Energy	
Velocity	

(2) **Draw lines to match the words to their definitions.** (4 marks, ★★★★)

1 Speed	**a** Has magnitude but no direction.
2 Velocity	**b** Has both magnitude and direction.
3 A scalar quantity	**c** Change in distance per unit time.
4 A vector quantity	**d** Change in displacement per unit time.

(3) **A boy is pulling a trolley along the ground. Moving the trolley requires him to exert a force on the trolley. The arrow represents the force. What two pieces of information does the vector tell you about the force?** (2 marks, ★★★)

....

....

(4) **An electrostatic force is a non-contact force.**

a **Describe the difference between a contact force and a non-contact force.** (2 marks, ★★★)

....

....

b **State two other non-contact forces.** (2 marks, ★★)

....

....

....

DO IT!

Learn the definition for scalar and vector and a couple of examples of each. Being asked to define vectors and scalars and provide examples of each is a common exam question.

NAILIT!

You need to be able to break a vector down into its vertical and horizontal components. This can be done graphically or by using trigonometry.

Gravity

(1) **State the formula and unit for weight.** (2 marks, ★★★)

....

(2) **Two students, Karen and Jane, are talking about mass and weight.**

Mass and weight are not the same and have different units.

Karen

Mass and weight are the same and are both measured in kg.

Jane

Explain which one of the students is correct. Compare mass and weight in your answer.
(6 marks, ★★★★)

....

....

....

....

....

(3) **An astronaut has a mass of 75 kg. He visits the Moon.**

The Moon has gravitational field strength of 1.6 N/kg

Calculate the astronaut's weight on the Moon. (2 marks, ★★)

....

....

....

 NAILIT!

Gravitational field strength is proportional to the mass of the planet the astronaut is on and inversely proportional to his or her distance from the centre of the planet.

The greater the mass → the greater the field strength.

The further from the centre of the planet → the lower the field strength.

DO IT!

Learn the difference between mass and weight. This is one of the most common misunderstandings in physics. Don't be the person who gets it wrong!

Resultant forces

(1) Match the left side to the right side to complete the sentences below. (4 marks, ★★)

1 A resultant force is	**a** One force that is the sum of all forces acting.
2 A force is	**b** The resultant force is zero.
3 When forces are balanced	**c** An object's motion or its shape.
4 A force can affect	**d** A push or a pull.
5 The unit of force is	**e** The newton (N).

H (2) Calculate the resultant force acting on each of the three boxes. (3 marks, ★★★)

(Arrows are not to scale and are only to indicate direction of the force.)

6 N → ← 3 N

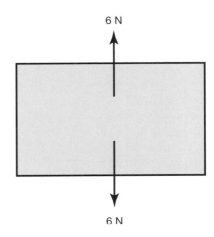

6 N ↑ ↓ 6 N

a ....

b ....

8 N ← → 2 N

c ....

DO IT!

Practise drawing free body diagrams. Make sure you can do this for objects that are in water, on a solid surface or falling through air.

NAIL IT! H

Remember that if an object is moving with constant velocity, or if it is stationary, the vector forces must be all balanced. Make sure you are familiar with all the different forces. Here are a few examples: normal contact force weight, drag, friction and upthrust.

(3) **A duck is moving across a lake at a constant velocity.**

H a **Add labelled arrows on the picture below to show the vector forces acting on the duck.** (3 marks, ★★★★)

| upthrust | air resistance | friction | weight | thrust |

b **The duck needed to accelerate to catch a tasty piece of bread.**

Describe and explain how these force vectors change. (4 marks, ★★★★★)

....

....

....

....

....

Work done and energy transfer

(1) **State the formula for work done.** (2 marks, ★★)

....

(2) **Which of the following units can be used for work done, as well as J or joules.** (1 mark, ★★★)

W	
Nm	

N/m	
J/s	

(3) a **A child pushes a go-kart with a force of 30 N. The go-kart moves 4 m along the floor. Calculate the work done on the go-kart.** (3 marks, ★★★)

....

....

....

....

 b **The child now does 240 J of work on the go-kart and pushes with the same force as in part a.**

   How far does the child have to push the go-kart to do 240 J of work? (3 marks, ★★★★)

....

....

....

....

 c **Would the temperature of the go-kart change? Explain your answer.** (2 marks, ★★★)

....

....

....

....

DOIT!

Learn the formula and units for work done. Remember work done is equivalent to energy transfer. Does this help you remember the unit for work done?

NAILIT!

Remember that the symbol for the displacement is **s**, and it is often used for distance as well.

Forces and elasticity

Ruler
Spring
Masses

① A student investigates by how much the extension of a spring changes when he suspends different slotted masses from it.

The student finds that the spring's extension increases by the same length each time an additional slotted mass is added, as long as he only adds one mass at a time. **Explain why.** (2 marks, ★★)

....

....

....

② a **Label the axes below, and sketch a graph to show the behaviour of a spring under tension/when a force is applied to it.** (3 marks, ★★★)

b **How could you work out the spring constant from the graph of results?** (2 marks, ★★★★)

....

....

....

(3) **The student uses the same experimental procedure but this time hangs slotted masses from an elastic band.**

They conclude that the elastic band's extension is not always proportional to the force applied and undergoes inelastic deformation.

Explain what is meant by the term *inelastic* deformation. (2 marks, ★★★)

....

....

....

DO IT!

Make sure you are familiar with all the key words in this topic. What is the difference between elastic and inelastic deformation?

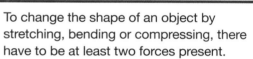

NAILIT!

To change the shape of an object by stretching, bending or compressing, there have to be at least two forces present.

Moments, levers and gears

(1) Complete the following sentence with the words below. (4 marks, ★★)

A force or a .... of forces can cause an object to .... The ....

effect of a force is also called the .... of the force.

momentum	rotate	system	turning	terminal	moment	float

(2) Tick the correct unit for a moment. (1 mark, ★★★★)

Nm			kg/m³	
Ns			kgm/s	

(3) A student predicts that the beam below would be balanced.

Use a calculation to show whether they are correct. (3 marks, ★★★)

....

....

40 N   50 N

10 m   8 m

....

DO IT!

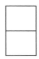

NAILIT!

A moment is the force multiplied by the perpendicular distance from the pivot.

Remember to state the conservation of momentum law:

anticlockwise moments = clockwise moments

All students find moments questions hard. The only solution is to keep practising the problems until you gain confidence.

Remember:

1 Choose a point on the beam.

2 Ignore the forces acting through that point.

3 Anticlockwise moments = clockwise moments.

WORKIT!

What distance must the 50 N weight be from the pivot to balance the beam? (3 marks, ★★)

State equation

Force × distance = force × distance (1)

Substitute in the values

4 N × 12 m = 50 N × y (1)

Solve equation

$y = \dfrac{4 \times 12}{50} = 0.96\,m$ (1)

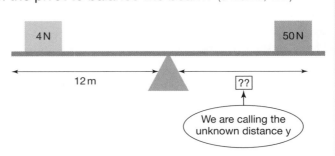

4 N   50 N

12 m   ??

We are calling the unknown distance y

Pressure and pressure differences in a fluid (1)

① **State the equation used to calculate the pressure exerted by the surface of a liquid on an object.** (1 marks, ★★★)

....

② **Tick one box. A fluid can be either:** (1 mark, ★★★)

A solid or a liquid	☐	A liquid or a gas	☐
A solid or a gas		A liquid or a cold metal	

③ **Complete the following sentences.** (3 marks, ★★★)

The .... in fluids causes a force .... to any .... The pressure at

the surface of any fluid can be calculated using the equation

.... = ... / ....

parallel   density   mass   pressure   perpendicular   surface   mass   force   area   volume

④ **The pressure at the surface of the Dead Sea is 106 kPa.**

A man floating on the Dead Sea has a surface area of 0.8 m² in the water.

Calculate the force exerted on his body by the water. (3 marks, ★★★★)

....

....

....

....

....

NAILIT!

The unit for pressure is either expressed as N/m² or Pa. Pa is the abbreviation for pascals. 1 Pa = 1 N/m².

NAILIT!

Make sure you can convert between the different units in area calculations.

1 000 000 mm² = 10 000 cm² = 1 m²

Pressure and pressure differences in a fluid (2)

H① A boy dives to the bottom of a deep swimming pool.

The pool has a depth of 3 m.

Calculate the pressure increase at the bottom of the swimming pool. (3 marks, ★★★)

Density of water = 1000 kg/m³

g = 10 N/kg

....

....

....

....

H② A mountaineer takes a bag of crisps up a mountain as a special treat for reaching the summit. When she reaches the top she pulls her crisps out and finds that the bag has puffed up like a balloon.

Why do you think this happened? Tick one box. (1 mark, ★★★★)

The air outside the packet has a higher temperature than the air inside the packet.	
The packet has a hole in it that allowed air from outside to enter.	
The increased ultraviolet on the bag gave the gas inside more energy.	
The air outside is now at a lower pressure than the air inside the packet.	

H③ Atmospheric pressure is approximately 100 kPa. Human ears contain air pockets.

Explain why the boy's ears, in question 1, might hurt when he is at the bottom of the pool. (3 marks, ★★★★)

....

....

....

H ④ A student has a large bottle full of water. The bottle has a long tube attached to the top.

She empties the bottle full of water into a bucket.

As the water pours out of the long tube the plastic bottle starts to crumple at the sides as shown in the diagram. **Explain why this happens.** (3 marks, ★★★★)

....

....

....

 DO IT!

If you can do this safely, swim to the bottom of a swimming pool. Pay particular attention to the pressure you can feel in your ears and nose. Why does this happen?

NAILIT!

We live at the bottom of a large mass of air called the **atmosphere**. It exerts a huge pressure on us called 'atmospheric pressure'.

Distance, displacement, speed and velocity

1. A bird flies from point A on one fence to point B on another. It travels a route that is 18 m long in total.

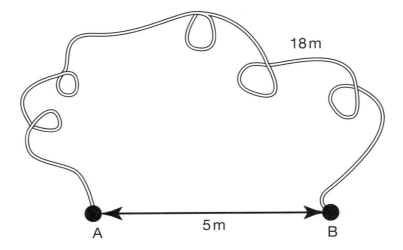

The diagram shows the route it took to get from A to B.

The 5 m route is the shortest way to get from A to B.

a State the term used for the 18 m route: .... (1 mark, ★★★)

b State the term used for the 5 m route: .... (1 mark, ★★★)

2. Label the following distance time graphs with the following words. (3 marks, ★★★)

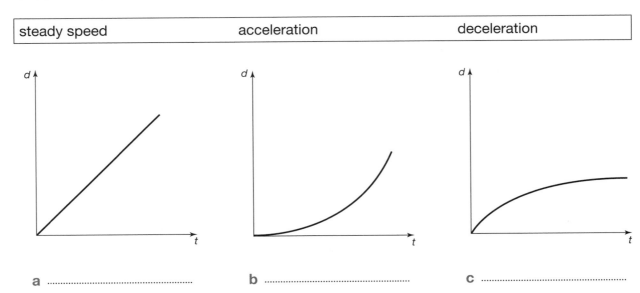

a .... b .... c ....

3 The following distance–time graph shows a car journey.

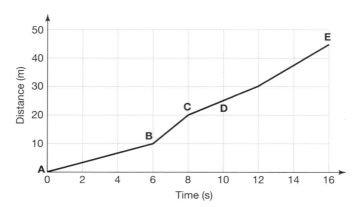

a What is the total distance travelled on the journey? (1 mark, ★★★)

....

b Work out the speed from A to B on the graph. (3 marks, ★★★)

....

....

c Without making a calculation, how can you tell that the speed from B to C is higher than A to B? (2 marks, ★★★★)

....

....

....

4 Match the following to their typical speeds. One has already been done for you.
(4 marks, ★★★)

1 An aeroplane	**a** 5 m/s
2 Olympic sprinter	**b** 30 m/s
3 Cheetah	**c** 200 m/s
4 Mouse	**d** 10 m/s
5 Snail ———————————	**e** 0.02 m/s

DOIT!

Practise drawing distance–time graphs and make sure you know how to represent the following: stationary or at rest, low steady speed, high steady speed, acceleration and deceleration.

NAILIT!

Learn the difference between distance and displacement. It's a classic exam question and comes up all the time.

Acceleration

1 a Label each of the following velocity–time graphs with one of the following. (3 marks, ★★★)

constant speed	acceleration	deceleration

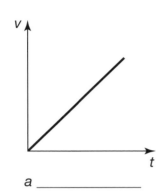

a _____ b _____ c _____

H 2 A car goes on a journey and the velocity–time graph below is made of a short part of the journey. Use the graph to answer the following questions.

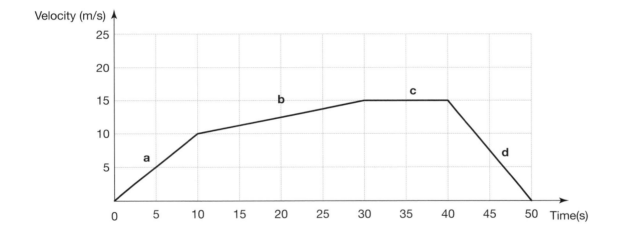

a Calculate the acceleration during part a. (2 marks, ★★)

....

....

....

b **Calculate the acceleration during part b.** (3 marks, ★★★★)

....

....

....

c **Describe the car's motion in part c.** (1 mark, ★★★★)

....

....

H(3) **Using the graph in question 2, calculate the distance travelled during parts a and b of the journey.** (3 marks, ★★★★)

....

....

....

....

NAILIT! H

In circular motion such as the Moon orbiting the Earth, the speed of the Moon is constant, but because its direction is constantly changing, its velocity is also constantly changing. This results in an acceleration, which acts towards the Earth. This acceleration is a centripetal or 'centre-seeking' acceleration.

Newton's laws of motion

H(1) **Complete the sentences with the missing words.** (3 marks, ★★)

The .... of an object will only change if there is a .... force acting on it.

When a car is at a .... speed the driving force and .... forces of friction and

.... are equal and act in .... directions.

steady	resistive	opposite	resultant	velocity
drag	balanced	high	upthrust	low

(2) **State Newton's second law in words. Use an equation in your answer.** (4 marks, ★★★★)

....

....

....

....

H(3) **Newton's first law is sometimes called the law of inertia. Define inertia.** (1 mark, ★★★★)

....

....

(4) **A boy jumps out of a boat. When he jumps out of the boat he pushes on the boat with a force of 100 N.**

a **The boat also pushes on the boy. Draw an arrow on the diagram to show the direction and size of this force.** (1 mark, ★★★)

← 100 N

....

....

b **Explain why you chose the value you did as your answer to part a.** (2 marks, ★★★)

....

....

c **Which of Newton's laws applies in this situation?** (1 mark, ★★★★)

....

....

H(5) **A 100 kg box has two forces acting on it.**

The forces are acting in opposite directions.

10 N acts to the left. 15 N acts to the right.

a **Work out the resultant force on the box.** (1 mark, ★★)

....

....

b **The box was initially at rest. Which way will it move?** (1 mark, ★★)

....

c **Calculate the acceleration of the box.** (3 marks, ★★★★)

....

....

....

WORKIT!

A car of mass 1200 kg accelerates from rest to 20 m/s in 10 s.

a Calculate the car's acceleration. (2 marks, ★★★)

$$a = \frac{v - u}{t}$$

Choose the correct equation and substitute in the values from the question.

$$a = \frac{20 - 0}{10} \quad (1)$$

Remember, from rest means 0 m/s.

$$a = 2 \text{ m/s}^2 \quad (1)$$

Remember to state your answer in the correct units.

b Calculate the resultant force acting on the car. (2 marks, ★★★)

$$F = ma$$

$$F = 1200 \times 2 \quad (1)$$

$$F = 2400 \text{ N} \quad (1)$$

6 A car has a mass of 800 kg and is travelling at a constant speed of 30 m/s.

a **State the resultant force acting on the car.** (1 mark, ★★★)

....

The driver applies the brakes and the braking force is 8000 N.

b **Calculate the deceleration of the car.** (2 marks, ★★★)

....

....

....

c **How long would it take the car to stop?** (3 marks, ★★★★)

....

....

....

NAILIT!

Newton's third law is the best known law, but probably the least understood. Remember the forces act in pairs but **never cancel each other out**. They are the same type of force but act on different objects.

DOIT!

Make sure you learn each of Newton's three laws. The basic idea of each law is actually very simple.

Stopping distance

(1) **Complete the following equation.** (2 marks, ★★★)

Stopping distance = ... + ...

(2) **The following graph shows how braking distance and thinking distance are affected by speed.**

DO IT!

Learn at least two factors that affect thinking distance and two factors that affect braking distance.

a **State two other factors that affect braking distance.** (1 mark, ★★)

....

b **i** **Using the graph, describe the relationship between thinking distance and speed.**
(1 mark, ★★★)

....

ii **Using the graph, describe the relationship between braking distance and speed.**
(2 marks, ★★★★)

....

....

③ **A student explains a simple experiment to compare the reaction times of different students in her class.**

One student drops the ruler.

The other student has to catch it as quickly as possible.

The shorter the distance that the ruler falls through the fingers, the shorter the reaction time of the student. Repeat the experiment twice and take an average.

Another student says: 'This experiment could be changed to see if texting on a mobile phone affects reaction time'. Explain how this new experiment would be conducted.

(6 marks, ★★★)

....

....

....

....

....

....

NAILIT!

Remember the thinking distance is equal to the speed of the vehicle multiplied by the reaction time of the driver. This is why thinking distance is proportional to speed. The braking distance is linked to kinetic energy, so is proportional to the square of the speed. For example, if speed doubles then the braking distance goes up by four times and if speed triples then braking distance goes up nine-fold. This explains why braking distance goes up so much at higher speeds.

Momentum (1)

H 1 **Which of the following is the unit for momentum?** (1 mark, ★★)

m/s
kg m/s
kg/ms
m/s²

H 2 **State the formula for momentum.** (1 mark, ★★)

....

H 3 **A 1000 kg car is driving along a racing track with a velocity of 400 m/s.**

Calculate its momentum. (3 marks, ★★★)

....

....

....

H 4 **A 3500 g labrador is running at 10 m/s.**

Calculate the dog's momentum. (4 marks, ★★★★)

....

....

NAILIT!
Momentum has two units. Make sure you learn them both, so you don't get caught out in exams.

NAILIT!
Momentum is a vector, so it has both magnitude and direction.

Momentum (2)

H① **Complete the following sentence with the missing words.** (2 marks, ★★★)

In a .... system (in which no .... forces act) the total momentum before an event

is equal to the total momentum after the event. This is called the .... of .... law.

external	moments	momentum	conservation
internal	closed	released	sum

H② **A speeding truck is approaching a stationary car at traffic lights.**

a **Calculate the momentum of the truck.** (2 marks, ★★★)

....

....

b **In an inelastic collision the two vehicles crumple together.**

Calculate the velocity of the truck and car as they move off joined together. (3 marks, ★★★★)

....

....

....

40 m/s →

Truck 2000 kg

0 m/s

Car 800 kg

H③ **Two cars have a head-on collision, their speeds and mass are shown in the diagram. Assume momentum is conserved in the collision.**

Both cars crumple together in an inelastic collision.

Calculate the velocity and direction of the cars as they move off together. (6 marks, ★★★★★)

....

....

....

40 m/s →   ← 30 m/s

800 kg   1000 kg

NAILIT!

When a force acts on an object that is moving, or able to move, a change in momentum occurs.

DOIT!

Make sure that you are confident with collision, recoil and explosion questions.

Momentum (3) H

H ① Explain, using physics ideas, why a crumple zone may prevent the driver in an accident from being killed during a collision. (6 marks, ★★★★★)

....

....

....

H ② A cricket ball of mass 200 g is struck with a force of 180 N for a period of 0.005 s.

Calculate the change in momentum. (3 marks, ★★★)

....

....

H ③ A golf ball of mass 50 g is struck with a force of 200 N for a period of 0.005 s. Calculate:

a The change in momentum. (2 marks, ★★★)

....

....

....

b The speed of the golf ball immediately afterwards. (3 marks, ★★★★)

....

....

....

NAILIT!

$F = \dfrac{m\Delta v}{\Delta t}$ is an important equation. It helps us to understand why increasing the time of impact by using crumple zones, for example, can reduce the forces suffered by the driver or passenger in a car collision.

DOIT!

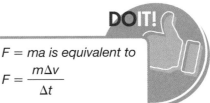

$F = ma$ is equivalent to

$$F = \frac{m\Delta v}{\Delta t}$$

Can you demonstrate how?

Transverse and longitudinal waves

(1) **Water ripples on a surface of a lake are an example of which type of wave?** (1 mark, ★★)

Longitudinal	
Transverse	

EM waves	
Rarefaction	

(2) a **What is a longitudinal wave?** (2 marks, ★★★)

....

....

b **Give an example of a longitudinal wave.** (1 mark, ★★)

....

....

c **Draw a diagram of a longitudinal wave.** (2 marks, ★★★)

(3) **A student is interested in waves.**

She takes a slinky and shakes it up and down while a classmate is holding the other end.

She observes this:

Direction of wave →

Vibration of coils

a **What type of wave does she observe? Explain your answer.** (3 marks, ★★★)

....

....

b **What could she do with the slinky to make a different type of wave?** (2 marks, ★★★)

....

....

c **Compare the two wave types. State their differences.** (2 marks, ★★★★)

....

....

DO IT!

Learn at least two examples of each type of wave.

NAILIT!

Waves can be either longitudinal or transverse. Make sure that you know the differences between them.

Properties of waves

(1) **Define the following:**

a **Amplitude** (2 marks, ★★★)

....

....

b **Frequency** (2 marks, ★★★)

....

....

c **Wavelength** (2 marks, ★★★)

....

....

DO IT!

Make flashcards to learn the definitions for **amplitude**, **wavelength**, **frequency** and **time period**.

(2) **The figure below shows an oscilloscope trace of a musical note.**

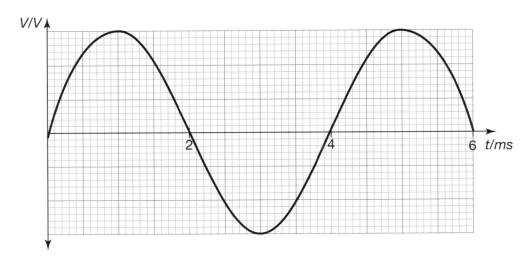

Work out the following:

a **The time period of the wave.** (2 marks, ★★★)

....

b **The frequency of the wave.** (2 marks, ★★★)

....

c **The amplitude of the wave. Each cm square represents 1 V.** (2 marks, ★★★)

....

③ **All EM waves travel at 300 000 000 m/s. BBC Radio 4 broadcasts at a frequency of 603 kHz.**
Calculate the wavelength of the radio wave. (4 marks, ★★★★)

....

....

....

....

NAILIT!

Make sure that you know how to label wavelength and amplitude on a wave diagram.

> Watch out for prefixes and powers. Remember that 1 MHz means 1 megahertz. This means 1 million hertz or 1 000 000 Hz.

WORKIT!

a Calculate the period of a radio wave that has a speed of 3 000 000 m/s and frequency of 1 MHz. (2 marks, ★★★)

Step 1 You do not have to use the wave equation, but you will instead need the following equation provided on the physics equation sheet:

$$\text{frequency} = \frac{1}{\text{time period}} = \frac{1}{T} \,(1)$$

Step 2 Rearrange and then substitute into the equation

$$T = \frac{1}{f} = \frac{1}{1\,000\,000}$$

> You can leave the number in standard form as it is very small, otherwise it is 0.000001 s.

$$= 1 \times 10^{-6} \text{ s } (1)$$

b Calculate the wavelength of the radio wave. The wave speed is 3×10^8 m/s. (1 mark, ★★)

Use formula $v = f \times \lambda$ and rearrange:

$$\lambda = \frac{v}{f} = \frac{3 \times 10^8}{1 \times 10^6}$$

$$= \frac{300\,000\,000}{1\,000\,000}$$

$$= 300\,\text{m } (1)$$

Reflection and refraction

(1) **A wave approaches a boundary. Which three things could happen?** (3 marks, ★★★★)

....

....

....

(2) **The diagram below shows a wave front approaching a hard flat surface.**

Complete the diagram to show reflection taking place. (3 marks, ★★★)

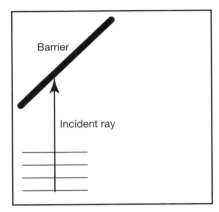

(3) **The light ray is moving from air into glass blocks a and b.**

Assume no reflection takes place.

Complete the path of the light rays:

  i **entering**

  ii **travelling through**

  iii **leaving the glass blocks**

On each diagram label the normal and direction of the rays.

a (3 marks, ★★★)   **b** (3 marks, ★★★★)

NAILIT!

Remember to add a normal when drawing ray diagrams.

If the wave is travelling from a less dense medium into a denser medium, it slows down and bends towards the normal. If it travels from a denser to less dense medium, it speeds up and bends away from the normal.

DOIT!

Practise drawing diagrams of wave fronts being reflected or refracted at the boundary between two different materials. Always use a ruler!

Sound waves (1)

H① **What is the normal audible frequency range for humans?** (2 marks, ★★★)

....

....

H② **A loudspeaker plays music. The sound waves reach the outer ear.**

With reference to the diagram to the right, explain how a human can 'hear' music.

(6 marks, ★★★★)

The ossicles

'Hammer' 'Anvil' 'Stirrup'

Cochlea

Nerve to brain

Ear drum

Oval window

....

....

....

....

H③ **A tuning fork is struck against a microphone connected to an oscilloscope.**

The sound wave can be seen on an oscilloscope screen.

Each horizontal square on the oscilloscope trace represents 1 ms.

Each vertical square represents 1 V.

Oscilloscope trace

a **What is the time period of the wave?** (2 marks, ★★★★)

....

b **Calculate the frequency of the wave.** (2 marks, ★★★)

....

c **What is the amplitude of the wave?** (2 marks, ★★★★)

....

DO**IT!**

Practise drawing diagrams of sound waves. Use the words **compression** and **rarefaction** in your labels to explain the ideas of low and high pressure air. Label the wavelengths.

NAILIT!

Sound behaves in a similar way to other mechanical waves. The wave transfers energy through matter such as solids, liquids and gases. The matter vibrates but does not actually move from one place to another.

For example, a wave travelling in water moves from one place to another, but the water doesn't. Each point on the water wave moves up and down perpendicularly to the direction of the wave.

Sound waves (2)

H(1) **Define the term 'ultrasound'.** (2 marks, ★★★)

....

....

H(2) **State two uses or applications of ultrasonic waves.** (2 marks, ★★★)

....

....

H(3) **Seismograph stations all over the world can detect P-waves and S-waves in the event of an earthquake.**

The diagram below shows the epicentre of an earthquake and the detection of P-waves and S-waves at different seismograph stations locations around the world.

Epicentre

1
2
3
4

→ P- and S-waves
→ P-waves only

a

b

a What is a P-wave? What type of wave is it?
(4 marks, ★★★)

....

....

b What is an S-wave? Describe what type of wave an S-wave is. (4 marks, ★★★)

....

....

c Explain why the waves that reach points 1, 2, 3 and 4 curve gradually as they pass through the Earth. (4 marks, ★★★★)

....

....

....

d Explain why only P-waves can be detected at points a and b. (2 marks, ★★★)

....

....

DO IT!

Make sure you know the difference between a P-wave and an S-wave. Which is transverse and which is longitudinal?

NAILIT!

Ultrasound can be used to measure distances without having to cut something open. Partial reflections of ultrasound take place at boundaries of different materials. It is possible to use an oscilloscope to work out the time it takes for the pulse reflection to return to the transducer. If the speed of ultrasound is known in the material, then you can calculate the distance to the different boundary. This technique can be used for many applications, for example, finding flaws in metal casings and measuring the size of eyeballs.

Electromagnetic waves (1)

(1) Complete the following table. (6 marks, ★★★)

Type of electromagnetic waves

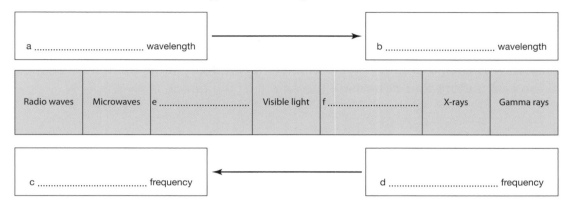

a .... wavelength → b .... wavelength

Radio waves	Microwaves	e	Visible light	f	X-rays	Gamma rays

c .... frequency ← d .... frequency

(2) State three properties of electromagnetic waves. (3 marks, ★★★)

....

....

H (3) Radio waves and microwaves are both used in communications.

Radio waves can be used to transmit television and radio programmes.

Microwaves are used for mobile phones and Wi-Fi.

The different properties of microwaves and radio waves make them suitable for these applications.

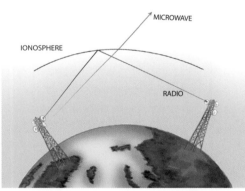

With particular reference to the diagram above, explain why microwaves and radio waves are suitable for these different applications. (6 marks, ★★★★)

....

....

....

....

....

DO IT!

You need to learn the electromagnetic spectrum in the correct order.

Here is a mnemonic:

Red **M**artians **I**nvade **V**enus **U**sing **X**-ray **G**uns

If you don't like it, make up your own one!

NAIL IT!

For waves, wavelength (λ) and frequency (f) are inversely proportional to each other. If the frequency has a very high value, then the wavelength has to be very short.

Electromagnetic waves (2)

H① Which of the following can be produced by oscillations in electrical circuits? (2 marks, ★★★★)

Ultraviolet waves	
Sound waves	

Gamma waves	
Radio waves	

② **Ultraviolet, X-rays and gamma rays can have hazardous effects on human tissue. Describe two factors that determine the extent of the effect.** (2 marks, ★★★★)

....

....

③ **Match the following EM spectrum waves to the application/use.** (6 marks, ★★★)

1 Radio waves	a Fibre optics and communication
2 Microwaves	b TV and radio
3 Infrared	c Heaters and cooking food
4 Visible light	d Sun tanning
5 Ultra violet	e Medical imaging and treatments
6 X-rays + gamma rays	f Satellite communications and cooking food

NAILIT!

Ultraviolet, X-rays and gamma rays are all ionising radiation. Over-exposure to any of them can lead to gene mutation and cancer.

DOIT!

This is real spider diagram and flashcard territory. It is important that you make an effort to learn at least two uses or applications for each member of the electromagnetic spectrum.

WORKIT!

A radio wave passes into a metal TV aerial.

Explain what effect the radio wave has on the metal TV aerial. (3 marks, ★★)

Radio waves can be absorbed by the metal TV aerial. (1)

The radio waves may induce an alternating current. (1)

The alternating current has the same frequency as the radio wave that induced it. (1)

Lenses

(1) a A lens forms an image by refracting light. State the two types of lenses. (2 marks, ★★★)

....

....

b State the types of images that can be formed by the lenses in part a. (2 marks, ★★★)

....

....

....

(2) Complete and annotate the diagrams below using the following labels: (6 marks, ★★★)

convex	concave	parallel	light	rays
principal	focus	focal		length

a

b

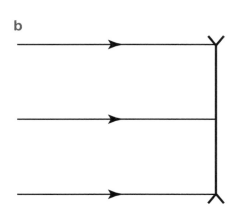

3 **a Complete the ray diagram below to show the image formed by the lens.** (6 marks, ★★★★)

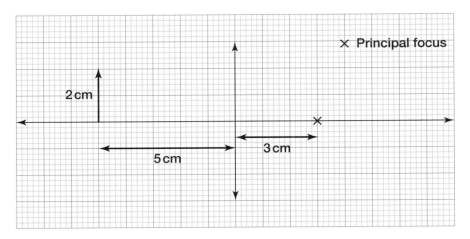

b State the type of image formed. (1 mark, ★★★)

....

....

c Calculate the magnification of the image formed. (2 marks, ★★★)

....

....

....

....

....

NAILIT!

Magnification is a ratio and does not have units.

DOIT!

Make sure you learn the two lens types in ray diagrams.

Visible light

(1) **Label the two types of reflection in the diagrams below.** (2 marks, ★★★)

 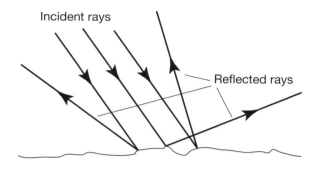

a .... **reflection**

b .... **reflection**

(2) **Complete the missing words in the sentences below.**

a **Objects that transmit light are either** .... **or** .... **.** (2 marks, ★★★)

b **The colour of an object that we observe is related to the different amounts of**

........................, ... **and** .... **of different wavelengths of light by**

the object. (3 marks, ★★★)

c .... **objects absorb or reflect the majority of the light incident on**

them. (1 mark, ★★★)

NAILIT!

Remember that a filter will absorb certain wavelengths of light (or colours) and will transmit certain wavelengths of light (or colours). A cyan filter, for example, will transmit green and blue light, but would absorb red light.

DOIT!

Learn the three primary colours for light and make sure you know all the different combinations. What combinations make magenta, cyan and yellow?

③ **A student considers the effect that using filters has on the colour of objects she observes.**

She shines white light from a torch. First the white light passes through a magenta filter and then the light passes through a red filter.

Then the student observes what colour some red poppies appear when the filtered light is shone on it.

The experimental set-up can be seen in the diagram below.

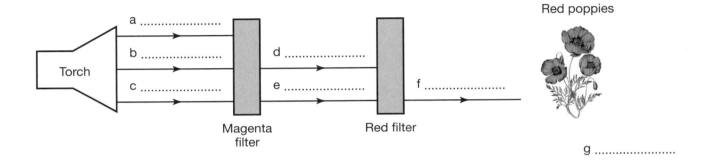

Label:

i **The missing primary colours on a, b and c that make up white light.** (3 marks, ★★★)

ii **The two primary colours on d and e transmitted by the magenta filter.** (2 marks, ★★★)

iii **The primary colour transmitted by the red filter.** (1 mark, ★★★)

iv **The colour that the red poppies will appear to the student on g.** (1 mark, ★★★)

Emission and absorption of infrared radiation and black body radiation

H(1) **If an object radiates and absorbs radiation at the same rate what does this tell you about the object's temperature?** (1 mark, ★★★)

| It is increasing | |
| It is decreasing | |

| It is constant | |
| It is impossible to know | |

(2) **A student carries out an experiment on the absorption and emission of infrared radiation.**

He paints one can white and another black.

He then fills them both with the same amount of boiling water.

He records the temperature change with a thermometer for each can 15 minutes later.

The student records that the black can's temperature goes down by 15°C, but the white can's temperature goes down by only 5°C. Explain why. (3 marks, ★★★★)

....

....

....

....

....

③ The student modifies the experiment and places an infrared heater equally spaced from both cans. He then fills both cans with cold water. He turns on the heater and records the temperature change after 15 minutes.

a Would the temperature of the water in each can increase or decrease by the same amount? Explain your answer. (3 marks, ★★★★)

....

....

....

....

....

b Describe the limitations of the experiment. (3 marks, ★★★)

....

....

....

....

WORKIT!

The student was only interested in finding out about absorption and emission of infrared radiation. What other factors may have affected his experiment? (1 mark, ★★)

The experiment will also be affected by conduction and convection. (1)

H④ An object has an increasing temperature. Which of the following statements is true? (1 mark, ★)

Absorption and emission of infrared are at the same rate	
Absorption and emission of infrared are at different rates	
Absorption of infrared is greater than emission of infrared	
Emission of infrared is great than absorption of infrared	

⑤ **The following graph shows the continuous spectra for stars that have different surface temperatures. The surface temperatures are given in kelvin (K).**

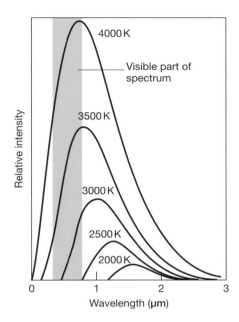

a **Each star has a peak wavelength. Define peak wavelength.** (2 marks, ★★★★)

....

....

b **State the relationship between the temperature of a star and the peak wavelength.** (2 marks, ★★★★)

....

....

H⑥ **Explain the factors that determine the temperature of the Earth.** (6 marks, ★★★★)

....

....

....

....

....

....

DO IT!

Learn the definition for a perfect black body.

'A perfect black body is an object that absorbs all of the radiation incident on it'

NAIL IT!

All objects emit infrared radiation, the hotter the object the more radiation it emits.

Magnetism

(1) **Complete the sentence. The poles of a magnet are the places where:** (1 mark, ★★)

the magnetic fields are the strongest	
the field lines are the furthest apart	
the magnetic fields are the weakest	
flux lines overlap	

(2) **a What is an induced magnet?** (2 marks, ★★★)

....

....

NAILIT!

Make sure you learn that magnetic materials are iron, steel, cobalt and nickel.

b What kind of force always exists between a permanent and an induced magnet? (1 mark, ★★★)

....

c Describe a simple test to check if a material is an induced or permanent magnet. (3 marks, ★★★★)

....

....

....

(3) **Draw the field lines on the following magnet combinations.** (6 marks, ★★★★)

a

N ___ S

S ___ N

b

N ___ S

N ___ S

DO IT!

The direction of a magnetic field at any point is given by the direction of the force that would act on another north pole placed at that point. Remember north pole really means north-seeking pole.

Electromagnetism

H

H① A student builds the circuit to the right. The circuit contains a dc power supply and a switch. He places a plotting compass near the wire.

a **When he closes the switch to complete the circuit what will he observe?** (2 marks, ★★★)

....

....

b **The student reverses the battery connection then closes the switch. What will he observe now?** (2 mark, ★★★)

....

....

H② The diagrams show a wire carrying current in the direction indicated by the arrow.

For each wire sketch the magnetic field that would be induced.
(6 marks, ★★★★)

H③ A current-carrying wire is placed between the two magnets below.

The current direction is indicated with an arrow.

a **Draw an arrow on the wire to show the direction in which it will experience a force.** (1 mark, ★★★★)

b **What is the name given to this effect?** (1 mark, ★★★★)

....

c **What changes could be made to make the wire move with a greater force?**
(3 marks, ★★★★)

....

....

NAILIT!

A wire shaped into a coil that carries a current is called a solenoid. A solenoid has the same magnetic field pattern as a bar magnet. The field inside a solenoid is strong and uniform (that is, the field lines are parallel and the same distance away from each other).
If you place a core inside the solenoid, you have created an electromagnet.

Motor effect

H 1 Add the following labels to the electric motor diagram below. Some labels are used more than once. (6 marks, ★★★★)

| force | split-ring commutator | rotating coil | dc power supply | brush |

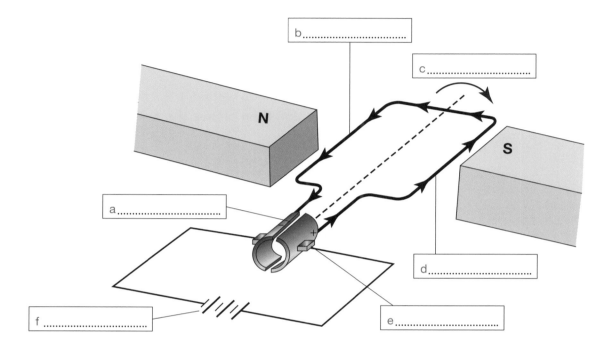

b.............................

c.............................

N

S

a.............................

d.............................

f.............................

e.............................

H 2 **a Explain the function of a split-ring commutator in a dc motor.** (2 marks, ★★★★)

....

....

b Explain the role of the brushes in an electric motor. (2 marks, ★★★★)

....

....

NAILIT!

Learn the different parts of the dc motor. Make sure you know the difference between a split-ring commutator and slip rings. Do you know why a split-ring commutator is used in a dc motor?

NAILIT!

Learn Fleming's left-hand rule. It comes up all the time. Remember that the left-hand rule is for motors.

(3) **The diagram below shows a student's design for a loudspeaker.**

The student will plug his MP3 player into the loudspeaker.

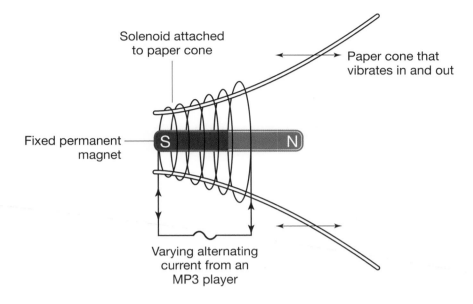

Solenoid attached to paper cone

Paper cone that vibrates in and out

Fixed permanent magnet

S   N

Varying alternating current from an MP3 player

With reference to the diagram, explain how the loudspeaker converts an electrical signal into sound waves. (6 marks, ★★★★)

....

....

....

....

....

....

....

NAILIT!

A loudspeaker uses the motor effect to convert variations in current to the pressure variations in sound waves. You need to be able to explain how a loudspeaker works. Remember to use bullet points and explain it stage by stage.

Electromagnetic induction

H(1) **Are the following statements true (T) or false (F)? Circle the correct answer.** (4 marks, ★★★)

a If a conductor moves at an angle to a magnetic field a potential difference   **T**   **F**
is not induced in the conductor.

b If a potential difference is induced across the ends of a conductor, a current   **T**   **F**
always flows.

c The left-hand rule is used for the motor effect and right-hand rule for the   **T**   **F**
generator effect.

d The generator effect can be used in a generator and a dynamo to generate ac.   **T**   **F**

H(2) **A student moves a metal conducting
rod between the poles of a horseshoe
magnet.**

**Both sides of the rod are connected
to a very sensitive ammeter (or
galvanometer).**

a **If she moves the rod up through the
field between the poles as shown in
the diagram what will she observe?**
(2 marks, ★★★★)

....

....

....

b **State the name of the phenomenon she observed in part a. Explain why it happens.**
(3 marks, ★★★★)

....

....

....

c **What will happen if she moves the rod down between the poles instead of up?**
(2 marks, ★★★★)

....

....

....

d **What will happen if she moves the rod up and down between the poles at a steady speed?** (3 marks, ★★★)

....

....

....

H③ **A boy has a dynamo on his bike. He connects it to a light bulb. When he cycles, the magnet rotates and the bulb lights up.**

Wheel

N S

Magnet

Coil on soft-iron core

Wires going to bulb

a **Explain why this happens.** (4 marks, ★★★★)

....

....

....

....

b **Why do you think dynamos are no longer legal on UK roads at night?** (2 marks, ★★★★)

....

....

....

NAILIT!

If you move a magnet into a coil, it will induce a current. The current flow will have an associated magnetic field that opposes the magnet's motion. For example, if you push a north pole into the coil, the coil's magnetic field will also be north. What will happen to the coil's field when you pull out the north pole?

DOIT!

You need to learn that if you double the speed of a coil in a magnetic field, not only will the frequency of the induced voltage double, but its amplitude will also double.

Transformers

H(1) **The diagram to the right shows an old-fashioned carbon microphone.**

If the carbon powder is compressed by pressure, its resistance changes.

a **With reference to the diagram, explain why the current changes when a person talks into the microphone.** (3 marks, ★★★★)

....

....

b **With reference to the diagram, explain why a changing current makes the metal plate vibrate back and forth.** (3 marks, ★★★★)

....

....

....

c **With reference to the diagram, explain why the coil is wound onto a magnet.** (2 marks, ★★★)

....

H(2) **The following diagram shows a transformer.**

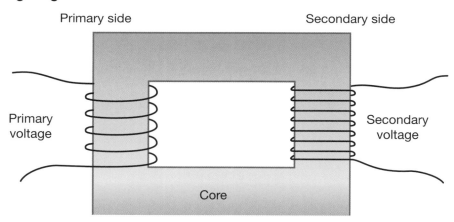

What type of transformer is shown in the diagram? Explain your answer. (2 marks, ★★★)

....

....

H (3) **Transformers are used in ac transmission.**

a **Explain how a transformer works.** (6 marks, ★★★★)

....

....

....

....

....

b **Explain why a transformer can only be used with ac, and not dc.** (3 marks, ★★★)

....

....

....

WORKIT!

A transformer is used in a laboratory. The voltage input to the primary coil is 230 V.

The primary coil has 200 turns and the secondary coil has 1000 turns.

a Calculate the potential difference output of the secondary coil. (2 marks, ★★★)

$$\frac{V_P}{V_s} = \frac{n_P}{n_s}$$ ⟵ Choose the correct equation.

$$\frac{230}{V_s} = \frac{200}{1000} \rightarrow V_s = \frac{230 \times 1000}{200} = 1150 \ (1)$$ ⟵ Substitute in the values.

Express answer with correct units Vs = 1150 V (1)

b If current in the primary is 3 A calculate the current in the secondary coil. Assume the transformer is 100% efficient. (2 marks, ★★★)

$$V_s I_s = V_P I_P \rightarrow 1150 \times I_s = 230 \times 3 \ (1)$$ ⟵ Remember to select the right equation and substitute in the values.

$$I_s = \frac{230 \times 3}{1150}$$

$$= 0.6 \ A \ (1)$$

c Explain why this current would be more suitable for transmission. (1 mark, ★★★)

Current is lower, so power losses would be lower. (1)

NAILIT!

Make sure that you know how to rearrange the transformer equations.

$$\frac{V_P}{V_s} = \frac{n_P}{n_s}$$

NAILIT!

Remember that transformers only work with ac. Transformers are very useful because when potential difference is stepped up, the current goes down. This can be explained with this formula: $V_s I_s = V_P I_P$. This means that there are less power losses in transmission. (This can be explained with the formula $P = I^2 R$.)

Our solar system

1 **Which galaxy is the Earth part of? Circle the correct answer.** (1 mark, ★★)

The solar system	The Milky Way	Andromeda	Orion's Belt

2 **a** **Fill in the gaps to provide a list of the planets of the solar system.** (4 marks, ★★)

Mercury		Earth		Jupiter		Uranus	

b **Why isn't Pluto included in the list above?** (2 marks, ★★★)

....

....

c **What is another name for the natural satellite of a planet?** (1 mark, ★★★)

....

d **What is the name of the nearest star to the Earth?** (1 mark, ★★)

....

3 **a** **Rank the following in order of size from 1 (smallest) to 7 (largest).** (6 marks, ★★★)

Planet	Moon	Dwarf planet	Solar system	Sun	Universe	Galaxy
	1					

NAILIT!

Learn the difference between polar and geostationary satellites. Geostationary satellites stay in a fixed position above the Earth and orbit at the same speed as the Earth. Polar satellites orbit around the poles and the Earth spins under them, so they get to see much more of the Earth.

WORKIT!

a Define the term nebula. (1 mark, ★★)

A nebula is a cloud of dust and gas. (1)

> Remember to include the keywords to hoover up those marks.

b How does a nebula go on to form a star? (4 marks, ★★)

Gravity pulls together the dust and gas in the nebula. (1)

> Structure your answer in short sentences, this will make it easier for the person marking it.

When pressure and temperature are high enough, fusion takes place. (1)

Outward pressure due to fusion energy is balanced by inward gravitational force. (1)

Stars remain in this stable state of equilibrium for a very long time (millions to billions of years). (1)

DOIT!

Learn the order of the planets. Try using a mnemonic. Here is an example: my very easy method just speeds up naming (planets).

Life cycle of a star

① **Complete the following sentences with the missing words.** (6 marks, ★★★)

When a star is a main-sequence star, this means the inward force of ....

is balanced with the outward radiation pressure caused by ....

This state of .... can last for millions to billions of years depending

on the star's .... When a star similar in size to our own runs out of

.... it grows in size and becomes a ....

red giant	equilibrium		hydrogen		fusion		neutron
stable	mass	supernova		white		dwarf	gravity

② **The following flow chart is a summary of the life cycle of stars. Complete the missing labels a–f in the flow chart.** (6 marks, ★★★★)

NAILIT!

There are three main paths of the life cycle of a star you need to learn:

1 Stars of a similar size to our Sun
2 Stars bigger than our Sun
3 Stars much bigger than our Sun

The beginning of each cycle is the same but the fate of the star is different in each of the three paths.

Small stars

Massive stars

Nebula

a

Main-sequence star

b

c

White dwarf

Supernova

d

e

f

③ **The universe contains an abundance of elements. Explain which stages of the life cycle of stars have made this possible.** (6 marks, ★★★★)

....

....

....

....

....

DOIT!

Practise drawing flow charts or spider diagrams of the life cycle of stars.

Orbital motion, natural and artificial satellites

(1) **Circle the force that allows planets and satellites to maintain their circular orbits.**
(1 mark, ★★)

Centrifugal forces	Circular forces	Planet and satellite forces	Gravity

(2) **Describe the differences and similarities between natural and artificial satellites.**
(4 marks, ★★★)

....

....

....

DO IT!

Make sure you learn the difference between an artificial and natural satellite and learn the correct meaning of the word moon. This word doesn't just belong to our Moon!

H(3) **The following diagram shows the path of Halley's Comet.**

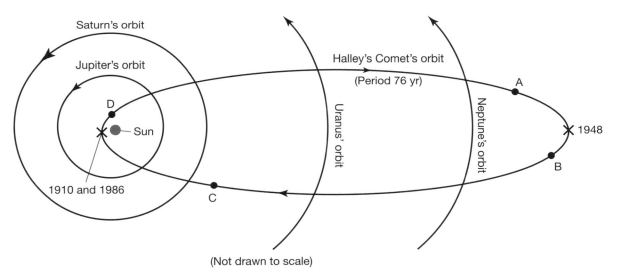

(Not drawn to scale)

a **What does period mean in this diagram?** (1 mark, ★★★)

....

b **What happens to the speed of the comet when it gets close to the Sun? Explain your answer.** (2 marks, ★★★)

....

....

H(4) Venus is the planet in our solar system with the most circular orbit.

Venus' orbital speed is constant, but its velocity is constantly changing.
Explain how this is possible. (3 marks, ★★★★)

....

....

....

(5) Jupiter's orbit is not circular, it is elliptical. This means it is not a perfect circle.

a **Describe Jupiter's distance from the Sun.** (1 mark, ★★★★)

....

....

b **What effect, if any, will this have on the orbital speed of Jupiter? Explain your answer.** (2 marks, ★★★★)

....

....

NAILIT!

Very few planets (if any) have a perfectly circular orbit. Most of them have an elliptical orbit. This is elongated and looks a bit like an egg.

Red-shift

1 **a** **What does the Big Bang theory suggest about the beginning of the universe?**
(2 marks, ★★★)

....

....

....

b **Which observations from 1998 onwards have provided evidence to support the Big Bang theory?** (1 mark, ★★★)

....

....

2 **The diagram shows emission spectra from two galaxies of approximately the same size and similar average temperature.**

Emission spectra from a nearby galaxy

Short wavelength ——————————————→ Long wavelength

Emission spectra from a distant galaxy

a **What observation can be made about the emission spectra from the distant galaxy?**
(2 marks, ★★★)

....

....

b **What does this observation reveal about the motion of the distant galaxy?** (2 marks, ★★★)

....

....

c **How does the observation support the Big Bang theory?** (2 marks, ★★★)

....

....

....

③ **The Big Bang theory does not provide information for two big unanswered questions in physics.**

These are:

- **Why is the rate of expansion of the universe increasing?**

- **Why does the universe have more mass than simply the sum of the mass of suns, planets, and other stellar material?**

State the two hypotheses that have been put forward by the scientific community to answer these questions. (2 marks, ★★★★)

a ....

....

b ....

....

NAILIT!

Make an effort to read up on the alternative theories to the Big Bang theory. The most popular one was the Steady State theory. This stated that the universe was eternal and had no beginning and galaxies were born from white holes. Like the Big Bang, the Steady State theory still had an expanding universe, but the discovery of cosmic microwave background radiation was the nail in the coffin of this theory!

DOIT!

We observe a similar effect to red-shift with sound. It is called the **Doppler effect**. If a car moves towards us, the sound waves get squashed together (making it high pitched). As it moves away, the sound waves get stretched out (making it low pitched). Watch a professional car race for a few minutes and you will hear this.

Paper 1

1 **a** State the formula for calculating the kinetic energy of a moving object. (1 mark)

....

A dog is chasing a cat in a field. Both the dog and cat are running at a steady speed of 10 m/s. The cat has a mass of 3 kg and the dog has a mass of 8 kg.

b Calculate the energy in the kinetic store of the cat. (2 marks)

....

....

c Calculate the energy in the kinetic store of the dog. (2 marks)

....

....

d The dog accelerates to a new steady speed and increases the energy in its kinetic store to 576 J. Calculate the dog's new speed. (4 marks)

....

....

....

....

e The cat maintains the same speed of 10 m/s. The cat is 10 metres ahead of the dog. Calculate the time it takes for the dog to catch the cat. (2 marks)

....

....

(2) **Complete the following with the different energy stores or energy pathways.** (6 marks)

a .... transferred from a torch.

b .... store of a stretched rubber band.

c .... from a singer performing.

d .... energy store of a battery.

e .... store of a moving bus.

f .... store of a boulder on the edge of a cliff.

(3) **Bradley has a breakfast of porridge followed by eggs.**

Bradley then goes for a bike ride up and then down a hill.

At the bottom of the hill he has to use his brakes to stop.

Use ideas about energy stores and systems to describe his journey. (6 marks)

....

....

....

....

....

....

4 a **Explain with the use of diagrams the particle arrangements of solids, liquids and gases.** (6 marks)

....

....

....

....

....

....

Sometimes models are put forward to describe particle behaviour.

A student has a tray of marbles and wishes to explain ideas about matter and particles.

b **Explain what the marbles represent in the student's model.** (1 mark)

....

c **The student wishes to use the model to demonstrate a solid. Describe how he could he do this.** (1 mark)

....

d **The student wishes to use the model to demonstrate evaporation. Describe how he could do this.** (2 marks)

....

....

(5) **A student lights a fire lighter and uses it to heat up 0.25 kg of water.**

When the fire lighter has all burnt away, the water temperature has increased by 10°C.

All of the energy in the chemical store of the fire lighter is transferred to the thermal store of the water.

The specific heat capacity of water is: 4200 J/kg °C.

Calculate the (energy) increase in the thermal store of the water in joules. (4 marks)

Clamp

Thermometer

Beaker

Gauze mat

Tripod

Fire lighter

....

....

....

....

(6) **Elena climbs up 3 flights of stairs. The total vertical distance she covers is 12 m.**

The energy in her gravitational store increases by 6 kJ.

The Earth's gravitational field strength is 10 N/kg.

Calculate Elena's mass. (4 marks)

....

....

....

....

....

7. **The current in a resistor and then in an unknown component X is measured for different voltages.**

The table shows the results.

Voltage/V	Current/A	
	Resistor	Component X
1	0.10	0.20
2	0.20	0.40
3	0.30	0.60
4	0.40	0.75
5	0.50	0.80
6	0.60	0.84

a **On the grid below and on the same axes, plot graphs of this data for the resistor and component X. Plot voltage on the x-axis and current on the y-axis.** (5 marks)

b **Draw lines of best fit for the resistor and component X.** (2 marks)

c **Determine what component X is and justify your choice.** (2 marks)

d **Use the graph to determine the resistance of the resistor.** (2 marks)

Resistance = _____

⑧ A carriage containing passengers on a roller coaster is raised through a vertical height of 90 m.

The combined mass of the carriage and the passengers is 2000 kg.

The Earth's gravitational field strength is 10 N/kg.

a The carriage is lifted 90 m vertically to point A on the diagram.

Calculate the energy increase in the gravitational potential store of the carriage in kJ.
(3 marks)

....

....

....

Increase in gravitational energy store = ... kJ

b During the ride the carriage drops from point A to point B as shown in the diagram.

Assume energy is conserved and friction or air resistance acting on the carriage are negligible and can be ignored.

Calculate the speed of the carriage at point B. (5 marks)

....

....

....

....

....

Speed of carriage at point B = ... m/s

(9) **Americium-241 is used commonly in smoke alarms around the world.**

Americium is an alpha emitter and has a half-life of 433 years.

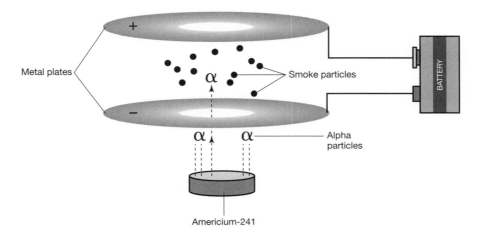

In normal use the alpha particles emitted ionise the air and cause a current to flow.

If the current continues to flow the smoke alarm will not sound.

a **Explain why an alpha emitter is used for this application.** (2 marks)

....

....

b **It is a criminal offence in the UK to tamper with smoke alarms that contain americium-241. Explain why.** (3 marks)

....

....

....

c **The half-life of americium-241 is stated as 433 years. Define the term half-life.** (2 marks)

....

....

....

d **Americium is used for the smoke alarm because it has a very long half-life.**

Ignoring background radiation, a G–M tube detects a count-rate of 30 counts per minute from the americium-241.

Calculate how many half-lives it would take the americium-241's count-rate to fall to $\frac{1}{4}$ of its original value. (2 marks)

....

....

e **How many years is this?** (1 mark)

....

10 a **Match the keyword to its definition.** (4 marks)

1 Nucleus	**a** An atom with the same number of protons and a different number of neutrons.
2 Isotope	**b** It is only composed of protons and neutrons.
3 Ion	**c** A neutral particle with the same mass as a proton.
4 Neutron	**d** An atom that has lost or gained an electron.

b **When a neutron inside a nucleus decays into a proton and emits an electron this is called:** (1 mark)

Beta decay	
Gamma decay	
Alpha decay	
Neutron emission	

c **An alpha particle is the same as:** (1 mark)

A hydrogen atom	
A neutral atom	
Gamma radiation	
A helium nucleus	

(11) **Explain using the following words what an electric field is and how it affects charged objects placed within it.** (4 marks)

electric	force	repulsive	same
attractive	charged	exerts	opposite

....

....

....

....

(12) **A teacher carries out a demonstration with protactinium-234 in a laboratory. Protactinium has a half-life of approximately 69 seconds.**

The nuclear equation below shows the changes to the atomic and mass numbers of protactinium when it undergoes decay, and the new element that is formed.

$$^{234}_{91}Pa \rightarrow\ ^{234}_{92}U + \text{radiation}$$

a **State the type of radiation released in the above nuclear equation.** (1 mark)

....

b **Describe the change that takes place in the protactinium nucleus before this radiation is released.** (3 marks)

....

....

....

c **The teacher wears gloves when handling the protactinium. Describe how this will this protect her.** (1 mark)

....

d **In what way will wearing gloves not protect the teacher? Explain your answer.** (2 mark)

....

....

e **How should the teacher move and store the protactinium once the experiment is over?** (2 marks)

....

....

(13) **The block in the image below is made of iron and has a mass of 192 g.**

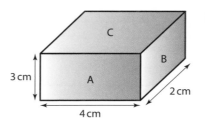

(Not drawn to scale)

a **Calculate the volume of the block in cm³.** (1 mark)

....

b **Calculate the block's density in g/cm³.** (2 marks)

....

....

c **Convert the density value to kg/m³.** (2 marks)

....

....

d **A student picks up the block and presses it down on the table first with face A and then with face B with the same force.**

Explain, without a calculation, which face (A or B) will exert the most pressure on the table. (2 marks)

....

....

e **Calculate the pressure exerted on the table in kilopascals if face A is placed on the table.** (4 marks)

....

....

....

.... **kPa**

Energy

Energy stores and systems

1 A system is an object, or group of objects. The **energy** in a system is a numerical **value** that tells us whether certain **changes** in the system could, or could not, happen. The total **amount** of energy in a system is always the **same** no matter what changes happen in the system, but the energy available can be **redistributed** in different parts of this system.

2 3–d; 4–g; 5–e; 6–c; 7– f; 8–a

3 1 – Chemical; 2 – Heating; 3 – Heating; 4 – Thermal; 5 – Thermal.

Changes in energy stores: kinetic energy

1 a Kinetic energy = 0.5 × mass × speed² Or $\frac{1}{2}mv^2$

 b J or joules

2 Kinetic energy = 0.5 × mass × speed²

 Kinetic energy = 0.5 × 1000 × 10²

 50 000 J or 50 kJ

3 Kinetic energy = 0.5 × mass × speed² rearrange to:

 mass = $\frac{\text{kinetic energy}}{0.5 \times \text{speed}^2}$

 mass = 800 000/0.5 × 10²

 16 000 kg or 16 tonnes

Changes in energy stores: elastic potential energy

1 E_e = 0.5 × spring constant × extension²

 or $E_e = \frac{1}{2}k\,e^2$.

2 E_e = 0.5 × spring constant × extension²

 Extension = 25 − 5 = 20 cm;
 Extension = 0.2 m

 E_e = 0.5 × 10 × 0.2²

 E_e = 0.2 J

3 $F = ke$, $k = \frac{F}{e} = \frac{2.5}{0.1} = 25$ N/m

4 E_e = 0.5 × spring constant × extension² : rearrange to

 extension = $\sqrt{\frac{E_e}{0.5 \times \text{spring constant}}}$

 Extension = $\sqrt{\frac{20\,J}{0.5 \times 10\,000}}$

 Extension = 0.063 m
 convert to cm = 6.3 cm

Changes in energy stores: gravitational potential energy

1 E_p = mgh or gravitational potential energy = mass × gravitational field strength × height.

2 E_p = mgh
 E_p = 4 × 10 × 4
 E_p = 160 J or joules

3 E_p = mgh
 E_p = 40 × 10 × 5
 E_p = 2000 J or joules

4 E_p = mgh rearrange to:

 $h = \frac{E_p}{m \times g}$; m = 300 g = 0.3 kg

 $h = \frac{90}{0.3 \times 10}$

 $h = 30$ m

Energy changes in systems: specific heat capacity

1 a Specific heat capacity is the amount of energy required to increase the temperature of 1 kg of a substance by 1 °C

 b Change in thermal energy = mass × specific heat capacity × temp change or $\Delta E = m \times c \times \Delta\theta$

 c J/kg °C.

2 Copper has a lower specific heat capacity than iron; The same amount of energy is delivered to each block; Copper will require less energy to raise its temperature.

3 $\Delta E = m \times c \times \Delta\theta$ rearrange to:

 $m = \frac{\Delta E}{c \times \Delta\theta}$; Temp change

 $= 35 - 25 = 10\,°C$

 $m = \frac{1500}{2400 \times 10}$

 $m = 0.063$ kg

Power

1 a Bill: $\frac{7500}{60} = 125$ W;

 $\frac{17\,800}{60} = 297$ W; $\frac{7200}{60} = 120$ W

 Ted: $\frac{6300}{60} = 105$ W;

 $\frac{20\,000}{60} = 333$ W; $\frac{8040}{60} = 134$ W

 b Ted; average power =

 $\frac{105 + 333 + 134}{3} = 191$ W,

 Bill average power =

 $\frac{125 + 297 + 120}{3} = 181$ W

 Therefore Ted is the most powerful.

2 Energy = power × time
 time = 7.5 × 60 × 60 = 27 000 s

 Energy = 50 × 27 000

 Energy = 1.35 MJ or 1 350 000 J

3 Time = $\frac{\text{energy}}{\text{power}}$

 Time = $\frac{2\,200\,000}{100\,000}$

 Time = 22 s

Energy transfers in a system

1 Energy stores can neither be created nor destroyed; but can be redistributed to other parts of the system via transfer or dissipation.

2 *Any sensible suggestion.* Battery-powered helicopter; MP3 player; electric fire.

3 a Gravitational potential to kinetic

 b Chemical to thermal

 c Elastic potential to kinetic (and thermal and vibrational)

 d Chemical to thermal and kinetic (and vibrational)

Efficiency

1 a Efficiency = $\frac{\text{useful output energy transfer}}{\text{total input energy transfer}}$

 b Ratio or percentage

2 Answers in order: initial; final. Gravitational; kinetic, thermal and vibrational. Chemical; kinetic, gravitational potential, thermal and vibrational. Chemical; Chemical, kinetic and vibrational.

3 Efficiency = $\frac{360}{500} = 0.72$ or 72%

4 Efficiency = $\frac{900}{5000} = 0.18$ or 18%

National and global energy resources

1 a Renewable: Wave; Solar; Wind; Hydroelectric [Remove 1 mark per incorrect response]

 b Requires burning: Oil and coal (both required)

2 Only renewable if extensive replanting takes place.

3 a 15 m/s

 b $\frac{\text{Total power output}}{\text{Max turbine power output}} =$

 $\frac{10\,000\,000}{1\,000\,000} = 10$ turbines

 c Wind supply fluctuates, is weather dependent.

4 Advantages: wind is renewable, doesn't emit greenhouse gases.

Disadvantages: wind is unreliable, requires a huge amount of land, is considered an eyesore.

Electricity

Standard circuit diagram symbols

1 Correct drawings of the following:

2 LDR	
3 Diode	
4 Variable resistor	
5 Fuse	

2 a Diagram includes a battery (or cell), variable resistor, ammeter and bulb connected in series; Voltmeter must be connected in parallel with the bulb.

b Connect bulb, ammeter, variable resistor and battery in series; Connect voltmeter in parallel to bulb; Vary current using variable resistor; Use the voltmeter and ammeter to measure potential difference and current, respectively; Record at least 5 values of potential difference and current. (If possible repeat results.); Plot graph with potential difference on the x-axis and current on the y-axis.

Electrical charge and current

1 Charge flow = current × time; or $Q = I \times t$

2 **Current** is the name given to the flow of negatively **charged** particles around a closed circuit. These particles are called **electrons**. Because of their charge they are attracted to the **positive** terminal of a cell or **battery**. In books we refer to the opposite direction and call this **conventional** current flow.

3 Time = $\frac{\text{charge flow}}{\text{current}} = \frac{40}{2} = 20$ s;

time = $\frac{\text{charge flow}}{\text{current}} = \frac{10}{2} = 5$ s;

current = $\frac{\text{charge flow}}{\text{time}} = \frac{100}{500} = 0.2$ A;

charge flow = current × time = 6 × 150 = 900 C

4 Time = $\frac{\text{charge flow}}{\text{current}}$; = $\frac{1800}{6} = 300$ s,

300 s; or 5 minutes

Current, resistance and potential difference and resistors

1 a Potential difference = current × resistance or $V = I \times R$

b Ohm's law

c Constant temperature

2 Series circuit; with resistor and variable resistor; and ammeter; Voltmeter connected in parallel with fixed resistor.

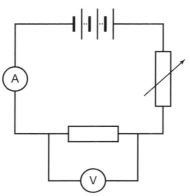

3 Vary current using variable resistor; Use the voltmeter and ammeter to measure potential difference and current respectively; Record at least 5 values of potential difference and current (If possible repeat results.); Plot graph with current on the x-axis and potential difference on the y-axis; Draw line of best fit; Calculate gradient of line to get resistance value.

4 a Thermistor

b Series circuit; with thermistor and variable resistor; and ammeter; Voltmeter connected in parallel with thermistor.

c i Thermometer; and kettle or Bunsen burner

ii 19 kΩ

iii Temperature sensor or thermostat to control central heating system

5 $R_{\text{total}} = R_1 + R_2$; = 10 + 5 = 15 Ω

6 $A_2 = 0.5$ A, $A_3 = 1$ A, $V_2 = 5$ V, $V_3 = 5$ V

Series and parallel circuits

1 In a series circuit, current is the **same** throughout the circuit and potential difference **splits** across the components. In a parallel circuit, **potential difference** is the same across each branch of the circuit and current splits through the parallel branches. An ammeter must be connected in **series** to work correctly. A voltmeter must be connected in **parallel** to work correctly.

2 a Cell in series with bulb and switch.

b Three bulbs in series with a battery/two cells and an ammeter connected in series.

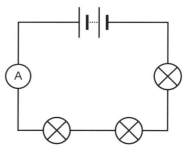

c Battery is series with bulb and thermistor. Voltmeter in parallel with thermistor.

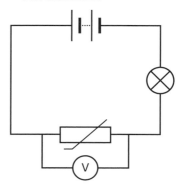

3 **a** Battery with two bulbs in parallel, switch correctly placed.

b Battery with three bulbs in parallel, switch correctly placed.

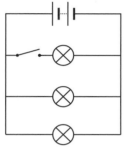

c Battery, bulb and thermistor in series bulb connected in parallel with thermistor.

4 Idea of ring main; and parallel circuit.

Mains electricity: direct and alternating potential difference (ac/dc)

1 **a** dc: direct current; and ac: alternating current

b Alternating current continually changes direction and can flow in two directions; Direct current flows in one direction.

2 Transformers needed to change voltage; Transformers only work with ac; Transmission requires large potential differences to minimise current; and reduce power losses.

3 dc, 5 V (± 0.5 V)

4 10 V

Mains electricity

1 The **electricity** supplied to our homes is called **mains** electricity and it is an **alternating** current supply. This type of current

changes direction many times per second. In fact the current goes forwards and back **fifty** times per second. This means it has a **frequency** of 50 Hz.

2 **a** fuse; **b** live wire; **c** neutral wire; **d** earth wire.

3 **a** Earth wire has zero potential difference/current unless there is a fault and ensures that any metal casing is safe to touch by also being at zero pd.

b Live wire is at 230 V and provides the potential difference which makes the current flow through the appliance.

c The neutral is at 0V this causes a potential difference between the neutral and the live wire; This causes a current to flow through the appliance.

4 **a** The live wire is still connected to the live terminal at 230 V and if touched the person will provide a path for charge to move to Earth; closing the circuit; A surge of current will flow through the person until the fuse melts.

b Device is double insulated; and the (plastic) casing is not a conductor.

Electric Power (with electrical devices)

1 $P = I^2R$ or $P = IV$ or $P = \frac{V^2}{R}$ or $P = Et$ or other correct answer

2 $P = VI = 20 \times 2; = 40;$ W

3 $P = I^2R = 0.1^2 \times 100; = 1$ W

4 $P = \frac{\text{energy transferred}}{\text{time taken}}$ rearrange to:

$t = \frac{E}{P} = \frac{36\,000\,000}{10\,000} = 3600$ s; or 1 hour

Energy transfers in appliances

1 $E = Pt$; or $E = VIt$ (or other correct answer)

2 Everyday electrical **appliances** are designed to bring about **energy** transfers. The **amount** of energy an appliance **transfers** depends on how **long** the appliance is switched on for and the **power** of the appliance.

3 **a** $E = QV = 500 \times 20; = 10\,000$ J or 10 kJ

b $t = \frac{Q}{I} = \frac{500}{2}; = 250$ s or 4 minutes 10 seconds

4 **a** $V = IR$ rearrange to : $R = \frac{V}{I} = \frac{12}{2} = 6;$ Ω

b $t = 120$ s; $Q = It = 2 \times 120 = 240;$ C

c $P = V \times I = 12 \times 2 = 24$ W
2 minutes = 120 s
$E = P \times t = 24 \times 120 = 2880$ J
2880 J

The National Grid

1 **a** 2.3 kV; **b** step-up transformer; **c** 675 kV; **d** pylon; **e** step-down transformer; **f** 230 V

2 Power is constant so if V goes up I goes down ($P = VI$); Power losses are proportional to the square of current ($P = I^2R$); Reducing the current reduces the power losses.

3 **a** Power losses due to comparatively high resistance of long power lines, so a lot of power is wasted on the power lines and relatively little is used to light the bulb. ($P = I^2R$).

b Student uses a step-up transformer for transmission; This increases the potential difference; and decreases the current and reduces the power losses; He uses a step-down transformer to reduce the potential difference and increase the current supplied to the bulb.

Static charge and electric fields (1)

1 **a** Negatively charged particles/electrons transferred by friction from the hair to the balloon; balloon becomes negatively charged.

b Hair becomes positively charged as it has lost electrons; Positively charged hair is attracted by and moves towards the negatively charged balloon; Unlike charges attract.

c Negative charges on the surface of the balloon repel negative charges in the wall; Force of attraction exists between remaining positive charges in the wall and negatively charged electrons; Unlike charges attract.

d (Water molecules are polarised so they attract charged particles.) The effect is that water is a better conductor than air and charge is able to escape the balloon.

Static charge and electric fields (2)

1 Charged, electric, friction, transferring, air, positive.

2 **a** Radial lines growing further apart; arrows pointing away from proton:

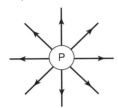

b Radial lines growing further apart; arrows pointing away from protons; lines showing repulsion effect:

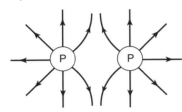

3 A lightning rod is made of a conductive material such as copper; The lightning rod is grounded or earthed; This provides a low resistance path to earth in the event of a lightning strike; The strong field around the lightning rod ensures that a lightning strike would pass through the low resistance copper generating less heat so it will not be as destructive.

Particle model

Particle model of matter and density of materials

1 The formula for density is **mass** divided by **volume** and the standard SI unit is **kg/m³**. Sometimes the values are very large so **g/cm³** are used instead. A density of **1000** kg/m³ is equal to the density of **1** g/cm³. This is also the density of water.

2 **a** Density $= \frac{mass}{volume} = \frac{56.5}{0.005}$; 11 300, kg/m³

b kg/m³ → g/cm³ = ÷1000
$\frac{11\,300}{1000} = 11.3$ g/cm³

3 Mass = density × volume
cm³ → m³ = 1 000 000 : 1 so 8000 cm³ = 0.008 m³
mass = 600 × 0.008 = 4.8 kg

4 Volume of stone = 27.5 ml – 20.0 ml = 7.5 ml; and 7.5 ml = 7.5 cm³
Density $= \frac{mass}{volume} = \frac{18}{7.5} = 2.4$ g/cm³

Changes of state and internal energy

1 A – solid; B – gas; C – liquid.
Solids: ordered, regular pattern, close together, vibration around a fixed point;
Liquids: Close together, disordered, multidirectional weaker bonds;
Gases: far apart, high speed, random motion.

2 Molecules in gases have higher average E_k than molecules in liquids; Change of state from gas (steam) to liquid (water) leads to drop in E_k of molecules; Condensation leads to steam transferring energy to glass as steam changes to water.

3 Physical

Changes of temperature and specific latent heat

1 Thermal energy change of state = mass × specific latent heat or E = mL

2 From −40 °C to 0 °C energy is supplied to the atoms by heating and it increases the energy in the kinetic store of the atoms, increasing temperature; During the melting stage energy continues to be supplied but there is no temperature change as the energy is being used to break the bonds as the substance changes state into a liquid; The energy store is called the latent heat of fusion; From 0 °C to 100 °C the energy in the kinetic store of the molecules increases; At 100 °C the energy is used to break the bonds and change the water from liquid into steam; This energy store is called the latent heat of vaporisation.

3 Thermal energy change of state = mass × specific latent heat = 33.4 kJ
Thermal energy change of state = 0.1; × 334 000 J; 33 400 J = 33.4 kJ

Particle motion in gases (1)

1 The molecules of gas are in constant **random** motion. The average **kinetic** energy of the **particles** is proportional to temperature on the **kelvin** scale. Changing the temperature of a gas in a container of fixed volume will change the **pressure** exerted on the sides of the **container**.

2 Random; with a range of speeds (or kinetic energies).

3 Total energy in the kinetic and potential stores; of all the particles that make up a system.

Particle motion in gases (2)

1 Pressure × volume = constant or pV = constant

2 **a** Initial temp in kelvin = K = °C + 273 = −23 °C + 273 = 250 K
Final temp = 477 °C + 273 = 750 K
Temp change = final temp – initial temp = 750 – 250 = 500 K

b Change in kinetic energy of the particles is proportional to increase in temperature on the kelvin scale; Increase from 250 to 750 is × 3 so E_k store triples

3 $p_1V_1 = p_2V_2$ so $V_2 = \frac{p_1V_1}{p_2}$;
$= \frac{120 \times 75}{225}$; = 40 cm³
(kilo prefix ignored as cancels out)

4 The work done on the gas leads to an increase in the internal energy store of the gas molecules; increasing their potential and kinetic energy stores; Subsequent increases take place in the thermal energy store of the tyre due to transfer in thermal energy stores.

Atoms

The structure of the atom (1)

1 **a** Protons; neutrons; and electrons. (in any order)

b Nucleus; protons, neutrons (protons and neutrons any order).

c Protons; electrons; neutral (protons and electrons any order).

2 Outer circle – electron; Inner circle with positive symbol – proton; Inner blank circle – neutron.

3 Row 1: 1; row 2: 0; row 3: 0, −1

4 Atoms are very small having a radius of about 1×10^{-10} m; The basic atomic structure is a positively charged nucleus; composed of both neutrons and protons orbited by negatively charged electrons; The majority of the mass of an atom is contained with in the nucleus; The nucleus is very small with a nucleus less than 1/10 000 of the radius of the atom; Protons and neutrons have considerably larger masses than electrons; or The electrons are arranged at specific distances from the nucleus.

The structure of the atom (2)

1 Order p, n, e: Li = 3, 4, 3;
Be = 5, 4, 5; Cu = 29, 34, 29;
Na = 11, 12, 11;
K = 19, 20, 19; Eu = 63, 89, 63

2 An **isotope** is an atom with the same number of **protons** and a different number of **neutrons**. **Isotopes** have the same chemical properties as the atom. If the **atomic** number is altered, the **element** changes.

3 **a** F

b T

c T

d F

Developing a model of the atom

1 Plum pudding is solid thereby atom is solid; Positive charge is thinly spread throughout atom (the dough); Negatively charged electrons are dotted throughout the pudding like currants.

2 Path A: A very small deflection confirms that the atom could be composed of thinly spread positive charge; This was predicted by and could be explained by the plum pudding model.

Path B: Results indicated that particularly in the case of the larger deflections that there could be a concentration of positive charge repelling positive alpha particle; This would not be predicted by the plum pudding model.

Path C: The deflections through large angles demonstrate that the atom has a concentration of positive charge and mass in a very small place; This was the first conclusive evidence for a nucleus, which was not included in the plum pudding model.

Radioactive decay and nuclear radiation

1 Some atomic nuclei are **unstable**. The nucleus gives out **radiation** as it changes to become more stable. This is a **random** process called radioactive **decay**. Activity is the rate at which a source of **radioactive** nuclei decays. Activity is measured in **becquerel** (Bq).

2 Row 1: helium nuclei, mm of paper or a few cm of air; row 2: high speed electrons, medium ionising effect; row 3: a few cm of lead or metres of concrete, low ionisation effect.

3 **a** Alpha not penetrative enough; gamma too penetrative.

b Signal indicates thickness of paper; Feedback controls whether rollers go closer or further apart to control paper thickness.

Nuclear equations

1 $^{214}_{82}\text{Pb} \rightarrow {}^{214}_{83}\text{Bi} + {}^{0}_{-1}\text{e}$

2 $^{214}_{84}\text{Po} \rightarrow {}^{210}_{82}\text{Pb} + {}^{4}_{2}\text{He}$

3 $^{230}_{90}\text{Th} \rightarrow {}^{226}_{88}\text{Ra} + {}^{4}_{2}\text{He}$

Half-life of radioactive elements

1 The half-life of a radioactive isotope is the time it takes for the number of radioactive nuclei in a sample to halve; or the time it takes for the count rate (or activity) from a radioactive sample to fall to half its initial level.

2 **a** $1 \rightarrow \frac{1}{2} \rightarrow \frac{1}{4} = 2$ half-lives;

$2 \times 5700 = 11\,400$ years

b $1 \rightarrow \frac{1}{2} \rightarrow \frac{1}{4} \rightarrow \frac{1}{8} \rightarrow \frac{1}{16} =$
4 half-lives; $4 \times 5700 =$ 22 800 years.

c x-axis and y-axis correctly labelled; with correct units;

First point 4000 cpm at time zero;

Plotting of 2nd, 3rd and 4th points showing 2000, 1000, 500 as count rates;

Points being plotted at times (approximately): 5700 years, 11 400 years, 17 100 and 22 800 years;

Smooth curve through plotted points.

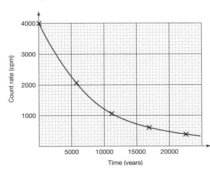

Hazards and uses of radioactive emissions (1)

1 Exposure can take place by contamination; Contamination is when the radioactive material is breathed in or ingested; Once inside the body the radiation can do damage by causing ionisation; Or irradiation; Irradiation is exposure to radiation directly; The radiation emitted can cause ionisation; Both forms can cause damage to DNA, cells and cause mutations that lead to cancer.

2 **a** Wearing film badges that monitor exposure; Limit exposure to as short a time as possible; Keep as far away from radioactive source as practical; This could be achieved by handling radioactive sources at arm's length (or by using tongs); Wearing protective clothing or working behind screens; Washing stations to ensure that any traces of radioactive material are removed from clothing or body to prevent later ingestion (or direct irradiation).

b It is important for the findings to be shared with other scientists; Then the findings can be checked by peer review.

3 **a** Radiation that is ever present emitted by man-made and natural sources.

b Atmosphere shields humans from cosmic rays; Astronauts travel above the atmosphere.

Hazards and uses of radioactive emissions (2)

1 Bismuth-214 has half-life of 20 minutes; 1 hour = 60 minutes.

Number of half-lives =
$\frac{\text{total time}}{\text{time per half-life}} = \frac{60}{20}$
= 3 (half-lives)

For 3 half-lives half 4000 3 times,

$4000 \rightarrow 2000 \rightarrow 1000 \rightarrow 500$

Count-rate 1 hour later is 500 counts/minute.

2 **a** To have $\frac{1}{8}$th of the original sample the sample must have undergone 3 half-lives

because $1 \rightarrow \frac{1}{2} \rightarrow \frac{1}{4} \rightarrow \frac{1}{8}$; is 3 half-lives.

b Radium-226 has a half-life of 1600 years; and $3 \times 1600 =$ 4800 years.

3 **a** 1 lead-210 for every 7 bismuth-210 means $\frac{1}{8}$th lead remains in sample

$1 \rightarrow \frac{1}{2} \rightarrow \frac{1}{4} \rightarrow \frac{1}{8}$ means 3 half-lives have elapsed

b $3 \times 22 = 66$ years

Hazards and uses of radioactive emissions (3)

1 Technetium-99; It emits gamma radiation that can be detected outside body; The half-life is short so as not to cause unnecessary irradiation but long enough to trace blood flow to liver.

2 **a** Xenon-133; Gamma radiation can be used in a gamma knife set-up; Individual rays do little damage due to the low ionisation of gamma, but their combined effect can destroy cells in a tumour; Gamma radiation is penetrative enough to reach the tumour.

   b Cobalt-60 can be reused several times; (As its half-life is much longer than that of xenon-133).

3 Risk of irradiation; and contamination; Chemotherapy and radiotherapy are aggressive treatments that also kill healthy cells, and can cause mutation that can also lead to cancer.

Nuclear fission and fusion

1 Fission

2 Mass number goes up by one; and atomic number remains unchanged.

3 Control rods absorb neutrons; and can slow down or stop the fission process completely; The fission rate or chain reaction can be controlled by inserting or withdrawing control rods.

4 **a** Two lighter nuclei are brought together in conditions of very high temperature and pressure; They join together to make a heavier atom and release energy in the process.

   b Similarities: Both are nuclear processes; both cause a transfer of (kinetic) energy; both release neutrons; both create different elements; both are related to $E = mc^2$; both have a mass defect.

   Differences: Fusion is the joining of small nuclei to form larger elements and fission is the splitting of large nuclei to form smaller elements; fusion occurs naturally in the Sun and fission is manufactured; fusion is safer as the waste products are not as dangerous as those of fission.

Forces

Forces and their interactions

1 Velocity

2 1– c; 2 – d; 3 – a; 4 – b

3 Direction; and magnitude/size/value.

4 **a** A contact force requires two surfaces to be touching for force to act; A non-contact force does not require surfaces to be touching for force to act.

   b Gravitational; magnetic; electrostatic, etc.

Gravity

1 Weight = mass × gravitational field strength or $W = m \times g$ and units: N or newtons.

2 Karen is correct; Mass is a measure of how much material (or how many atoms) something contains; Mass cannot be changed unless some of the material is removed; Weight is a force; A force due to an object's position in a gravitational field; Mass is measured in kg and weight is measured in N.

3 $W = mg$
   $W = 75 \times 1.6; = 120\,\text{N}$

Resultant forces

1 1 a; 3 b; 4 c; 5 e

H2 **a** 3 N →

   b 0 N

   c 6 N ←

H3 **a** Vertical and horizontal arrow pairs should be approximately the same size, if not subtract one mark from total; Friction and air resistance can be represented as two separate arrows.

   b To accelerate there needs to be a resultant/unbalanced force; It is not possible for weight or upthrust to change; The duck needs to paddle faster to make the thrust force larger; The resultant force will now be greater than zero so the duck can accelerate.

Work done and energy transfer

1 Work done = force × distance or $W = F \times s$

2 Nm

3 **a** Work done = force × distance
   Work done = $30 \times 4; = 120$; N;

   b Work done = force × distance
   rearrange to
   distance = $\frac{\text{work done}}{\text{force}}$
   distance = $\frac{240}{30} = 8\,\text{m}$

   c Yes; friction between the go-kart and surface would increase the temperature of the wheels.

Forces and elasticity

1 Extension is proportional to force; provided the spring is not stretched beyond elastic limit.

2 **a** Straight line through the origin; Axes are force and extension.

   b Label force on y-axis and extension on the x-axis; then calculate gradient or reverse axes and reciprocal of gradient.

3 Inelastic deformation means the material has been permanently; stretched or squashed and will not return to its original length or shape.

Moments, levers and gears

1 A force or a **system** of forces can cause an object to **rotate**. The **turning** effect of a force is also called the **moment** of the force.

2 Nm

3 $40\,\text{N} \times 10\,\text{m}; = 50\,\text{N} \times 8\,\text{m}$;
   $400\,\text{N m} = 400\,\text{N m}$; So she is correct.

Pressure and pressure differences in a fluid (1)

1 Pressure = $\frac{\text{force}}{\text{area}}$

2 A liquid or a gas

3 The **pressure** in fluids causes a force **perpendicular** to any **surface**. The pressure at the surface of any fluid can be calculated using the equation **pressure = force/area**

4 Rearrange: pressure = $\frac{\text{force}}{\text{area}}$ to: force: = pressure × area;

   Force = pressure × area = 106 000; × 0.8 = 84 800; N; or 84.8 kN

Pressure and pressure differences in a fluid (2)

H1 Pressure difference = height × density × gravitational field strength

   pressure difference = 3 × 1000 × 10; Pa or N/m²

H2 The air outside is now at a lower pressure than the air inside the packet.

H3 Pressure in a fluid is proportional to depth; because Pressure difference = height × density × gravitational field strength; Pressure exerted by water on his ears is (three times) higher at the bottom of pool, causing discomfort.

H4 As water pours out of the bottle it creates a vacuum inside; Atmospheric pressure outside the bottle is higher than the pressure inside the bottle; Atmospheric pressure pushes the sides of the bottle in.

Distance, displacement, speed and velocity

1 a Distance
   b Displacement
2 a Steady speed
   b Acceleration
   c Deceleration
3 a 45 m
   b Distance travelled = speed × time, rearrange to

   $speed = \frac{distance\ travelled}{time}$,

   $= \frac{10}{6}$,

   $= 1.67\,m/s$

   c B → C has steeper gradient/slope than A → B
4 1 – c; 2 – d; 3 – b; 4 – a

Acceleration

1 a Acceleration
   b Constant speed
   c Deceleration
2 a $Acceleration = \frac{change\ in\ velocity}{time\ taken}$
      $= \frac{10}{10} = 1;\ m/s^2$
   b $Acceleration = \frac{change\ in\ velocity}{time\ taken}$
      $Acceleration = \frac{15-10}{30-10}$
      $= 0.25\,m/s^2$
   c Steady or constant speed
H3 Triangle area = $0.5 \times b \times h$
    rectangle area = $b \times h$
    triangles: $0.5 \times 10 \times 10 = 50\,m$
    and $0.5 \times 5 \times 20 = 50\,m$
    rectangle: $10 \times 20 = 200$
    Total distance = 50 + 50 + 200
    = 300 m

Newton's laws of motion

H1 The **velocity** of an object will only change if there is a **resultant** force acting on it. When a car is at a **steady** speed the driving force

and **resistive** forces of friction and **drag** are equal and act in **opposite** directions.

2 The acceleration of an object is proportional; to the resultant force acting on the object the object; and inversely proportional to the mass of the object; $F = ma$.

H3 Measure of how difficult it is to change an object's motion.

4 a Arrow is equal and opposite.
   b The force exerted by the boy on the boat; is the same magnitude as the force exerted by the boat on the boy.
   c This is an example of Newton's third law.

H5 a 15 – 10 = 5 N
   b → or 'right'
   c Resultant force = mass × acceleration rearrangement:
      $acceleration = \frac{resultant\ force}{mass}$
      $acceleration = \frac{5}{100} = 0.05\,m/s^2$
6 a Zero
   b Resultant force = mass × acceleration: rearrangement:
      $acceleration = \frac{resultant\ force}{mass}$
      $acceleration = \frac{8000}{800};\ = 10\,m/s^2$
   c $Acceleration = \frac{change\ in\ velocity}{time\ taken}$
      rearrangement:
      $time\ taken = \frac{change\ in\ velocity}{acceleration}$
      $time\ taken = \frac{30}{10};\ = 3\,s$

Stopping distance

1 Thinking distance; + braking distance
2 a Condition of brakes; tyres; and condition of road surface (wet, icy, etc.).
   b i Thinking distance is proportional to speed.
      ii Braking distance increases more and more with each increase in speed; Braking distance is not proportional to speed but to the square of speed.
3 One of the students could be looking at a mobile phone; A second student could drop the ruler without warning between his fingers; They could check how far the ruler falls through the finger to indicate reaction time; The further the ruler falls the longer the reaction time; The test could be repeated several times (possibly with other students); They could then compare the results with

the mobile phone to those results taken without a mobile phone.

Momentum (1)

H1 kg m/s

H2 Momentum = mass × velocity or $p = m \times v$

H3 $p = mv;\ = 1000 \times 400$
   $= 400\,000;\ kg\ m/s$

H4 $p = mv;\ = 3.5;\ \times 10 = 35;\ kg\ m/s$

Momentum (2)

H1 In a **closed** system (in which no **external** forces act) the total momentum before an event is equal to the total momentum after the event. This is called the **conservation** of **momentum** law.

H2 a $p = mv = 2000 \times 40 = 80\,000;$ kg m/s
   b Momentum = combined mass × velocity
      combined mass of car and truck = 2000 + 800 = 2800 kg
      $velocity = \frac{momentum}{combined\ mass};$
      $= \frac{80\,000}{2800} = 28.6\,m/s$

H3 Momentum of car 1: $p = mv$
   $= 800 \times 40 = 32\,000;\ kg\ m/s$
   (momentum direction →)
   Momentum of car 2: $p = mv$
   $= 1000 \times 30 = 30\,000;\ kg\ m/s$
   (momentum direction ←)
   Combined mass of car 1 and 2
   $= 800\,kg + 1000\,kg = 1800\,kg$
   Final momentum = momentum of car 1 – momentum of car 2
   $= 32\,000 - 30\,000 = 2000;\ kg\ m/s$
   $Velocity = \frac{momentum}{combined\ mass} = \frac{2000}{1800}$
   $= 1.1\,m/s\ →$

Momentum (3)

H1 The car is made of material that is not too hard, so it will crumple in a collision; Force felt by occupants in a collision is $F = \frac{m\Delta v}{\Delta t}$ (expressed as formula or words); Crumple zones effectively make the time of the collision longer; If time is made longer; force experienced by occupants is made smaller; The force can be reduced to a level that will result in a less serious/non-fatal injury.

H2 $F = \frac{m\Delta v}{\Delta t}$ rearrangement required: change in momentum = $F\Delta t$
   change in momentum = 180 × 0.005 = 0.9; N s or kg m/s

H3 a Change in momentum = $F\Delta$
      $= 200 \times 0.005 = 1;\ N\,s$ or kg m/s

Answers

b $\frac{m\Delta v}{\Delta t}$ rearrangement required:
$$\Delta v = \frac{F\Delta t}{m}$$
$$= \Delta v = \frac{200 \times 0.005}{0.050} = 20\,\text{m/s}$$

Waves

Transverse and longitudinal waves

1 Transverse

2 **a** Vibrations of molecules or particles are parallel; to direction of wave motion/energy transfer.

b Sound waves, P-waves, any other correct response.

c Wave fronts closer together; and wave fronts further apart:

Compression   Compression
Rarefaction   Rarefaction

3 **a** Transverse; because vibrations are at right angles; to direction of wave motion/energy transfer.

b Instead of up and down push it in and out; so that vibrations are same direction as wave motion.

c In longitudinal waves particles vibrate parallel to wave motion, energy transfer; whereas in transverse waves vibrations are at right angles (to wave motion/ energy transfer).

Properties of waves

1 **a** The distance from the rest position/mid-point/equilibrium/ undisturbed position; to the maximum displacement of a wave.

b The number of vibrations; per second; (of a wave) or number of waves passing a point per second.

c The distance from a point on the wave; to the equivalent point on the adjacent wave.

2 **a** 4 ms

b Frequency $= \frac{1}{\text{time period}} = \frac{1}{0.004}$
$= 250\,\text{Hz}$

c 3 squares and each 1cm square $= 1\text{V}; 3 \times 1\text{V} = 3\text{V}$

3 $v = f \times \lambda$ rearrangement required:
$\lambda = v/f; = \frac{300\,000\,000}{603\,000} = 497.5; \text{m}$

Reflection and refraction

1 Absorption; reflection; transmission (accept refraction also).

H2 Angle reflected wave makes with incident ray should be 90°; Reflected ray should be horizontal and have an arrow showing direction; Wave fronts should be perpendicular to horizontal reflected ray.

Barrier   Reflected ray

After reflection

3 **a** Ray inside block refracted towards normal in glass; Ray leaving the block must be refracted away from the normal; Angle ray makes with normal leaving block must be very close to angle ray made with normal before entering the block. (Rays must be labelled with an arrow and drawn with a ruler).

b Ray bends towards the normal when entering the block; Ray bends away from the normal when leaving the block; Ray leaving the block and entering the block are both horizontal. (Rays must be labelled with an arrow and drawn with a ruler).

Sound waves (1)

H1 20 Hz; to 20 000 Hz (or 20 kHz)

H2 Air molecules are compressed or pushed together by speaker; Air molecules spread out or rarefaction takes place; Sound waves are collected by outer ear and channeled into inner ear; Ear drum vibrates; Small bones (ossicles) in ear vibrate; at same frequency as original sound; Fluid in cochlea vibrates; Auditory nerve converts vibrations to electrical impulses sent to brain.

H3 **a** 7 squares and each square = 1 ms 1 × 7 = 7 ms

b Frequency $= \frac{1}{\text{time period}} = \frac{1}{0.007};$ f = 143 Hz

c 4 squares and each square = 1V; 4 × 1V = 4V

Sound waves (2)

H1 Sound above; 20 kHz (or accept above human hearing range).

H2 Medical imaging, destroying gall or kidney stones, industrial imaging or other correct response.

H3 **a** A P-wave is a primary wave/It is the first wave to arrive in an earthquake; It is a longitudinal wave. A longitudinal wave is one where the vibrations of the wave are parallel to; its motion.

b An S-wave is a secondary wave/It the second wave to arrive in an earthquake; It is a transverse wave. A transverse wave is one where the vibrations of the wave are perpendicular/at right angles/at 90 degrees; to its motion.

c Density of the rock changes; so speed changes; Density changes gradually, so the paths are curved; This is a refraction effect.

d The core is liquid; and only P-waves can travel through liquids.

Electromagnetic waves (1)

1 **a** Long
b Short
c Low
d High
e infrared
f ultraviolet

2 Transverse; travel through a vacuum/space; all travel at the speed of light through a vacuum (accept other sensible responses).

3 Radiowaves have longer wavelengths than microwaves; Radiowaves can be reflected by the ionosphere; The ionosphere is an ionised/charged layer of the upper atmosphere; Radiowaves can be transmitted to points where receiver is not in line of sight; Radiowaves can be transmitted with this method around the globe; Microwaves have shorter wavelengths and can pass through the Earth's atmosphere; Microwaves can be used to transmit information to and from satellites in orbit; Microwaves need to be transmitted to points where the receiver is in the line of site; Microwaves can be used for telephone, television and internet.

Electromagnetic waves (2)

H 1 Radio waves

2 The type of radiation; and the size of the dose.

3 1– b; 2 – f; 3 – c; 4 – a; 5 – d; 6 – e.

Lenses

1 a Convex/converging; Concave/diverging

b Real and virtual

2 a Parallel lines correctly labelled and middle line continues horizontally; Focal length and principal focus correctly labelled; Labelled convex and top and bottom rays converging as per diagram.

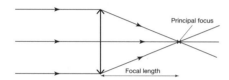

b Parallel lines correctly labelled and middle line continues horizontally; Focal length and principal focus correctly labelled; Virtual lines passing through principal focus as dotted lines on the left side of lens; Lines then continued as continuous lines on the right side of the lens (light rays must be drawn with a ruler).

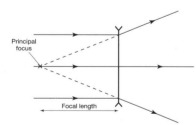

3 a Horizontal line from object to lens; line from top of lens passing through focal point; distance to image must be 8 cm +/− 10%; line from top of object through centre of lens to intersection point; intersect of at least two lines; image drawn with arrow. (Allow the construction lines through focal point on object side and parallel line to principal axis).

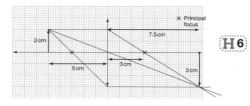

b Real, enlarged and inverted (upside down).

c Magnification = $\frac{\text{image height}}{\text{object height}}$

$= \frac{3}{2.0}$; $= x$; $\times 1.5 \pm 10\%$

Visible light

1 a Specular

b Diffuse (or scattering)

2 a Translucent; transparent.

b Absorption; transmission; and reflection.

c Opaque

3 i red, green and blue (in any order).

ii red and blue (answer must be consistent with choices in part i).

iii red

iv red

Emission and absorption of infrared radiation and black body radiation

1 It is constant.

2 The black can is a better emitter of radiation than the white can; The black can is able to radiate more infrared radiation than the white can (in the 15 minutes); The temperature drop is less for the white can as it radiates away less infrared radiation.

3 a Both of the cans will increase in temperature; The black can will increase to a higher temperature; because black is a better absorber of infrared radiation than white.

b In both cans the absorption of infrared will not be the only factor that affects temperature, both cans will increase their thermal store via conduction; Also the dissipation will take place (from the can) to the thermal store of the surroundings and table due to conduction and convection; When the water has evaporated the results will become meaningless.

H 4 Absorption of infrared is greater than emission of infrared.

5 a The wavelength at which the greatest intensity of radiation is emitted.

b As temperature increases; the peak wavelength decreases.

H 6 The Earth absorbs infrared radiation from the Sun, this increases the temperature of the Earth; The Earth then radiates infrared (IR) back into space. This decreases the Earth's temperature; The Earth radiates IR back into space that is a lower frequency that the IR from the Sun (the Sun has a higher temperature than the Earth); The IR radiation emitted by the Earth is absorbed by greenhouse gases such as methane or carbon dioxide; The greenhouse gases re-radiate this IR in all directions but some of the IR goes back to Earth; The atmosphere acts as an 'insulating-layer', preventing the Earth from depleting its thermal store during the night; The correct amount of greenhouse gases maintains the correct temperature and prevents it getting too cold; Too many greenhouse gases would lead to an increase in temperature.

Electromagnetism

Magnetism

1 The magnetic fields are the strongest.

2 a An object that becomes a magnet; when placed in a magnetic field.

b Attractive

c Take a known magnet and push the north pole at one end of the material; Push the same north pole towards the other end of the material; If attraction always takes place, the object is an induced magnet. If both repulsion and attraction take place in the above test, the object is a permanent magnet.

3 a

b

Answers

Electromagnetism

1 **a** The needle will deflect in one direction; and then go back to the centre position.

    b The needle will deflect in the opposite direction; and then go back to the centre position.

2 At least 3 concentric rings; distance between rings increases the further out you go; arrow direction of magnetic field lines anti-clockwise.

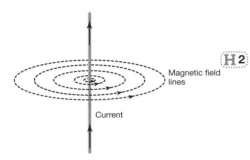

At least 3 concentric rings; distance between rings increases the further out you go; arrow direction of magnetic field lines clockwise.

3 **a** Arrow out of the page

    b Motor effect

    c Magnet with greater field strength; larger current; wire in a coil.

Motor effect

1 **a** split ring commutator; **b** force; **c** rotating coil; **d** force; **e** brush; **f** dc power supply.

2 **a** Current direction changes every half turn; to keep the coil spinning in the same direction.

    b The brushes connect the wire to a power supply; and make contact with the split-ring commutator.

3 The MP3 player converts the sounds into an alternating current to the solenoid; The current in the solenoid induces a magnetic field; The solenoid magnetic field is constantly changing; The solenoid is repelled and attracted by the permanent magnet; The solenoid is attached to the paper cone; As the solenoid moves back and forth it makes the paper cone vibrate producing sound waves; The compressions and rarefactions of the sound waves produced match the frequency and amplitude of the original recording.

Electromagnetic induction

1 **a** F
    b F
    c T
    d T

2 **a** Needle deflects to one side of the galvanometer; then returns to zero deflection.

    b Generator effect; If a conductor moves at right angles to a magnetic field; when the conductor cuts through the flux lines; a potential difference is induced across the ends of the conductor; If there is a complete circuit a current is also induced in the conductor.

    c The needle will deflect in the opposite direction; then return to zero deflection.

    d The needle will rock from side to side; The student will be generating an ac voltage; The frequency of the output voltage/current will match the frequency of the vibrations.

3 **a** A magnet rotates near a coil of wire; The coil is cutting through the changing field/flux lines of the magnet; An alternating potential difference is induced in the coil; The circuit is complete so the bulb is supplied with an alternating current.

    b If you go very slowly or stop completely you will no longer have a light on; This is obviously very dangerous and could impair your visibility to other road users.

Transformers

1 **a** The circuit contains a battery which supplies a current to the circuit; If somebody talks into the microphone its resistance changes; If the resistance goes down the current goes up, and vice versa.

    b The coil wrapped around the permanent magnet is a solenoid; If it is supplied with a changing current then the solenoid's magnetic field changes with it; This means that the solenoid will be repelled or attracted by different amounts by the permanent magnet; This changing attraction/repulsion makes the metal plate vibrate.

    c The coil needs to be wrapped onto a magnet, otherwise it would not be repelled; or attracted, and would not vibrate the metal disk.

2 Step-up transformer; because it has more coils on the secondary than on the primary coil.

3 **a** A changing potential difference in the primary coil induces a changing magnetic field in the core; The changing magnetic field in the core means that flux lines are constantly being cut by the secondary coil; A changing potential difference is induced in the secondary coil; The size and direction of this potential difference change as the voltage applied to the primary coil changes; If there is a complete circuit an alternating current will flow in the secondary coil.

    b A transformer will only work with ac supply as without a changing magnetic field in the core no potential difference can be induced in the secondary coil.

    For a transformer to work a changing magnetic field must be induced in the core; to induce an alternating potential difference in the secondary coil; A constant dc voltage will not induce a changing magnetic field in the core.

Space physics

Our solar system

1 The Milky Way

2 **a** Venus; Mars; Saturn; Neptune.

    b Pluto has been reclassified; as a dwarf/minor planet.

    c Moon

    d The Sun

3 Dwarf Planet – 2; Planet – 3; Sun – 4; Solar System – 5; Galaxy – 6; Universe – 7.

Life cycle of a star

1 When a star is a main-sequence star, this means the inward force of **gravity** is balanced with the outward radiation pressure caused by **fusion**. This state of **equilibrium** can last for millions to billions of years depending on the star's **mass**. When a star similar in size to our own runs out of **hydrogen** it grows in size and becomes a **red giant**.

2

Nebula
↓
Protostar
↓
Main-sequence star

Small stars ———————————————— Massive stars

Red giant ———— Red super giant

White dwarf ———— Supernova

Black dwarf ———— Black hole ———— Neutron star

3 Most of the early Universe was hydrogen and a smaller amount of helium; The Sun and other stars use fusion to release energy; Hydrogen nuclei fuse to form helium and heavier elements; Fusion reactions can make elements up to iron; Heavier elements are formed when a star larger than ours collapses and there is a supernova; A supernova casts matter into the Universe.

Orbital motion, natural and artificial satellites

1 Gravity

2 Similarities: both are objects that orbit another object; that is larger or has a larger mass.

Differences: artificial satellites have been launched by people into orbit; whereas a natural satellite is one that is already orbiting a planet and people did not put it there.

H 3 a The time it takes the comet to make one orbit of the Sun.

b Speed increases due to an increase in the gravitational field strength when the comet is closer to the Sun.

H 4 Direction is constantly changing;, so velocity is also changing; Acceleration is change in velocity per unit of time, so acceleration is taking place.

5 a It is not constant (or it is changing).

b It will change as the forces on it change; Speed will be greatest when the force of gravity is greatest or when object is closest to the Sun.

Red-shift

1 a The Universe started from a very small region (a singularity); that was very hot and dense.

b Observations of supernovae.

2 a The light from the distant galaxy; has been shifted to the red end (longer wavelength) of the spectrum.

b The galaxy is accelerating away from us; and the acceleration is greater than the nearby galaxy.

c The red-shift observation supports the idea that the Universe is expanding and the rate of expansion is increasing.

3 a Dark energy

b Dark matter

For answers to the practice papers, visit www.scholastic.co.uk/gcse